I0820300

338
Accutronic
ACCEL
PENNZOIL
GUMOUT
WEBER
GENERAL KINETICS CAMS
GAPP & ROUSH
SPEED PRO
MOROSO

CarTech®

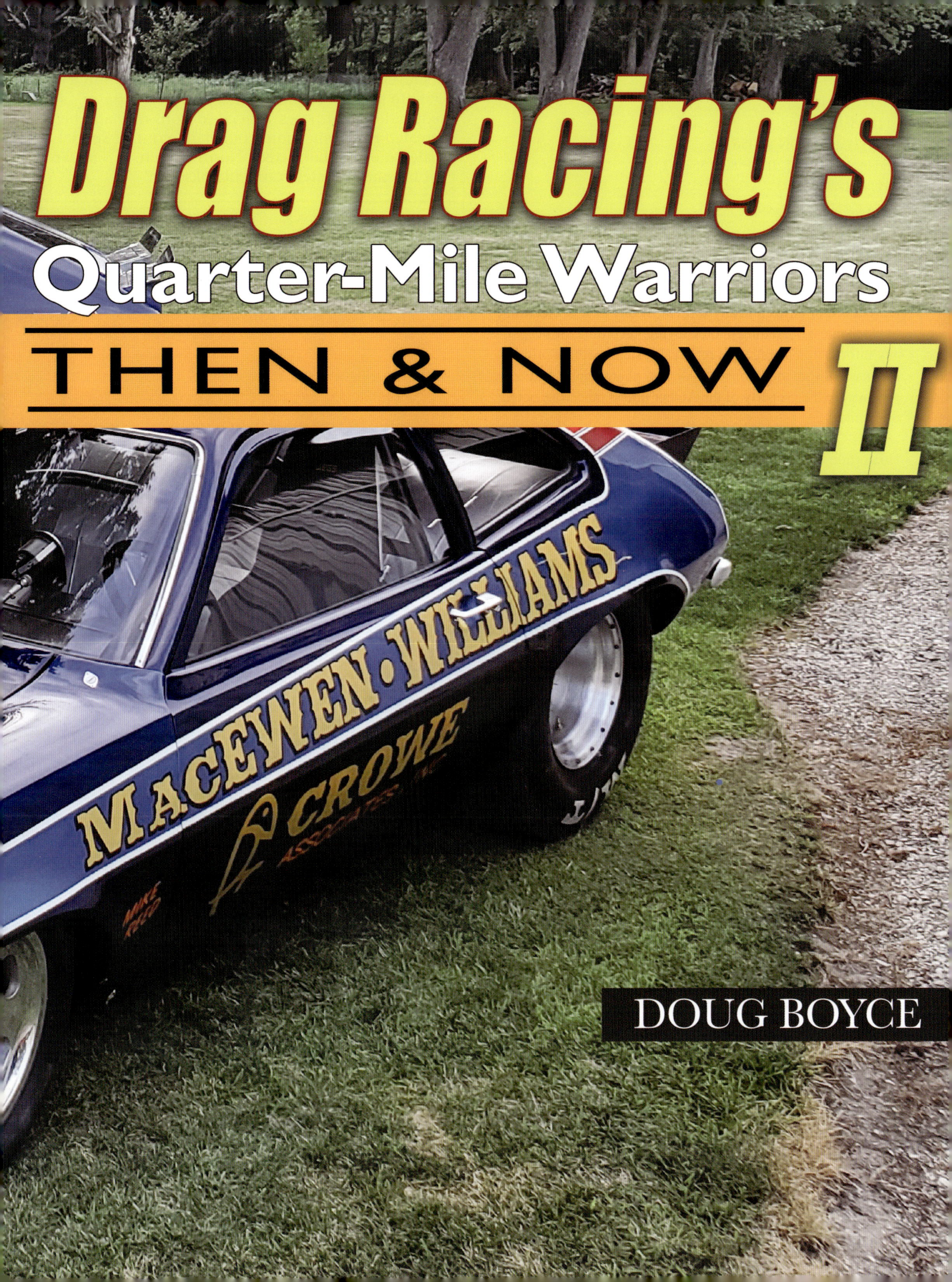
Drag Racing's
Quarter-Mile Warriors
THEN & NOW
II
MACEWEN • WILLIAMS
CROWE
DOUG BOYCE

CarTech®

CarTech®, Inc.
6118 Main Street
North Branch, MN 55056
Phone: 651-277-1200 or 800-551-4754
Fax: 651-277-1203
www.cartechbooks.com

Edit by Bob Wilson
Layout by Connie DeFlorin

ISBN 978-1-61325-865-1
Item No. CT702

Library of Congress Cataloging-in-Publication Data Available

Written, edited, and designed in the U.S.A.
Printed in China
10 9 8 7 6 5 4 3 2 1

Many of the vintage photos in this book are of lower quality. They have been included because of their importance to telling the story.

DISTRIBUTION BY:

Europe
PGUK
63 Hatton Garden
London EC1N 8LE, England
Phone: 020 7061 1980 • Fax: 020 7242 3725
www.pguk.co.uk

Australia
Renniks Publications Ltd.
3/37-39 Green Street
Banksmeadow, NSW 2109, Australia
Phone: 2 9695 7055 • Fax: 2 9695 7355
www.renniks.com

Canada
Login Canada
300 Saulteaux Crescent
Winnipeg, MB, R3J 3T2 Canada
Phone: 800 665 1148 • Fax: 800 665 0103
www.lb.ca

TABLE OF CONTENTS

Acknowledgments

Each car that is featured in this book has a history that needs to be shared. To get the story for each one, it took a significant amount of research, chasing leads, and many interviews. I made my cell-phone provider happy by racking up the hours. In addition to acknowledging individuals in the photo attribution, I want to give a special shout out to the individuals who went above and beyond to help me with this project: John Bloom, Michael Pottie, Steve Reyes, John T. Francis, Jim Baughman, Jack Gillett, Paul Schavrien, Paul Kennedy, Charlie Morris, John Norris, and Don Nicholson.

In addition, publications, such as *Car Craft*, *Super Stock & Drag Illustrated*, *Drag News*, and *Drag Sport Illustrated*, provided a wealth of information. Helpful websites included Hearst Digital Media (motortrend.com), nhra.com, cacklefest.com, and mecum.com.

Introduction

The *Oxford English Dictionary* defines the word *nostalgia* as, "a sentimental longing or wistful affection for the past, typically for a period or place with happy personal associations."

We all can be nostalgic when reminiscing about a time that we'd love to return to—if only briefly. In those days, life seemed easier, less chaotic, and, of course, we were all a little younger. Life was good, the music was great, and the drag racing was fantastic!

To many fans, the sport of drag racing today has lost much of its flavor. The Fuelers no longer race to the 1,320 mark, it's difficult to differentiate one Funny Car from another, and Pro Stock lost me when rules stated that an engine from any manufacturer was okay to use in any car.

Apparently, I'm not the only one who misses drag racing the way it was—not by a long shot. The interest in the sport's past has never been stronger. In increasing numbers, the cars that we once cheered on are being resurrected, restored, shown, "cackled" (fired up and run), and raced.

This book focuses on the original, surviving, and restored drag cars of yesteryear. About 85 cars are featured, covering each category from drag racing's glorious past. These vehicles are not museum pieces or cars that have been tucked away from prying eyes. Instead, they see the light of day and are shown proudly by their owners. The cars in this book are placed in easy-to-follow chronological order, which allows you to see how the sport evolved over time.

CHAPTER ONE

DRAGSTERS

TODAY'S TOP FUEL CARS INCORPORATE YARDS OF CHROMOLY TUBING AND A 500-CI AFTERMARKET HEMI FOR POWER. SPEEDS ARE APPROACHING 340 MPH IN 1,000 FEET.

Within the sport of drag racing, no category of car evolved more than the dragster. When Wally Parks incorporated the NHRA in 1951, dragsters were being created using original equipment manufactured (OEM) chassis. A carbureted flathead Ford or an overhead valve (OHV) Oldsmobile or Cadillac engine provided the power. Speeds peaked at around 95 mph in the quarter mile. Today's Top Fuel cars incorporate yards of chromoly tubing and a 500-ci aftermarket Hemi for power. Speeds are approaching 340 mph in 1,000 feet.

Above: Tony Nancy campaigned his Sizzler from 1970 into 1972. It was runner-up at the 1970 NHRA Winternationals and won the March Meet at Bakersfield the same year. The canards show that this car was restored to how it appeared in 1971. Nancy set the class record that year with a 236.22-mph top speed. The Woody Gilmore–chassis, Ed Pink–powered car was restored by Nancy with the help of Harry Hibler and Bill Carter. Today, the Sizzler is owned by John Neas. (Photo Courtesy John Neas)

Galt Strokers

In the mid-1950s, the drag racing scene was exploding in popularity. Here, Andy Marsh races the **Purple People Eater** *at Ontario's Kohler Dragway. The track later became Cayuga Dragway. (Photo Courtesy Mark Rogerson)*

Drag racing has always been a sport where inspiration and influence has come from many sources. That is no more apparent than when looking at Top Fuel. From its humble beginnings to today, no category has gone through greater change.

From Day 1, aerodynamics played a role in how dragsters are built. In the early 1950s, racers used sheet metal, aluminum, and even plywood to direct air over the rails. This was followed by formed bodies and enclosed cockpits. The *Glass Slipper,* which was built in 1956 by Roy and Ed Cortopassi, and the *Purple People Eater* of the Galt Strokers, a car club based in Ontario, Canada, come to mind. The *Purple People Eater* was directly influenced by the *Glass Slipper*, and it is evident due to the beautiful craftsmanship.

In 1951, the Galt Strokers car club was founded. In 1954, the club's name became official, and it was led by club President, Al Howett. The club assisted in organizing drag races in southern Ontario, so it made sense to pool resources from its members and build a car of its own.

The dragster wasn't their first choice, as they previously batted around the idea of building a Competition Coupe. However, after seeing the *Glass Slipper* on the pages of the January 1956 issue of *Hot Rod* magazine, that all changed.

The dragster was pieced together by the club members whose background allowed them to build the chassis and form the skin. Early dragster building was primitive. For example, the floor pans were made out of old street signs and chassis tubing was bent by heating and bending it over random objects. One of these random objects was a nearby telephone pole that caught fire and required the local fire department to extinguish.

When it came to the engine, club member Doug Lovegrove secured a DeSoto Hemi from the local salvage yard. Club members opened the bores and added a four-carburetor setup and an Isky 5-cycle camshaft. Lighting the mixture of alcohol and nitromethane was a magneto that was shipped all the way from England. Behind the Hemi rode a LaSalle 3-speed transmission and a Ford truck rear end. A 1935 Ford front axle supported the spoked rims.

The *Purple People Eater* (as it came to be known) made its debut on October 8, 1957, at Kohler Dragway, sans bodywork, and Lovegrove ran a 12.09 elapsed time (ET) at 115 mph.

The 1958 season saw the addition of the full body

These are the remains of the Galt Strokers **Purple People Eater** *dragster. Thankfully Mark Rogerson was up to the challenge to restore it. (Photo Courtesy Mark Rogerson)*

The Purple People Eater ***looks right at home in Mark Rogerson's garage, which features memorabilia from drag racing's glorious past. (Photo Courtesy Mark Rogerson)***

shell and belly pan. It was a tough year that saw the *Purple People Eater* crack a block and break the rear end. However, ETs eventually improved to an 11.59 at 128.57 mph. The biggest win of the season came at the Ontario Championship Drags, where the *Purple People Eater* was victorious.

The season ended on a downer, as the car blew a clutch and ran off the end of Kohler Dragway. A vote by club members was taken shortly after, and the decision was made to end the venture. Club members Al Howlett and Andy Marsh made repairs to the car, removed the damaged body, and took it to the NHRA Nationals at Detroit in 1960. The car failed inspection and never ran. It was sold after that and was briefly campaigned by its new owner with a flathead engine under the name *Jiggs Fat*.

Unfortunately, the *Purple People Eater* was soon parted out and the chassis was reportedly ditched. The

The driver of the Purple People Eater didn't see a "No Dragsters" sign anywhere. This is the oldest streamline dragster in Canada, as it was built in 1957. (Photo Courtesy Kenny Kroeker)

This is a prime example of what a late-1950s dragster interior looked like. Drum brakes are the only thing stopping this car. (Photo Courtesy Mark Rogerson)

Powering the dragster is a 364-ci Hemi (derived from a 354 engine that was bored 0.060-over). Twin 500-cfm carburetors rest on an early aluminum Weiand intake manifold. (Photo Courtesy Mark Rogerson).

body ended up miles away in outside storage. It was a chance online meeting with Shawn Currie in 2015 that current owner, Mark Rogerson came into possession of the remains of the *Purple People Eater*. Little remained of the car, but Rogerson made the promise to restore the piece of history.

The car sat for a few years while Rogerson gathered missing parts. Russ Moore of Moore's Blacksmith Shop was brought in to duplicate the original chassis from old pictures, and Richard Hilton of Rich Refinishing tackled the restoration of the fiberglass body. As Rogerson planned on making passes in the car, a few upgrades were necessary. Along with a fresh Hemi, the original Ford banjo rear end gave way to a 4:11-equipped Ford 9-inch, which also provided better braking. Since LaSalle transmissions are extremely rare today, Rogerson used a Powerglide.

The restoration was completed in 2022, and the *Purple People Eater* made its first trip down the track in 2024, when Rogerson recorded some low-13-second ETs at Ohio's Dragway 42.

Richard Hilton's Rich Refinishing Auto Restoration painted the car, duplicating the original color by using an original 1950s Strokers Club plaque. Dan "Danno" Drouin laid on the pinstriping and the "Strokers" lettering. (Photo Courtesy Mark Rogerson)

Scotty's Muffler Service Special

This car, which was known as the Scotty's Muffler Service Special, *was built by Robert White in 1953. The chassis was constructed using PBY aircraft wing struts. (Photo Courtesy Scott Cochran)*

Scott Cochran seemed like he was destined to own the *Scotty's Muffler Service Special*. In 2015, he received a text from a friend, Tom Duttrey, who sent him a for-sale advertisement for the dragster. Duttrey was well aware that Cochran was in the market for an early-1960s front-engine dragster, and seeing that this one already had his first name on it, Duttrey told Cochran that Cochran should buy it. The name was just one of the weird coincidences that came to light. Another was that Cochran himself operated a muffler shop. Cochran wasted little time calling the seller, Dave Long. Long had been entertaining a few offers and listened to Cochran as he made his pitch and shared his own story.

Cochran's dad, who was suffering from the effects of leukemia, stressed to him the importance of pursuing what makes you happy. Cars make Cochran happy—drag racing and front-engine dragsters to be precise. His interest in the sport came by way of his father, who visited tracks many times in his life and likely caught a glimpse of the *Scotty's Muffler Special* racing in his youth.

At 30 years old, Cochran decided to heed his dad's advice. He quit his job as an electrician and opened his own muffler shop that specialized in custom exhaust work. It was quite the learning curve for a man with no experience. However, in 2015, a year after his dad passed, Cochran's company, which was named the Cochran Garage Exhaust Shop, was born.

Long listened to Cochran's story, and although Long had been entertaining other offers, he decided that the car had to go to Cochran. Cochran hooked up the trailer and hit the road, driving the 1,200 miles from his home in Washington state straight through to California. Cochran's wife, Kelly, came along for the trip, and his friend Tony sharing in the driving.

Long remembered the *Scotty's Muffler Service Special* well, having watched it race many times. He said that many years ago he would hang out at Scotty's Muffler Service, which was located in San Bernardino, California.

Mike Snively, the first into the 5s, got his start in this dragster. Snively consistently ran 8.50 ETs at 180 mph. (Photo Courtesy Scott Cochran)

The chassis needed little more than a quick cleanup. Scott Cochran disassembled the car and only replaced what was necessary. (Photo Courtesy Scott Cochran)

The nose and tail of the car are formed from fiberglass, whereas the belly and cowl are magnesium. The dragster features the original front wheels, and the rear wheels are ultra-rare Romeo Palamides magnesium slots. (Photo Courtesy Scott Cochran)

Many have referred to the Scotty's Muffler Service Special *as the most original dragster (that has not been restored) in existence. (Photo Courtesy Scott Cochran)*

Charles "Scotty" Scott was the original owner of Scotty's Muffler Service, which was a business that he opened with his wife in 1946. He gained a name for himself racing at the drag strip and on the dry lakes. The couple was blessed with two boys, Billy and George, who, when they were old enough (5 years old in Billy's case), raced quarter midget cars.

In 1962, with Billy at age 14, his father figured that it was time to put him in a real car. To the horrors of his wife, the real car turned out to be a well-used dragster. Well, there was no way that she was going to let her juvenile son ride off to certain death in a blown dragster. She laid down the law, saying that until Billy was 16, he would not be driving the dragster. In stepped Billy's older buddy, Mike Snively.

Being 16 years old, Snively was game to give it a go. The car that would be labelled the *Scotty's Muffler Service Special* was originally campaigned by San Bernardino's Robert White. White built the car himself in 1953, which was his last year of high school. He made the chassis using wing struts from a PBY sea plane, and the body was built using a combination of fiberglass and magnesium panels. He raced the dragster with an Ardun-headed flathead, direct drive, and a Halibrand quick-change rear end. White raced the car until early 1962, when he parked it.

Into the aging chassis, Scott placed a blown and punched-out 377-ci Chevy engine. Replacing the quick-change rear was a stronger 1957 Oldsmobile housing. Snively drove the car through the 1963 season, running a best ET in the 8-teens at more than 180 mph. He gained a significant amount of experience in

The fully functional interior looks just as it did when the car was last raced in the mid-1960s. The rear end is a 1957 Oldsmobile unit. Nothing has been polished or repainted. (Photo Courtesy Scott Cochran)

Built in 1953, this car survived running Top Fuel into the mid-1960s. Atop the Chevy engine is an old-school Hampton GMC 6-71 blower. It's a genuine piece of drag racing history. (Photo Courtesy Scott Cochran)

this car, and many took notice. In 1966, Snively was hired by Roland Leong to drive his famed *Hawaiian* AA/FD. In doing so, Snively won the NHRA Winternationals and Indy Nationals that year. In addition, Snively later became the first to run a 5-second ET in a Top Fuel car.

In 1964, Billy Scott turned 16 and was ready to drive himself. His dad had a new car built and installed the 377-ci engine from the now-obsolete *Scotty's Muffler Special*. Ralph Fuller purchased the old dragster and ran it briefly with an injected Chevy. By the mid-1960s, the car was way past its prime and ready for retirement. Fuller parked the car in his mother's chicken barn while he and his wife took on a life as missionaries. In the barn, the *Scotty's Muffler Special* sat for the next 30 years or so until Long came along in the 1990s.

Working as a telephone lineman, Long had been searching everywhere for the car, keeping his eyes peeled, talking with people and posting classified advertisements. One day when he was out on a house call in Indio, California, he walked around the corner of the building, and there sat the *Scotty's Muffler Special*. The car was in great shape, and Long made a deal and hauled it home. Although the car was missing the engine, everything else was there and in great shape. Long hung onto the car for about 20 years, using it as a show piece in his garage/man cave before deciding to part with it.

Shortly after Cochran purchased the car from Long, he received a phone call from Billy Scott.

"It was a call completely out of the blue," Cochran said. "I thought he was dead."

The pair developed a great rapport, and over the next months, they talked regularly. Billy, who missed the opportunity to buy the car in the past, offered to buy it from Cochran more than once. Cochran relented and accepted an offer, as he felt that the car belonged with Billy.

Plans were laid to bring the car down to Billy's place, where the deal would be sealed. Sadly, it was not to be. Billy passed away in April 2017. With his passing, Cochran was determined to honor Billy's legacy and bring the car back. He installed a blown small-block between the rails and moved forward with plans to build a correct 377 engine.

In 2016, the car made its debut as a static display at the California Hot Rod Reunion. Jaws dropped upon seeing the car. It had been tucked away for 50 years, and everyone who was familiar with the car assumed that it was junked years ago.

Cochran returned to the Reunion in 2017, this time with a blown small-block between the rails. The *Scotty's Muffler Special* draws the crowds, especially when Cochran fires it up. A 60-percent load of fuel brings smiles to the faces and tears to the eyes.

The *Sidewinder* Cars

Here, in the summer of 1958, Jack Chrisman put the original Sidewinder *through its paces. Six carburetors are atop the GMC blower. (Photo Courtesy J. R. Bloom)*

When it comes to dragster design, there isn't really a layout that hasn't been tried. One of the most unusual designs is where the engine is mounted in the rear in a transverse position. Although the design rarely worked (due to the unequal distribution of power to the two drive wheels), a few gave it a try. One of those was Paul Nicolini. With the help of Tony Capana and backing from his father in-law, Harry Duncan, Nicolini began the build of the *Sidewinder* during the first week of 1958.

Nicolini fabricated the 98-inch-wheelbase chassis in his South Gate, California, shop while Joe Maillard built the 456-ci blown Hemi that powered the car. Power from the Hemi ran via a chain to the left wheel. To equalize power, a drive axle ran to the right wheel. Ted Cyr, Jack Chrisman, and others drove the *Sidewinder*. On gas, the car produced a best ET of 9.03 at 150 mph. At some point, the *Sidewinder* was sold back East and lost in time.

Nicolini built the *Sidewinder II* in mid-1959. This car featured a longer, 108-inch wheelbase and was campaigned by Jim Camboor and Chuck Jones. Chrisman once again took the wheel of the Maillard Hemi-powered car and raced it in conjunction with the *Sidewinder*.

Both cars appeared at the NHRA Nationals at Detroit in 1959, with Jack Chrisman driving both. The best ETs recorded for the *Sidewinder II* were produced when nitro was added. On the juice, ETs of 8.50 at 185 mph were realized. Adding nitro increased breakage, with the drive chain and axle being the weak links.

At some point in the 1970s, Nicolini began to build the *Sidewinder III*. The new car used a 117-inch-wheelbase chassis and incorporated many parts that were salvaged from the *Sidewinder II*. *Sidewinder III* was never completed, though, and it somehow ended up in the hands of a gentleman named John Fell. Fell owned an aluminum foundry business across the alley from Nicolini's shop. He held onto the car for a few years, and it appears that he did little with it before selling the car to Jim Travis. Travis added the body panels and a nose and tail that were created by Bob Melley.

In 1995, Travis displayed the *Sidewinder III* at the March Meet, as he continued his quest of gathering original parts. The project stalled again, and the *Sidewinder III* switched hands again. This time, it was bought by Don Ferguson. In April 2013, current owner Jack Gillett purchased the project from Ferguson.

When Gillett bought the car, he put his years as a machinist to work. The *Sidewinder III* was far from being in operating condition, and several key pieces were missing and had to be fabricated. So, while Gillett fired up the lathe to make a new axle, sprocket drive system, and brakes, he hired Fred Muehlenhort at Racetec Motorsports in Oxnard, California, to clean up the

The Sidewinder II *featured slight revisions, including a longer wheelbase, a taller roll bar, and fuel injection (instead of carburetors).*

well-worn, original body.

To build a fresh Hemi for the car, Gillett called on Cliff Roa, an old friend, to lend a hand. Together, the two pieced together a stroked 465-ci Hemi. It took Gillett and company 18 months to get the *Sidewinder III* to this point.

In 2017, Gillett made the decision to have a new aluminum body created. The original aluminum was barely hanging on, suffering badly from the ravages of time. Terry Hegman in Fountain City, California, was tasked with building the new shell, and he knocked it out of the park. Hegman was provided with a few photos of the *Sidewinder II* from 1959 to use as a template. Then, he spent 2-1/2 months welding and forming the new aluminum body. Gillett had Ed Whippi at Team Auto apply 1965 Corvette Metallic Blue paint before Jamie Stormes added the lettering and pinstripes.

As rough as it was, Jack Gillett used the original aluminum body when restoring the Sidewinder III. *M&H slicks on magnesium slotted rims are on the rear, while new, stainless spokes are mounted to the original* Sidewinder II *hubs. (Photo Courtesy Steve Reyes)*

The restored Sidewinder III *features a Cliff Roa–built Hemi that measures 465 inches. The heads are the better-breathing 331-Hemi units. Doug Robinson crafted the exhaust. (Photo Courtesy Steve Reyes)*

The Sidewinder II, *and* Sidewinder III *were designed with the crankshaft centerline 4 inches below the axle centerline. Jack Gillett fabricated almost everything in this photo. (Photo Courtesy Jack Gillett)*

Jack Gillett incorporated the salvageable parts from the Sidewinder II *when it was time to complete the* Sidewinder III. *The car runs on an 82-percent load of nitro. (Photo Courtesy Jack Gillett)*

Ed Whippi did a fantastic job of mimicking the blue paint and scallops that the famed Ed "Big Daddy" Roth laid on the Sidewinder II *in 1959. (Photo Courtesy Jack Gillett)*

The *Western Mfg. Special* and *Little Fuller*

Pete Starrett led the restoration of the Little Fuller *dragster. Eric Hayes performed many aspects of the restoration. Hayes and Fred Vosk both get credit for the beautiful bodywork and paint. (Photo Courtesy Jim Baughman)*

As told by cacklefest.com, Kent Fuller built the *Western Mfg. Special* in early 1962, in a very similar fashion to the famed *Greer, Black, & Prudhomme* car that was so dominant during the period. This dragster was built very light (about 900 pounds). It was campaigned with a blown Chevy fuel motor that was built by Vic Hubbard's Speed Shop in Northern California. Fuller especially liked the car, so the next year, when Hubbard wanted a new car built, Fuller took this one back on trade. He then dropped in an Ardun-headed flathead and ran more than 180 mph in the car. According to cacklefest.com, this is considered to be the fastest ET ever turned by an Ardun.

In 1965, Fuller sold the car to Jon Halstead. Bob Keith drove the car while Pete Starrett pulled the wrenches. They competed in AA/GD with a freshly built, blown small-block Chevy. In 1967, the car was bought by Jim Laing. Laing had his own automotive business, but, although intentions were to campaign the car himself, he never got around to it. For the next 30 years, the dragster sat disassembled in Laing's garage.

Over the years, Starrett kept track of the dragster's whereabouts. In 2000, he contacted Laing about restoring the car. Laing was on board, and the two became partners in the build. Starrett hauled the dragster to Kirkland, Washington, where it spent the next 5 months going through its restoration.

The restoration of the *Little Fuller*, as the car has come to be known, was completed in 2001, thanks to the helping hands of Kent Fuller; Fred Vosk; Eric Hayes, who laid the metal-flake silver and candy red paint; and Rick Evans, who completed the lettering. The efforts paid off when the dragster won best paint honors at the Grand National Roadster Show in California.

The gas-powered small-block Chevy was assembled by Pete Starrett and features a mix of period-correct and modern parts. Eric Hayes once again gets credit for the car's polished components. (Photo Courtesy Jim Baughman)

Looking through the cage, the ultra-rare Halibrand rear end is in full view. Its total weight is 74 pounds. The brakes are by Airheart. (Photo Courtesy Jim Baughman)

In 2020, Laing passed away at age 85. His widow, Diane, held onto the dragster until she had found the right buyer. That turned out to be Jim Baughman, who became the caretaker of this historic Fuller dragster in June 2021.

Restored in 2001, the Little Fuller *was rebuilt and improved by Pete Starlett in 2006. It features candy red paint over a Silver base, using real metal flake. (Photo Courtesy Jim Baughman)*

The Little Fuller *was cackled for the first time in 2001. The car was unique for a Fuller car, featuring a short wheelbase. (Jim Baughman)*

The *North-Wind* 1962

The North-Wind *was campaigned by members of the Slo Poks Car Club and mainly driven by Earl Floyd. This was the first A/FD car that was built by Gasser legends Jack Coonrod and Jim Albrich. (Photo Courtesy Jeff Miller)*

The Northwest has produced its share of legendary drag racers. Jack "the Bear" Coonrod, who is based in Vancouver, Washington, immediately comes to mind. Coonrod is forever associated with Gassers, because he ran in the category starting in the late 1950s. In 1962, he decided to dabble, although it was briefly, with a Fuel Dragster.

Coonrod partnered with fellow Slow Poks Car Club (established in 1952) member, Jim Albrich and fielded the candy red Scotty Fenn dragster. Albrich would build the 354-ci Chrysler Hemi, which ran power to a mid-1950s Oldsmobile rear end. Fellow club member Earl Floyd was brought in to drive the dragster.

The *North-Wind* was campaigned throughout the Northwest in 1962. In 1963, a new Kent Fuller–chassis *North-Wind* was built, and the old car only had sporadic use before it was retired in 1964. Coonrod, who felt that running the Fueler was a losing venture, returned to his first love: the Gassers after 1962. The best ETs turned for the *North-Wind* were an 8.50s at 189 mph.

Coonrod retained ownership of the *North-Wind*, and when it was retired, he put it into storage at his home in Vancouver. There it sat unchanged until 1983, when he decided to dust off the car and make some appearances with the car. Coonrod also planned to make a few passes down the track, so several things had to be freshened up. The brakes, fuel lines, and related rubber parts were replaced.

Current owner, Jeff Miller purchased the *North-Wind* from Coonrod in 2022, and outside of going through the original 354 engine, little has been changed.

"When I first bought it from Jack, I showed it about a half dozen times, but it was starting to leak and lose compression," Miller said.

Miller refuses to make any other changes to car, choosing to keep it all original.

In addition to the line of North-Wind *dragsters, Portland-based Columbia Racing Engines had more high-profile northwest legends, including Whipple & Goodell, Jack Coonrod, and Mark Coletti.*

For approximately 40 years, Jack Coonrod displayed the North-Wind at his home in Washington. It's amazing that so little of the car has changed. (Photo Courtesy Jeff Miller)

The North-Wind is a great glimpse into the past, featuring rare items, such as the Enderle "barn door" injector and a chain-driven blower. (Photo Courtesy Jeff Miller)

The current owner has changed little, aside from necessary safety upgrades. After being cleaned and polished, the North-Wind looks just as nice as it did more than 60 years ago. (Photo Courtesy Jeff Miller)

A Chassis Research gauge cluster is in the center of the cockpit. The long arm to the right is the brake handle. This is all original from 1962. (Photo Courtesy Jeff Miller)

North-Wind owner Jeff Miller attends as many shows as he can with the dragster. The reaction has always been positive. The pedal car hides the battery for the dragster. (Photo Courtesy Jeff Miller)

The *Northwind* 1965

The Northwind *was a unique Kent Fuller–built car that ran well and looked good. This photo was captured at Bakersfield, California, in 1965. (Photo Courtesy Mike Channing Collection)*

Mike Channing's *Northwind* was campaigned by Jim Albrich, Steve Krieger and Ed "the Ace" McCulloch. The team formed in 1964, with Albrich and his Columbia Racing Engines shop supplying the Hemi, Krieger supplying the funding, and McCulloch picking up the Kent Fuller chassis. Southern California's Dave Jeffers was hired to drive, as McCulloch's accident the previous year in his Junior Fueler made him reluctant to climb behind the wheel.

The *Northwind* was one of three unique dragsters that were built by Fuller. Tagged with the name "Magicars," Fuller's chassis differed from the traditional build practices of the day in several ways, one being the rear suspension. Unlike the majority of dragster chassis of the period that were built with the rear end solidly mounted, Fuller's three Magicars incorporated a live rear axle that used ladder bars and coil springs. Fuller felt that his design worked better to plant the tires.

The front suspension lacked the typical torsion bars and spring support. Instead, Fuller incorporated rubber biscuits that allowed the axle to pivot. Thus, both front wheels would remain planted during chassis twist.

Jeffers's time as the driver was brief, as commuting north to Washington was just too inconvenient and expensive. McCulloch was then convinced to give the car a try. With a few uneventful passes at Woodburn under his belt, McCulloch took over the reins. One issue McCulloch had with the car was its sprung rear suspension. He didn't care for it, and, in short order, the ladders bars and springs disappeared in favor of a solid-mounted rear.

The *Northwind* was raced up and down the West Coast, as there was never a shortage of Top Fuel events. After laying down a Northwest top-speed record of 206.88 mph against Sid Waterman at Woodburn Dragstrip in Woodburn, Oregon, McCulloch had an opportunity to challenge for the top spot on the *Drag News* top-10 list. At the time, "Sneaky" Pete Robinson of Atlanta, Georgia, held the number-one spot, and had defended it a reported five times previously. The two combatants agreed to meet at Woodburn on what turned out to be a rainy June 13 afternoon. In front of a reported crowd of 10,000 spectators, McCulloch defeated Robinson in a best-of-three match to win the coveted title of the nation's top A/Fuel Dragster. McCulloch's best ET of the day was a tire-melting 7.50 at 206.42 mph.

As the summer progressed, the wins for the *Northwind* continued, including two unsuccessful challenges for the *Drag News* top spot against "TV" Tommy Ivo. With the speed in which Top Fuel cars were evolving, it was time to move on. The *Northwind* was listed for sale in

The Northwind *name lives on, thanks in part to Mike Channing, who owns the final* Northwind *dragster that was tied to the Slo Poks Car Club. (Photo Courtesy Mike Channing)*

This is the restored cockpit of Ed "the Ace" McCulloch. McCulloch's climb to becoming one of drag racing's elite drivers began right here. The butterfly wheel was reproduced by Kent Fuller. (Photo Courtesy Mike Channing)

Just like it had in the past, the 392 Hemi uses the best of parts, including an Enderle injection, a Mickey Thompson intake and rocker covers, and a Delta blower drive. (Photo Courtesy Mike Channing)

The Northwind *features gold metal-flake paint. Being No. 1 on the* Drag News *1320 list was a huge deal. (Photo Courtesy Mike Channing)*

the fall and eventually sold to Terry Major of Longview, Washington.

Fast-forward to 2005. With McCulloch battling colon cancer, it was decided that the *Northwind* needed to be found and restored. Jack Coonrod, a longtime friend of McCulloch, and Earl Floyd set out to find the car that started McCulloch on the road to fame. After months of searching, they were able to track the car to British Columbia, Canada, where it was being stored in the rafters of a barn. It had been up there for more than 30 years, having last raced in the early 1970s as a Gas Dragster.

A deal was struck to buy the car, and it was hauled south to Washington, where the restoration began in January 2006. Jack Coonrod headed up the restoration. At some point, the 140-inch chassis had been lengthened (an additional 13 inches were tacked on). The original front axle was no longer on the car, nor were the body panels that enclosed the roll cage. Coonrod called in several favors to get the car completed. Fuller, who was a tremendous help throughout the restoration, stepped up to duplicate the front axle and the suspension that he

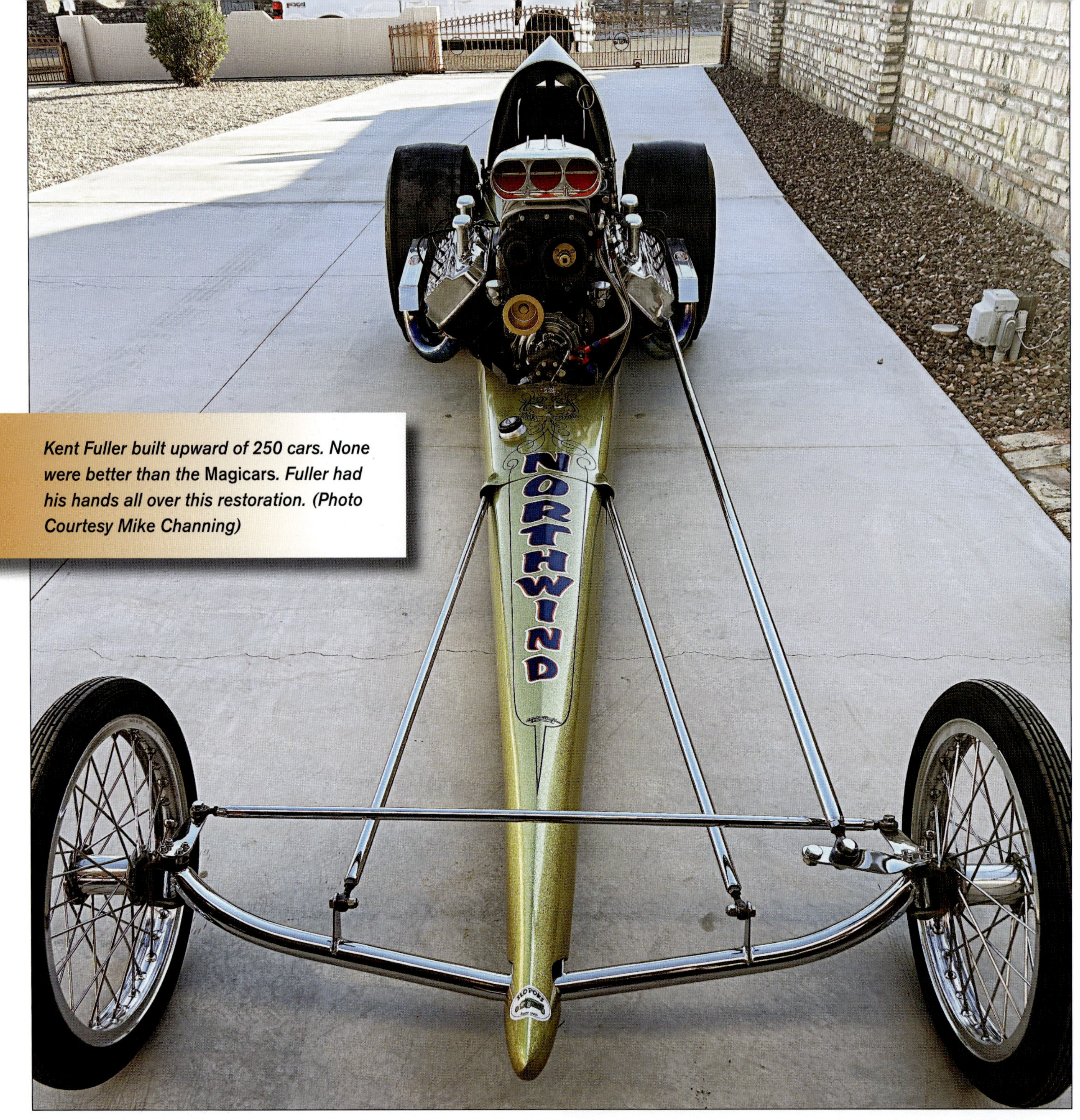

Kent Fuller built upward of 250 cars. None were better than the Magicars. Fuller had his hands all over this restoration. (Photo Courtesy Mike Channing)

had created four decades ago. Bruce Cassidy of Cassidy Manufacturing in Vancouver, Washington, was tasked with restoring the chassis. To do so, Cassidy relied on Fuller and old images.

When it came to the engine, Bucky Austin, among others, stepped up with several difficult-to-find parts, before Albrich, the original engine builder, began building the 392. Mike Channing, who has owned the *Northwind* since 2021, has since gone through the engine to make it a little more user friendly.

Dale Withers of Estacada, Oregon, was handed the responsibility of forming the new tail section. Relying on old images, Withers was able to work his magic, recreating the tail to perfection. While attempting to install the tail section, it was discovered the main roll cage hoop had been changed at some point. Kent Fuller once again helped out, supplying the proper measurements.

Wrapping up the package, Dave Jacobus applied the period-correct gold paint that incorporates a little extra metal flake, and Don Pennington did the lettering. The restored *Northwind* made its debut in the summer of 2007, with McCulloch once again taking the seat.

Poison Ivy

Ted Miller and Robert Martinez pose with their Poison Ivy *car, which was still under construction at the time. The AA/FD became one of Southern California's nicest-looking cars. (Photo Courtesy Ted Miller/Bob DeBurn Collection)*

By 1964, drag racing was all the rage in Southern California. Radio stations blared out advertisements to entice racers and spectators to go to any one of the tracks that dotted the region. The Martinez brothers, Robert and Gilbert, were tired of watching from the sidelines. They partnered with Ted Miller and jumped into the action with both feet.

They went straight to AA/Fuel Dragster. Robert built a 125-inch, 2x3 rectangular chassis and had the Cope brothers build a 354 Hemi. Being body and paint experts, the brothers and Miller formed their own body panels and applied the green paint. Some would question their choice of color, seeing that green was supposed to be bad luck on race cars, but it worked for these guys. The name they chose for the car, *Poison Ivy*, seems appropriate in this instance.

The guys competed with the car around Southern California into 1966 and saw some success. Being on a limited budget, the car was raced infrequently and retired

The chassis, which was designed and fabricated by Gilbert Martinez, gives the Poison Ivy *a wide-body look. Phil Whetstone of Miracle Design completed the lettering. (Photo Courtesy Bob DeBurn)*

The beautifully formed tail section was prepared by Larry Storck, who also hammered out the rest of the body. (Photo Courtesy Bob DeBurn)

partway through the season. Then, the car sat until 2002, when Bob DeBurn came along.

DeBurn, who was born and raised in Southern California lived a life that many dreamed of with surfing, women, and fast cars. He surfed and was a regular spectator at Lions Drag Strip, Irwindale Raceway, and Carlsbad Raceway. In 2000, with the emergence of the "cackle" car festivities, DeBurn had to get in on the action. A friend pointed him to an ideal candidate for a car to purchase: the *Poison Ivy* dragster. The car was rough, having sat outdoors for 15 years. Between the rails sat a carbureted Hemi. What sold DeBurn was the *Poison Ivy* name that was painted across the body. He remembered watching the car run at Carlsbad decades earlier.

"It was a beautiful car and not [one that was] easy to forget," DeBurn said.

DeBurn set a deadline for himself to have the car completed in time for the 2003 California Hot Rod Reunion, and he made it. The car was "cackled" there (to fire the car and run it at idle) with NHRA division director Don Irvin in the seat. DeBurn had topped the tank with a full load of nitro, and it sounded great! Little did he realize that he was only supposed to use a 50-percent mixture of nitro. No wonder the crowds came running. Nothing sounded better. In 2004, *Poison Ivy* won the Best Competition Car award at the Grand National Roadster Show. DeBurn sold the car in 2005 and moved on to the next project. As of this writing, the *Poison Ivy* dragster is owned by Sam Harding, who attends cacklefest events with the car.

Bob McKray Performance built this period-correct 354-ci Hemi. California Plating added the brightwork. The front axle is a Willys unit. (Photo Courtesy Bob DeBurn)

Tom Hoover's *Fishbowl*

In 1965, Tom Hoover put Minnesota on drag racing's map with his Woody Gilmore–chassied Fishbowl. *The chassis initially measured 156 inches, but over the winter of 1965–1966, it was stretched to 182 inches. (Photo Courtesy Steve Andersen)*

For any doubters, the Minnesota-based Hoover family proved that a family that drag races together stays together. Driver and tuner Tom Hoover held the spotlight while his mother and father (Ruth and George) worked behind the scenes. For more than 50 years, "Hoover" was one of the sport's most recognized names.

Success came as early as 1960, as Tom took Gas class honors at the NHRA Nationals at Detroit. The Hoovers' early success led them into the world of Fuel Dragsters. They purchased a Rod Stuckey chassis in 1964, and Tom used the Hemi-powered car to win his first national event by defeating Dean Turk in the final round of the 1965 AHRA Winter Nationals. A new Woody Gilmore, Race Car Engineering (RCE)–chassis car followed midseason, but it was stolen six months later.

To help the Hoovers get back on their feet for the 1966 season, Woody Gilmore built a new 156-inch-wheelbase chassis and Tom Hanna added the tin work. Bob Meyers later stretched the chassis to 182 inches. Hanna was called upon once again to form the new body.

According to cacklefest.com, "Hanna fashioned a recessed, teardrop-shaped hole in the tail for a decorative wood panel, and when a visiting reporter queried Hanna midway into the body build about the holes, Hanna responded that Tom Hoover was into aquariums and wanted live fish swimming in the tail. Thus, the *Fishbowl* was christened."

Rounding out the chassis was a candy red fade paint and a matching red upholstery by Imperial Customs.

Initially powering the new car was a 392 Hemi. After exploding a block in 1966, it was decided to make a swap and install a Ford Cammer. Issues with the Cammer, including the fact that it seemed to be too much power for the chassis, resulted in returning to the Hemi. Tom

Tom Hanna (left) is shown in 1965, and Corey Conyers (right) is shown working for Hanna in 2012. The opening in the panel looked like a great place for a fishbowl. (Photo Courtesy Steve Andersen)

When a new car was built for the 1968 season, the Fishbowl *was sold to a buyer in Canada. It eventually came back to the United States, where it was discovered in 2005. (Photo Courtesy Gord Barr)*

The restored chassis (minus the Tom Hanna skin) exposes the remarkable workmanship performed by Woody Gilmore. Nothing was spared to ensure that the restoration was done correctly. (Photo Courtesy Mike Chase/Steve Andersen)

Long-wheelbase 1960s Fuel dragsters looked good. Aside from safety modifications, this car appears just as it did in 1966. (Photo Courtesy Mike Chase/Steve Andersen)

The attention to detail here is second to none. All of the controls are a finger's reach away. Power from the Hemi ran through a Schiefer clutch to a Woody Gilmore–produced, cast Chrysler rear end. (Photo Courtesy Mike Chase/Steve Andersen)

competed at numerous regional meets and national events through 1967. At the 1966 AHRA Grand American race in Illinois, Tom was runner-up to Cliff Zink in the *Zink & Witz* car, losing with a quicker 7.91 ET. At the end of 1967, the decision was made to build a new car, and the *Fishbowl* was sold.

Denny Darragh, a resident of Winnipeg, Canada, became the new owner and campaigned the car at least through the 1971 season. He eventually sold the car, but where it went had long been forgotten. In 2005, after years of searching, Steve Andersen discovered the car in Coeur d'Alene, Idaho.

Andersen, a former member of the Cogs Car Club remembered the car and had spent time in the seat of the Hoovers' first two dragsters after they had been purchased by the Gopher State Timing Association club. It was the rekindled friendship with chassis builder and driver Pat Foster that started him on his search for the *Fishbowl*.

Jim Swedberg of Grand Forks, North Dakota, built the 392 engine, which carries parts by Enderle, Cragar, Venolia, Cerillo, and Donovan. J&B Plating is credited with the beautiful chrome plating. (Photo Courtesy Mike Chase/Steve Andersen)

The beautiful lines of the Tom Hanna/Corey Conyers body were prepped and painted candy red by Vescio's Customizing in Rogers, Minnesota. Lenni Schwartz added the lettering. (Photo Courtesy Mike Chase/Steve Andersen)

The car that he discovered for sale in Idaho had been advertised as a Don Long–chassis car with a Donovan 392 Hemi. Well, the seller had the Hemi part right but the chassis wrong. It was a Gilmore chassis. The chassis had been front halved (again), and, at one time, a Chevy engine and Powerglide transmission had been used. A Ford 9-inch rear end was out back.

Numerous telltale signs confirmed that this was indeed the *Fishbowl*. The high mount for the parachute, the scars on the chassis from the relocated chute release, and the fuel shutoff on the left side of the chassis were all there. Full of confidence, Andersen, with help and guidance from Foster, Tom Hoover, and Hanna, began working on the restoration in 2006.

Things got off to a shaky start as the shop that was selected to do the metalwork had ideas of its own. Andersen retrieved the car, and it sat at his own garage, untouched for a while. He had lost interest in the project, and, during that time, Pat Foster passed away. Hanna stepped in and gave Andersen the push that was needed to blow the dust off the stalled project and move forward.

Steve Davis and Steve "Opie" Elliot brought the chassis back to originality, and Corey Conyers at Tom Hanna's shop got busy on the body. While all of this was taking place, Andersen was busy gathering the parts that were needed to complete the project. One of his finds was the original Gilmore-built 8.75 Chrysler rear end that belonged with the car. Being a direct-drive car, little more was needed to complete the driveline than to build a correct Donovan Hemi. Thankfully, the car was purchased with the "right" block and heads. Jim Swedberg was responsible for building the Hemi.

The restored *Fishbowl* debuted at the 2014 Hot Rod Reunion in Famoso, California. Tom Hoover was on hand to cackle the car. Tom noted the originality and how little the restoration deviated from how the car appeared when he campaigned it in 1966. The only changes that current-owner Glen Barta made to the *Fishbowl* were related to safety.

The restored* Fishbowl *sits next to a John Dearmore tribute car. The market is saturated with original, restored, and tribute cars, as the desire for drag racing the way that it used to be continues to grow. (Photo Courtesy Steve Andersen)

Daryl Greenamyer boils the hides of the Smirnoff *Fueler at Nevada's Stardust International Raceway. The short-lived track opened in 1965 sanctioned by the AHRA and ceased operations about 5 years later. (Photo Courtesy Don Prieto)*

Joe Passalaqua had a passion for cars, and he and his wife, Julie, owned several rare, numbers-matching muscle cars. During the restoration of one, Passalaqua met Rick MacDonald, whose talents included building engines for vintage Top Fuel dragsters. It was through this friendship that Passalaqua gained an interest in the "cackle" cars. When he decided that he had to own one, his preference leaned toward something that was all original and unrestored. These kinds of cars are few and far between. However, one name that came up in conversation was the *Smirnoff* rail that had been campaigned by Daryl Greenamyer.

In the mid-1960s, Greenamyer was a test pilot who also raced airplanes, including a very fast Grumman Bearcat that was sponsored by Smirnoff. Greenamyer became interested in drag racing through a friendship with engine builder Dave Zeuschel. He met Zeuschel at an air race and was convinced to watch the Fuelers run at Lions Drag Strip. It took only one run for Greenamyer to exclaim that he needed one. Immediately, he began the planning process to build his own Fueler.

Greenamyer reached out to Ralph Hart, who was chairman of the board at Smirnoff, and negotiated a sponsorship deal for the car. Apparently, Hart loved drag racing and was "all in." The sponsorship allowed Greenamyer to build the car with the finest parts available. Zeuschel built the stroked 392 Chrysler Hemi, Roy Fjastad's Speed Products Engineering fabricated the chassis, and the eye-popping body was formed by Bob Sorrell using a sketch by Steve Swaja. Over the controversial body went

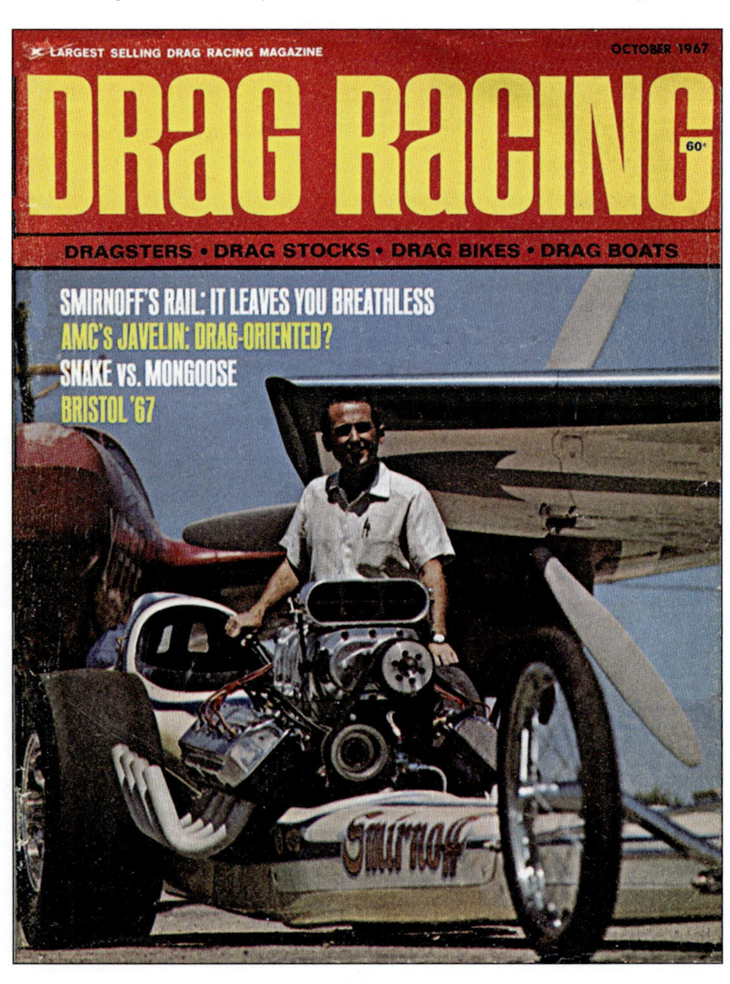

Daryl Greenamyer poses proudly with his Smirnoff *rail. This photo was published on the cover of the October 1967 issue of* Drag Racing *magazine. His Smirnoff-sponsored Bearcat is in the background.*

The restored Smirnoff *is seen here in 2017 at the first annual Nitro Revival at Barona Drag Strip in Barona, California. Graphics, including the Smirnoff bottle on the cowl, were completed by an artist known as Mikhi. (Photo Courtesy Dave Kommel)*

Car owner Joe Passalaqua (in the Zeuschel Racing Engines T-shirt) listens to the big Hemi cackle. There's a good chance that his wife, Julie, is the one sitting in the Tony Nancy–upholstered seat. (Photo Courtesy Dave Kommel)

pearl white paint and blue stripes by "Rueben" and lettering and details by Ted Miller.

According to a cacklefest.com interview with renowned chassis builder and driver Pat Foster, Sorrell took liberties while forming the rear body panels.

"In the course of the body fabrication, Bob decided the roll bar was too high and at the wrong angle for how he felt the body should appear," the article said. "Race cars are a strange breed when it comes to form and function. Car builders, as a rule, think and cater to function. Also, as a rule, the body masters tend to put form ahead of function. Sorrell took that at least one step too far when, without informing any of the principals of his decision, he cut off the entire cage, built the rear half of the body, never reattached the cage in any way, and told them to come get 'er—it's a wrap. [Chassis builder] Roy went insane and blamed Zeuchel as much as Sorrell. Zeuchel shrugged and said, 'We'll get a smaller driver.' And Daryl, who was small, thought she looked bitchin' and finished it the way she sat!"

Zeuschel asked Foster to test the car, but because of the modified cage, he no longer fit the car. It was never a good fit for Greenamyer, nor Larry Dixon Sr., who, by the time that Bakersfield rolled around in March, was sharing the driving chores.

Greenamyer made the inaugural passes in the car at Las Vegas. His first pass netted a tire smoking, crossed-up, 183-mph top speed. It was definitely a handful. Then, the car proved that it could run as good as it looked during the 1967 United States Professional Dragster Championship meet at Lions Drag Strip in July. At this event, more than 90 of the nation's fastest Fuelers competed in hopes of making the 64-car field, and Dixon tied James Warren for low ET of the meet with a 7.01 while driving to 222.23 mph.

Greenamyer drove the dragster during the 1968 season, qualifying at several NHRA and AHRA events. Late in the 1968 season, the Smirnoff sponsorship deal ended. Prior to the 1969 season, Greenamyer gave the dragster a new coat of blue paint.

Greenamyer entered the car in the 1969 NHRA Winternationals but failed to qualify. Shortly afterward, he retired the car. For the next 37 years, it sat

The Smirnoff *dragster is shown in 2009 at Beech Bend in Bowling Green, Kentucky. The Bob Sorrell–designed tail leaves nothing to be desired. (Photo Courtesy Paul Hutchins)*

untouched and protected from the elements in its home in the Mojave Desert. Over the years, Greenamyer entertained many offers to sell the car but refused until Joe Passalaqua came calling in October 2006. Passalaqua met Greenamyer's asking price and made a promise that the car would be restored, shown, and cackled.

Although the dragster was remarkably well preserved, the Zeuschel Hemi was long gone. Zeuschel was one of the best builders of the period, so it came as no surprise that the engine would end up elsewhere. In this case, it went into a drag boat, which eventually sank. Rick MacDonald, who helped throughout the restoration, was tasked with building a new "cackle" Hemi. The 392 that he was provided with came with the purchase of the car and was an engine that Daryl had stashed away years ago as a spare for the dragster.

Because the rail was in such remarkable condition, its restoration was fairly straightforward. The Fjastad chassis was stripped, sandblasted, and powder coated by R. J. Little. Before Passalaqua attached the original parts, they were either repainted or rechromed. Passalaqua did the majority of work in his home garage in California. This included stripping the paint and straightening panels before applying the pearl white paint and blue trimming. The gold leaf and lettering were applied by Bob Thompson, and the airbrushing, including the Smirnoff vodka bottle on the cowl, was completed by an artist known as "Mikhi."

The final touch was reinstalling the Tony Nancy upholstery and Surfer Bob butterfly steering wheel. Passalaqua got to know Surfer Bob (Bob Knight) during the car's restoration and asked him to replicate the missing brake handle that matched the steering wheel. Surfer Bob then offered to sell Passalaqua his business. Passalaqua not only bought the business but started making butterfly steering wheels of his own and gave them to his drag racing buddies.

Passalaqua displayed the car in as-found condition at the California Hot Rod Reunion in 2006 and returned the following year with the restored car.

"This car was semi-blessed in the way it came back together," Passalaqua said. "All these ghosts out of the past would appear and help make this thing."

Passalaqua and his wife, Julie, became enthusiastic cackle participants.

Sadly, Passalaqua succumbed to a massive heart attack in October 2022 at the age of 58.

"We didn't talk about death a lot, but when we did, Joe told me to not sell the dragster. He wanted it in a museum," Julie said.

Former drag racer Bruce Larson advised her to donate the dragster to the Petersen Automotive Museum.

"They'll treat it like it should be," Larson said.

"It was hard for me to part with it, but I knew that I wanted to fulfill Joe's wishes," Julie said.

The Poachers

The Poachers dragster frequented Southern California tracks and instilled fear in its opponents. The new "lizard nose" is an identifier that this photo was taken in 1971. (Photo Courtesy Paul Schavrien)

In 1968, Frank Huszar, the owner of Race Car Specialties (RCS) in Tarzan, California, was commissioned by a young man to build a Junior Fuel dragster. With a deposit in hand, Huszar and his team, which included seasoned driver, Walt Stevens, got busy on the construction. However, the young man who commissioned the build quickly ran out of money, leaving Huszar with a partially built Junior Fueler. Then, Downey, California, resident Jack McCloud came into the picture.

McCloud had experience racing in Top Gas but was looking to step up to AA/Fuel Dragster. He swung a deal with Huszar to buy the car and convert it over to a AA/Fuel Dragster. To save himself some money, McCloud would come in after-hours and assist in the build. Tubing was swapped out, and several design changes were made. The rear end uprights were moved back 6 inches, and a float rear end was designed and created by McCloud and Paul Rick. The wheelbase was 184 inches, which was on the short side for a typical AA/FD of the period. Walt Stevens built canards that were mounted to the chassis in front of the slicks to provide additional downforce. After the chassis was complete, famed tin-man Tom Hanna formed the body panels.

McCloud, with help from his friends, built a stroked 460-ci Hemi. Power was transmitted through a two-disc Hays clutch that was tucked inside a Huszar aluminum "can" to an 8.75 Chrysler rear end. Best ETs were in the 7s at 220 mph.

After being restored, The Poachers rail's initial runs were made on an 86-percent load of nitro. (Photo Courtesy John Beard/ Paul Schavrien Collection)

Mike Kuhl built the cast-iron 392 engine, which features a brand-new, stock, stroked, billet crank, Brooks rods, pistons from Venolia Pistons, and a Mike Kuhl camshaft that was straight out of 1969. The Enderle injector and 6-71 blower was courtesy of Mike Kuhl. (Photo Courtesy Paul Schavrien)

of the hippie, he painted a red Vans shoe; on his left foot was a green Vans shoe. This is what McCloud himself often wore. Wrapping it all up was the image of a frog smoking from a hookah pipe.

As with many racers, McCloud had little money to run the car and only raced at local Southern California tracks. In 1970, he had another tin man, Kenny Ellis, added full body panels with a "lizard nose." Orval Cerny then painted the car candy red and black, with a candy blue border. According to Walt Stevens, Cerny was airbrushing the blue border and began at the nose of the car with a Dixie cup. He quickly abandoned that idea and used a 3x5 index card to finish air brushing the border.

Walt Stevens took over driving the car after McCloud, who loved his fire burnouts but suffered serious burns to his legs when the ritual went awry. Stevens drove the car through 1972, at which time McCloud decided to build a rear-engine dragster. *The Poachers* dragster was sold to a gentleman in Texas, who campaigned the car with a big-block Chevy for power in the Econo Rail category. Later, the car went to Florida, where its next owner raced it for several years, again with a big-block Chevy.

McCloud chose to name the car, *The Poachers*, because he was fond of poaching frogs at the time. He was also fond of taking an occasional puff of "the devil's weed." McCloud hired famed artist, Nat Quick to paint an image of a marijuana plant and a long-haired hippie with a knife in his hand on the car. On the right foot

With Mike Leach at the wheel,* The Poachers *rail is pushed off to fire. No expense was spared in this restoration. (Photo Courtesy Paul Schavrien)

The Poachers *rail belches nitro flames during in October 2014 during the Nitro Nights event in Escondido, California. (Photo Courtesy Pam Conrad)*

In 2000, the dragster was purchased by Tim Calhoun in Prairieville, Louisiana. At that time, the car was sporting rattle-can black paint. Calhoun began stripping the black paint, and underneath he found the original Cerny paint and lettering that striper Tom Kelly had applied.

In 2002, Calhoun hauled the dragster to the ninth-annual Hot Rod Reunion, where Stevens and Hanna verified that it was indeed the RCS-built *The Poachers* car. With this newfound information, Calhoun took the car home with the intention to restore it. Accessing what would be required, he quickly realized that it would take more money to complete the restoration than what he could afford.

In 2003, Calhoun listed the dragster on eBay. There, it was spotted by 16-year-old Ryan Schavrien. Ryan, the son of Pam and Paul Schavrien, rushed to tell his dad that he found a great father-and-son project. Paul never looked at the auction but told his son to buy it.

"Just don't spend too much money on it," Paul told Ryan.

Ryan won the auction and the journey began.

The Schavriens took delivery of the car in January 2004 and set the goal to have it completed in time for the Hot Rod Reunion in November. Work began by removing all the modern changes that had been made to the car, including the five-point roll cage. Bruce Dyda of Torrance, California, was brought in to perform the restoration. After collecting original parts needed to build a proper 392 engine, Paul handed the responsibility to his good friend, Mike Kuhl. Paul's intentions were to make full passes in the car, even though the NHRA disallowed it.

Tom Kelly painted and lettered the car, matching the original Mitch Kelly–applied paint. Kelly also mimicked the Nat Quick hippie artwork on the cowl.

Although it was behind schedule, *The Poachers* car made its debut at the Pomona finals in 2004. The car had participated in most of the Hot Rod Reunion events and entertained the crowds with epic half-track burnouts. It was just like it was 1969 all over again.

The Poachers car is no longer owned by the Schavrien family. It has passed through the hands of a few owners and today is owned by the Swanson family of Nebraska. Joel and Aaron Swanson brought it to Irwindale in November 2024 and entertained the fans once again.

Kuhl & Olson

The Kuhl & Olson Fueler features a 183-inch Woody Gilmore chassis. Seen here at the NHRA Springnationals in June 1971, the team debuted a new rear-engine dragster in August. (Photo Courtesy Carl Olson)

The story of the restored *Kuhl & Olson* Top Fuel dragster was graciously shared by Carl Olson. Olson relayed the story of how he and Mike Kuhl became one of the most feared Top Fuel teams of the era.

Carl Olson and Mike Kuhl made a formidable team during the early 1970s. Olson started driving Kuhl's car again at an Orange County International Raceway All-Pro event early in 1971, which he won. (Photo Courtesy Carl Olson)

In 1968, Kuhl was campaigning his second Top Fuel Dragster, a beautiful ride featuring a Woody Gilmore chassis, an aluminum body by Tom Hanna, paint by George Cerny Jr., and lettering by Nat Quick.

"Kuhl's chosen driver was 'Captain' Billy Tidwell, who had gained experience driving a Junior Fuel dragster," Olson said. "The pair enjoyed success, winning events at Lions, Irwindale, and Orange County. Unfortunately, in 1969, the car was destroyed in a crash at Lions after the engine exploded. Tidwell suffered non-life-threatening injuries, which put him out of action for some time."

Kuhl immediately commissioned an identical replacement car utilizing the services of the very same craftsmen. With Tidwell still recovering from his injuries, Kuhl secured the services of several drivers, including Olson, who ran two events over the Fourth of July weekend in 1970, before returning to his regular *Ewell-Bell-Olson* ride.

Eventually, Tidwell was medically cleared to return to action and once again joined Kuhl. Unfortunately, at the 1970 NHRA Nationals in Indianapolis, Tidwell experienced a parachute failure. He ran off the end of the track and impacted a television camera, which resulted in a broken collarbone and other injuries. Kuhl repaired the car and then secured the driving services of Dick Rosberg. The two raced primarily in Southern California.

In March 1971, Kuhl learned that Olson, who was then campaigning his own Top Fuel dragster, had crashed and destroyed the car at Fremont. Due to a falling out with Rosberg, Kuhl proposed that Olson could drive his car until Olson was able to put his own operation back together. Their first race was at the Orange County All Pro Series final, where Olson earned the pair a well-deserved win.

The pair immediately recognized that their talents complemented each other, and that it might be in their best interest to combine forces. The two competed together at several local events (winning several) and then traveled to Texas to participate in the NHRA

Don Thoren took ownership of the former Kuhl & Olson car. Here is competing at the March Meet at Bakersfield in March 1972. (Photo Courtesy Tom West/Lou Hart Collection)

The restored Kuhl & Olson *Fueler* debuted at the California Hot Rod Reunion in 2000. This was the first year for the "push-start cacklefest." Olson is behind the wheel. (Photo Courtesy Carl Olson)

Springnationals in Dallas. Olson qualified well and made it through several rounds of eliminations.

It was around the time of the Springnationals that Kuhl and Olson recognized that the rear-engine dragster was the future of Top Fuel racing and agreed to pool their resources and form a partnership. They met with Woody Gilmore, who agreed to build them a new rear-engine chassis.

"The front-engine car was put up for sale and was purchased, complete, by a gentleman named Don Thoren, who christened it *Plum Crazy*," Olson said. "Thoren campaigned the car until he ran out of funds. Thoren then sold the car (with no engine or drivetrain) to a racer named Dick Krieger, who modified it to accept a small-block Chevy engine and Powerglide transmission. Krieger had his own success with the combination, winning Comp Eliminator at the 1974 NHRA Sportsnationals and other events. He then turned to running the brackets with the car before selling it to a gentleman in El Centro, California. From there the car disappeared."

Around 1989, Kuhl decided to search for his old car.

"Because the name *El Centro* was the only information that he had to go on, he decided to make the drive from his shop in Santa Ana, three hours away in hopes of locating his old dragster," Olson said. "Kuhl checked on several businesses in town but was getting nowhere. He was about to give up when a local told him about a dragster that had been purchased by a friend of his. This friend had passed away before he had been able to get it running, and, to the best of his knowledge, it was sitting in the backyard of a local residence with nothing more than a tarp over it.

"Armed with the address, Kuhl immediately drove to the residence, where he was greeted by a woman who confirmed the presence of a dragster in her backyard. She knew little about it but referred Kuhl to a gentleman who she said would be able to answer his questions."

Kuhl contacted the gentleman but was unable to strike a deal for the car.

"He left the man his business card in hopes he would change his mind and then headed home," Olson said.

A few months passed and to Kuhl's surprise, the same gentleman pulled up to his shop with the dragster on a trailer. The man told Kuhl that if he could meet his price, the car and trailer would be his. With cash on hand, the deal was struck.

Kuhl, with the help of Darryl Woods, and longtime crew member, Don "Fats" MacKay, immediately began the process of restoring the car. Kuhl had Woody

Mike Kuhl restored his car in 1999. The 392 engine, which is belching flames at Escondido Nitro Nights in 2019, produces 2,500 hp. (Photo Courtesy Pam Conrad)

Gilmore restore the chassis to its original configuration, he commissioned talented fabricator Steve Davis to do the same with the body, and he had local artist "Swede" duplicate the original paintwork. While all of that work was taking place, Kuhl went to work building a period-correct, blown, nitro-burning 392 Hemi, adding the multi-disc clutch and completing the drivetrain.

Following a series of static appearances at various vintage drag racing events in the late 1990s, the car made its grand debut at the 2000 California Hot Rod Reunion at the Famoso Drag Strip near Bakersfield. There, Olson took the wheel and was one of the original nine restored or recreated cars to participate in the first push-start "cacklefest" exhibition.

Following Kuhl's passing in 2020, the car appeared at a handful of events until it was finally put on permanent display at the Lions Drag Strip Museum in Rancho Dominguez, California.

This dragster is shown in Columbus in 2004. It was originally painted by George Cerny Jr., and lettered by Nat Quick. When Mike Kuhl restored it (because Cerny Jr. had passed away), it was painted and lettered by David Earle "Swede" Savage. (Photo Courtesy Carl Olson)

Walton, Cerny, & Moody

The Walton, Cerny & Moody *Don Long car featured a 224-inch chassis. A Cerny tuned, iron-block, 426 Keith Black Hemi powered the car. (Photo Courtesy Rich Carlson/Grant Bittner Collection)*

The rear-engine dragster configuration had been around since the beginning of the sport. However, it took until 1971, when guys such as Bernie Schacker, Duane Ong, and Don Garlits found success, that the rear-engine configuration really took hold. One of the more successful rear-engine cars of the period was the Don Long–chassied car that was campaigned by Doug Walton, Wes Cerny, and Don Moody.

The 1972 season didn't get off to a great start for Walton, Cerny, and Moody. They debuted a new car at the NHRA Winternationals but an engine explosion put them out of commission. The car was repaired and sold to the team of Creitz, Dill, and Brown, and a new Don Long car was built. It took until the AHRA National Challenge race over Labor Day weekend before the team saw success. With Don Moody behind the wheel, the team won the event and the $25,000 that went with it by defeating Dennis Baca in the final with a 6.21 ET at 229 mph. Until this point, this was the largest payout in drag racing history.

The Supernationals in November would feature drag racing's first class-legal 5-second pass. Mike Snively in "Diamond" Jim Annin's Fueler hit a 5.97 ET in a semifinal loss to Vic Brown, who ran a 6.03 ET in the *Creitz & Dill* car. In round two, Moody was extremely close, running a 6.005 ET to defeat Gary Beck. In the semifinals, Moody backpedaled with a 6.01 ET at 202 mph to defeat a broken Carl Olson. In the final round against Brown, Moody let it all hang out, recording a 5.91 ET at 235.91 mph for the victory.

At the Last Drag Race at Lions Drag Strip on December 2, fans hoping for drag racing's first 5-second pass had to settle for Moody's 6.02 ET. This was the event's low ET and the last Top Fuel track record for Lions Drag Strip.

Car owner Wes Cerny sold the car at the end of 1973. Moody's last pass was a single at Orange County International Raceway, where he rolled the car, damaging the wing and scraping the chassis. The repairs were made to the car before it was sold to Larry Sorg.

According to research performed by Bill Schneider, Sorg campaigned the dragster through 1978. A falling out with his racing partners led to a lawsuit that resulted in the Tom Hanna–built body and Don Long chassis being separated. Sorg retained the chassis and had Hal Canode build a new body. In a turn of events, a later lawsuit saw the body and trailer returned to Sorg, but the body was never reunited with the chassis. According to Schneider, the last pass that the chassis made (with the new body) was in 1988. That ended with a blown engine.

The car sat in Sorg's barn for the next 10 years before he sold it at a swap meet to Mike McGee, who campaigned it briefly as a bracket car. Sorg retained the original Hanna body.

Jim Bell was the next owner of the dragster, and he sold it in 1996 to an unknown buyer. However, Bell recalled seeing the car for sale in a 1998 edition of *National Dragster* magazine.

So, Schneider, now joined by Sorg and Hal Canode poured over editions of *National Dragster* magazine in search of the advertisement. The advertisement was found and had been placed by Chicago's Kevin Connor. Schneider called the phone number that was listed in the ad, but it was no longer in service. At that point, Schneider reached out to Phil Burgess at *National Dragster*

Larry Sorg campaigned the old Walton, Cerny, & Moody *car through 1978. Sorg had his own success with the car running in events from multiple sanctioning bodies.*

Current owner Hal Sanguinetti loves to share the history of the **Walton, Cerny & Moody** *car, and he cackles it wherever possible—from Arizona high schools to Nitro Night (shown here) in Escondido. (Photo Courtesy Marc Gewertz)*

Outside of the side panel on the **Walton, Cerny, & Moody** *car, the paint remains 1972 fresh. (Photo Courtesy Hal Sanguinetti)*

Inside, the seat is original and unpadded—just as George Cerny Jr. liked it. The seat belt is also original. It's also believed that the butterfly steering wheel is original to the car. The oil-pressure gauge was an add-on by the current owner. (Photo Courtesy Hal Sanguinetti)

magazine. It was through Burgess that they were able to locate Connor, who was a Division 3 racer and still owned the dragster. The authenticity of the car was verified with the help of Don Long.

The chassis, which was now together with the original body, was purchased by Hal Sanguinetti, who proceeded to restore the car in 2016 with help from many people, including Andi Huminek and those at Don Long's shop. Today, the car retains 90 percent of its original tubing, with changes coming when the modern roll cage was removed.

"Double A" Dale Armstrong built the Hemi not for cackling but for racing. A new steel block was procured from Chrysler, which was fitted with Venolia rods and pistons, and the crankshaft was courtesy of Michigan's Ramchargers. Parts came from every corner of the nation; a new, unused magnesium Cragar blower manifold was found in Ohio, a period-correct Mallory Super Mag 1 was found in Pennsylvania, and, Mark Engle at Engle Cams in California provided a camshaft with the proper specifications.

Sorg provided the original headers and push bar. When it was all buttoned up, Armstrong made it clear that this engine would turn a 5.91 ET, just as it had in 1972. Sadly, Armstrong passed away before having the opportunity to hear the motor run. This was the last fuel engine that was built by Armstrong.

Outside of the two magnesium side panels that were damaged, the car retains the original Cerny orange that was applied in 1972. The completed car debuted in 2017 at Rick Lorenzen's museum in Long Beach, California.

The Hemi was built by famed Comp racer Dale Armstrong. It is cackled on a 90-percent load of fuel. (Photo Courtesy Hal Sanguinetti)

The restored car is all but buttoned up in this late 2017 photo. Many people were involved with the restoration of this significant piece of drag racing history. (Photo Courtesy Hal Sanguinetti)

CHAPTER TWO

FUNNY CARS

THESE CARS EVOLVED QUICKLY, AND IN SHORT ORDER, ALTERED WHEELBASES, BLOWERS, AND NITROMETHANE BECAME THE RULE RATHER THAN THE EXCEPTION.

The Funny Car category was born out of the Stock class, match-race cars of the early 1960s. These cars evolved quickly, and, in short order, altered wheelbases, blowers, and nitromethane became the rule rather than the exception. In 1965, the term "funny car" was born to describe these radical-looking cars.

In 1966, the first flip-top body, tube-chassis Funny Cars appeared, and a category was established. Unlike today, they weren't all powered by a derivative of the Chrysler Hemi. In the 1960s, when brand loyalty meant a lot more than it does today, a Chevy usually was powered by a Chevy and a Ford was powered by a Ford. Of course, there were always exceptions to the rule.

Above: The Chi-Town Hustler *1972 Dodge Challenger was restored in 1997 by Bob Gibson. The racing team was one of the sport's most popular, consisting of Austin Coil, John Farkonas, and Pat Minick. (Photo Courtesy Bob Gibson)*

Dodge Chargers

The exhibition **Dodge Chargers** *cars of 1964 were built for Dodge by Dragmaster's Dode Martin and Jim Nelson. Blown 480-ci Wedge engines powered the cars. (Photo Courtesy Richard Kinistry)*

Many claim (and few will argue) that the first Funny Car appeared in March 1964 in the form of Chrysler's three supercharged Dodge Chargers. Promoter Don Beebe can take credit for selling Chrysler on the idea of placing a Gas Dragster engine in a stock-body sedan. With a reported budget of $250,000, the build of these cars was left to the trusted hands of Jim Nelson and Dode Martin of Dragmaster in Carlsbad, California.

When completed, the cars were nearly identical, right down to the blown 480-ci Max Wedge engines. Once the driveline was installed, famed customizer Dean Jefferies went to work on the bodies. He added front and rear rolled pans, enlarged the rear wheel openings for tire clearance, cut an opening in the hood and scoop for blower clearance, and created a rear opening for the drag chute. Jefferies then applied the eye-catching candy red paint and blue and white stripes. Although the story of the Dodge Chargers is confusing, it's believed that a fourth car was built after the third car was smashed into a bridge while it was parked on the top tier of a car hauler. That fourth car was said to have ended up in the hands of drag racer Charlie Allen, who used it as a display in his Chrysler dealership decades ago. Historians doubt that this car has survived. The photos in this chapter of the

Two **Dodge Chargers** *prepare for an exhibition pass on opening day at Tucson Dragway (April 12, 1964). Out of the gate, the cars recorded 10-second ETs at 140 mph. (Photo Courtesy J. R. Bloom)*

"FARMER" BESWICK'S PONTIAC TEAM
DRAG RACING
SEPTEMBER 1964 50c
Why The FIFTH WHEEL?
Action at DETROIT SAN DIEGO LAS VEGAS
Can the FOUR-SPEED be SAVED?
16 PAGES OF FULL COLOR!
A-B-C's of Dealer Sponsorship

A Dodge Chargers *car's Diest drag chute flies in the breeze after another successful run. This is the cover of the September 1964 issue of* Drag Racing *magazine. Many people acknowledged that the* Dodge Chargers *cars were drag racing's first Funny Cars.*

restored car are believed to show the second car that was built, which was driven by Jimmy Nix.

The Chargers fit no existing drag racing class and were usually driven side by side on exhibition runs by Nix and Jim Johnson. The cars were a sight to behold. Low-11-second, smoke-filled ETs at 140 mph were capped off by the deployment of the Deist red, white, and blue parachute.

The Dodge Chargers seemed to open the floodgates for blown exhibition stock-bodied cars. Jack Chrisman ushered in the days of mid-10-second, 150-mph Stockers when he unleashed his blown, nitro-fed, 427-equipped Comet in the summer of 1964. Many more soon followed.

By August, the team of Nix and Johnson ran out of spare parts and money. They were cannibalizing the Johnson car to keep the Nix car running. At the same time, they were cutting into Johnson's car with the intention to install a Hemi to take on Chrisman.

The last showing for the remaining Dodge Charger was in August. Shortly after, Dodge recalled the cars. Some say that this was due to the fact that Chrisman was showing up at tracks the Dodge Charger was booked to run and embarrassing Dodge by running quicker ETs.

In 1965, the team of Bud Roche and Don Mattison bought the two cars from Dodge. They completed one build with a nitromethane-fed 392 Hemi and direct drive, which managed a reported best ET of 10.20 at 150 mph. The *Guzler* Charger, as they had branded the car, was believed to have been Dodge Charger number one. As the *Guzler*, the car's life was short-lived. It was destroyed in a crash at Cordova in August at the World Series of Drag Racing. Roche and Mattison had enough of the Dodge Chargers and sold off the remaining parts of the car.

Skip ahead to 1980, and Tom Jones had got wind of the remaining car. In a *Hot Rod* magazine article, Tom said that he had heard about a broken and abused 1964

This is how the sole remaining Dodge Chargers *car appeared in 1988. The owner wasn't sure about what he had. (Photo Courtesy Frank Spittle)*

A little scraping of the paint on the roof revealed the blue stripes from the car's* Dodge Chargers *days. The tinted windows were added at some point after 1965. (Photo Courtesy Frank Spittle)

"I wasn't sure what it was until I started removing paint and revealed the colors," Jones said.

Jimmy Nix confirmed that the car was the Dodge Charger he had driven. When the parts ran out, Nix had torn into the car with the intention of going the same route as Johnson. This, of course, was before Chrysler retrieved the cars.

Jones initiated the restoration on the survivor, taking it as far as prepping the body for paint before funds ran low. The car went on the auction block and was purchased by music promoter C. K. Spurlock.

Spurlock owned the Dodge Charger for the next 9 years, making further progress on the restoration. He added the candy paint and stripes as well as a Brad Anderson–built 480-ci engine. With the restoration nearly 75 percent complete, the car was sold to Frank Spittle. Spittle had tried to buy the car at the time Jones was selling it but was outbid by Spurlock. Spittle told Spurlock at the time that if he ever wanted to sell it, to give him a call. That call came in 1996.

Dodge 330 sedan that was resting 30 miles from his Madison, Wisconsin, home. He also heard vague rumors from local gearheads about the car's distant past as some sort of factory race car, after which it ran ET brackets in the Midwest and Canada.

In the same article, Jones said, "The previous owner had the car for 13 years. It came with a 440 and a 4-speed. He ran it one time, around 1975, and broke an axle. He replaced the axles, but before he could get back to the track, someone broke in and stole his cylinder heads."

The car didn't move again until Jones purchased it in 1988.

"I'm one of the lucky ones who was around for the birth of the Funny Car, so I couldn't believe that one of the original cars still existed," Spittle said.

Spittle completed the restoration around 2007. In 2018, he was offered more for the car than he could refuse and sold it to Gary Kuck of Nebraska.

This* Dodge Chargers *car is a significant piece of drag racing history. It is also believed to be the last Max Wedge–powered car that Dodge built. (Photo Courtesy Frank Spittle)

Chevamoco

The Chevamoco *took on a few different guises during its tenure as a drag car. This image is from around 1968, and the car features its second paint job/color. The front magnesium wheels are still with the car. (Photo Courtesy David Paine)*

Bobby Lagana Sr. chose to join the Funny Car fray in 1966, when he built the Chevamoco match-race car. Lagana Sr. had a fondness for Chevys, and when the manufacturer introduced its new 427 engine in the fall of 1965, he was all in. Lagana Sr. wasn't the only family member afflicted with the drag race addiction. His brother Bill also was knee-deep in the sport. He had campaigned a match-race 1963 Impala before he landed a deal with Mercury in 1964 to campaign an A/FX 427-Wedge-head Comet. Bill eventually went the match-race route with the Comet, altering the wheelbase and adding fuel injection.

It was Lagana Sr.'s altered Comet that influenced his choice as to where to plant his 427 Chevy. Now, if you haven't figured it out by the name "Chevamoco," Lagana Sr. decided to use a lightweight Ford Falcon. Before taking on fellow match bashers, both the Falcon and Chevy were going to need some reworking.

There was no need to dig deep into the Chevy, as from the factory it was built with pretty stout parts. Lagana Sr. added the Enderle short-stack injection and ran straight alcohol. Lighting the fire was a Vertex magneto. Out the gate, ETs were in the mid-10s and the top speeds were close to 140 mph. Lagana Sr. trialed a mix of fuel, consisting of 85-percent nitro, 10-percent alcohol, and 5-percent hydrazine

After sitting in the elements for 30 years, the Chevamoco *was in rough condition. However, it was amazing how complete the car was when it was discovered. (Photo Courtesy Randy Dunlap)*

Nothing was left untouched during the restoration. Previous repairs, including a new roof, were revisited. At this stage, the Chevamoco *is nearly ready for paint. (Photo Courtesy Randy Dunlap)*

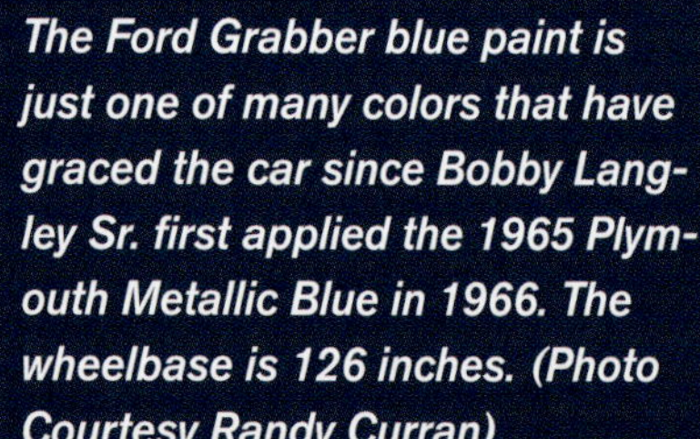

The Ford Grabber blue paint is just one of many colors that have graced the car since Bobby Langley Sr. first applied the 1965 Plymouth Metallic Blue in 1966. The wheelbase is 126 inches. (Photo Courtesy Randy Curran)

The Chevamoco *appears just as Bobby Langley Sr. raced it back in the 1960s. Although the interior was restored, the aluminum firewall was left as is. Just visible is the gas pedal, which is a Ludwig bass drum pedal. (Photo Courtesy Randy Curran)*

In place of the original 427 Chevy engine is a 496-ci big-block. This image shows how far back the engine sits. (Photo Courtesy Randy Curran)

(the highly unstable additive). He was awarded with a hair-raising run that was said to net him 198 mph and a barrel full of exploded 427 parts. Expelling the spent gases from a now-fresh engine were a set of 1-7/8-inch "weed burners" that Lagana Sr. fabricated himself. Backing the Chevy was a Muncie transmission and a relocated Ford 9-inch rear with 4.57 gears. Suspending the rear were leaf springs and a fabricated set of traction arms.

The body itself, a recovered rolled wreck, was straightened and stripped to the bare minimum as a means of dropping weight. The chassis was boxed and extended forward of the firewall. A straight axle was installed, and over the few years that Lagana Sr. campaigned the car, it was bumped up to where it could be seen today. The engine was set back into the cowl, requiring a new firewall be fabricated.

Lagana Sr. sold the *Chevamoco* at the end of the 1968 season to a local racer but continued to help with the tuning. Like most old drag cars, this one switched hands numerous times. Somewhere along the way, it ended up in Michigan. In 2001, it was discovered by the brothers Jim and Spanky Sandlin. The pair had been hunting for an old drag car when they came across the remains of the *Chevamoco* while checking out a Ford Thunderbolt. Although the Falcon was rough from years of sitting out in the elements, it was remarkably complete. All of the key parts were there, including the front and rear suspension, wheels, and even the seats. Everything was ready to be refurbished.

As the car went through numerous changes during the years in which Lagana Sr. raced it, the brothers chose to incorporate various facets at each stage. Lightning's Custom can take credit for restoring the body, chassis, and applying the paint. Steve "Freakin" Fairman recreated the lettering.

Sadly, both Lagana Sr. and Spanky Sandlin passed before the restoration was completed. The car was sold to Randy Dunlap by Spanky's brother Jim, and the restoration was completed.

From the rear, we can see how the rear Lexan window has been drilled out to relieve air pressure. The same goes for the taillights. (Photo Courtesy Bob Wenzelburger)

Tiger II

Jimmy and Andy Adcock built this Tiger II *Chevelle at their A&B Machine Shop and match raced it extensively throughout the Southern states in 1965 and 1966. (Photo Courtesy Connell Miller)*

Jimmy Alcock had a hankering to join the growing match-race Stocker scene, so he built himself a 1965 Chevelle. Now, don't be confused by the 1964 Chevelle fiberglass front clip. The 1965-model Chevelle was so new when Alcock went to work that no 1965 Chevelle fiberglass parts were available.

Experimental Stock was the early form of the Funny Car category. Power at this point was provided by a Dickie Harrell 427 engine. (Photo Courtesy Dave Giles)

The *Tiger II* came by way of Plains Chevrolet in Amarillo, Texas. Interestingly enough, Alcock received the car as a rolling chassis direct from the assembly line. It has never had a VIN, and there was never any paperwork assigned to the car. It was an unusual way to receive a car from the factory in 1965, but it became a fairly common practice in the beginning days of Pro Stock.

The bare bones of the Tiger II *were good, but when it was found, the Chevelle needed a significant amount of work. Owner Dave Giles had to think twice on this one. (Photo Courtesy Dave Giles)*

The restoration of the Tiger II was not a high-dollar operation. The majority of work was performed by Dave Giles, his wife, and his daughter in their home garage. (Photo Courtesy Tommy Lee Byrd)

The metal body panels and the original Fibercraft fiberglass parts needed attention prior to the paint being applied. The front wheels are rare American Racing magnesium spindle mounts. (Photo Courtesy Tommy Lee Byrd)

Changes came quickly in the early days of Funny Car, and the *Tiger II* was no exception. Alcock initially campaigned the Chevelle with a stock wheelbase, supported by a straight-axle front end and a leaf-spring-supported Pontiac rear end. In NHRA-legal competition, the *Tiger II* was campaigned in the NHRA's B/Experimental Stock class. By the end of the season, the rear suspension had been shifted forward. Powering the Chevelle through the first year was an Enderle-injected, 376-ci small-block Chevy that was running on a 30-percent load of nitromethane.

At the close of the 1965 season, Alcock hauled the Chevelle to T-Bar Chassis in Dallas to have an altered-wheelbase tube chassis fabricated for the car. This is in the books as possibly the first full-tube-chassis, center-steer Funny Car that was built. During the winter break, the Chevelle was stripped of excess weight. Fiberglass doors and a fiberglass decklid were added along with a Lexan rear window.

Around the same time, the 376-ci engine gave way to a Hilborn-injected 427 that was running on a load of fuel anywhere from 85 to 95 percent. Dick Harrell supplied a fresh engine after he destroyed the existing engine while out on a trial run.

To keep the car competitive, Alcock removed additional weight. The B-pillars were part of the second round of weight reduction, and it gives the car the look of a hardtop. At the same time, the paint went from gold to blue, and the *Tiger II* name was dropped in favor of *Blitzer*. The quickest and fastest run that the car produced, as Alcock recalled, was an ET in the 8.90s at 165 mph. Alcock tried a GMC blower on nitro during one test session late in 1967, but the NHRA refused to allow the combination. Alcock parted out the Chevelle shortly after.

Alcock sold the engine to future NHRA announcer, Dave McClelland, who dropped the engine into a flat-bottom boat. The body ended up in the hands of J. C. Sizemore of Alabama, and it last raced in 1973 as the *Funny Money* of Jerry Rhodes.

In 2006, Tennessee-resident David Giles found the car in Alabama. Giles went to look at some old-style magnesium wheels that were for sale. Discovering a set of spindle-mount rims, Giles asked the seller where the rest of the Funny Car was. The seller responded that it was just down the road. The pair took a drive and viewed the remains of the *Tiger II*, which were sitting out in someone's backyard. Giles made an offer, the seller accepted it, and Giles hauled the car home.

The car was rough from years of neglect and abuse. Feeling overwhelmed by the immensity of the project, Giles sold the car. However, he would regret that decision.

The Tiger II is now powered by a punched-out 427 that now measures 439 ci. Internals include a Velasco crankshaft, a Comp Cams camshaft, and 13.5:1 compression. (Photo Courtesy Tommy Lee Byrd)

In 2018, when the opportunity to buy it arose, he jumped at it.

The restoration was a painstaking endeavor that was made easier with the help of his wife, Stephanie, and his daughter Faith. Thankfully, the key pieces of the car remained, although everything needed to be freshened.

The dashboard's aluminum inserts are original pieces, and they were cleaned by Faith, who also cut and shaped all-new aluminum interior panels. When it came to the body, the original Fibercraft panels needed a lot of attention, and new quarter panels were required. The paint was matched as closely as possible using scrapings of the original color that were found on the car. Trick Paint & Custom in Washington did flawless body prep and applied the House of Kolor, gold metal-flake paint over the silver base.

The aluminum panels within the dashboard are original. The seat is by Fibercraft. Controlling the Turbo-400 transmission is a Hurst shifter. (Photo Courtesy Tommy Lee Byrd)

The metal-flake paint really pops in the daylight. Restoration of the Chevelle was completed in 2023. (Photo Courtesy Tommy Lee Byrd)

Chevoom

The year 1966 was a year of transition for the so-called Funny Cars. Fiberglass bodies and tube chassis became the norm. The 1966 Chevelle of Maynard Rupp, which is shown here, was impressive. (Photo Courtesy James Handy)

Maynard Rupp, the 1965 NHRA Top Fuel World Champion, caught some fans by surprise when he retired his fuel dragster and built himself a match-race Funny Car for the 1966 season. Rupp had worked at Logghe Chassis and was one who could think outside of the box. So, when it came to building his own match-race car, it was going to be something unique.

Rupp chose to build a Chevy because it was the most popular brand with the spectators. Instead of using the popular Chevy II bodystyle, Rupp went with the longer-wheelbase Chevelle. The all-fiberglass Chevelle was laid up by Dayton, Ohio's B&N Fiberglass using a new 1966 Chevelle as a plug (a model that is used to make a mold). Bob Marianich at the Carriage Shop prepped the body, applied the Mooneyes yellow paint, and installed the tin work. To finish off the body, Paul Hutton did the lettering.

Going against the grain of running an engine that was the same brand as the car, Rupp used an early Chrysler 354-ci Hemi. What really made Rupp's setup unique was that the Hemi wasn't placed under the hood. Instead, it was mounted where the rear seat was usually located. Rupp's theory was that the mid-engine configuration would aid in traction. Another advantage was that he would not have to suffer like he did in the fuel dragster with the engine blowing up in his face.

The car featured an Art Carr TorqueFlite transmission and a solid-mounted Chrysler rear end that rode on a 2x3 rectangular cradle. The cradle was bolted to the round chromoly tube chassis. The length of the drivetrain pushed the rear end farther back, helping to grow the Chevelle's wheelbase from the factory's 115 inches to 128 inches. The front suspension consisted of a tube axle located 4 inches forward (compared to the stock configuration) and was supported by a transverse leaf spring and torsion bars.

Rupp debuted the Chevelle in January at the Detroit Autorama, where the engineering marvel earned the Best in Show Ridler Award. At its NHRA Winternationals debut the following month, the Chevelle won the Best Engineered Car award. The

This is how the Chevelle appeared after sitting for 20 years. Ken Bigham, the current owner, hired Greg Cook at Cook's Restorations in Gettysburg, Pennsylvania, to do the restoration. (Photo Courtesy Bob Snyder)

The restored cradle and chassis are mated together, and they await the body. The workmanship was second to none. (Photo Courtesy Greg Cook)

Bob Foote of Cook's Restorations was responsible for a substantial part of the restoration. (Photo Courtesy Greg Cook)

The restored Chevoom *rides on timeless Cragar S/S wheels. It harks back to a more innovative era of drag racing. With Moon Equipment as a sponsor, it was appropriate to paint the car yellow.*

Only the bare necessaries were used, including a bank of gauges, toggle switches, a Hurst shifter, and a Moon fuel pedal. The ring (shown below the steering wheel) is the release for the Diest drag chute. (Photo Courtesy Greg Cook)

Chevelle competed in Experimental Stock and recorded a reported best ET in the 8.40s at more than 170 mph.

Although the Chevelle was loved by the fans, it failed to meet Rupp's expectations and was sold at the end of the 1966 season. He moved into an STP-sponsored flip-top Cougar Funny Car in 1967, and the Chevelle was sold to a buyer in Ohio. Apparently, the new owner blew the engine and parked the Chevelle. It sat outside until the 1980s, when it was purchased by the current owner, Ken Bigham. In 2017, the Chevelle was finally restored by Cook's Restorations.

Maynard Rupp was speechless when he first viewed the finished restoration in 2017. (Photo Courtesy Greg Cook)

Kenz & Leslie Comet

Funny Cars (as we know them today), with their flip-up bodies and tube chassis, first appeared in 1966 when Mercury released its revolutionary Comets. The team of Kenz & Leslie hailed from Wheat Ridge, Colorado, and ruled the High Country in their Comet. (Photo Courtesy Randy Hernandez)

Unlike Ford, which supported drag racing as far back as 1962, Lincoln-Mercury didn't enter the game until 1964. Who would have thought that, in just a few short years, they would revolutionize the sport? In 1966, they did just that by introducing the first tube-chassis, flip-top Funny Car. Immediately, the design made all existing renditions of the Funny Car obsolete.

Mercury dished up four flip-top cars to their assigned drivers: Don Nicholson, Jack Chrisman, the team of Ed Schartman and Roy Steffey, and the Colorado-based team of Bill Kenz and Roy Leslie.

Based upon the Comet's bodystyle, these Funny Cars were the brainchild of Chrisman. The pair was conversing with Gene Mooneyham one night in 1964 about the success that Chrysler was having with their altered-wheelbase cars.

"If we set the engine back like Mooneyham's 25 percent with a tube chassis and a fiberglass body on it, we would kick their ass!" Turner said.

That was the beginning of the whole thing. The following year, Chrisman returned with his rebuilt Comet carrying a Cammer that was set back in the chassis 25 percent. The Comet Funny Cars of 1966 were a natural progression.

The Logghe brothers, Ron and Gene, were hired to build the tube chassis, retaining the Comet's 116-inch wheelbase. Plastigage Corp. of Jackson, Michigan, was hired to form the required bodies, doing so by using a design plug that was provided by Mercury. The initial plan for the Comets was to have the bodies lift off, but when the shells returned from Plastigage, they were heavier than expected. It was Ron Logghe who came up with the idea of hinging the bodies at the rear, thus creating the flip-up design.

The team of Kenz & Leslie should be familiar to anyone who knows automotive racing history. The pair teamed up in the mid-1950s and was successful in

Kenz & Leslie's success led to the team receiving a new Comet in 1967. Refinements to the new model spurred further success. (Photo Courtesy Randy Hernandez)

Although it may seem primitive by today's standards, this setup was great in 1967. The Cammer engine was designed for NASCAR use, but when it was banned, it found a home on the drag strip. (Photo Courtesy Randy Hernandez)

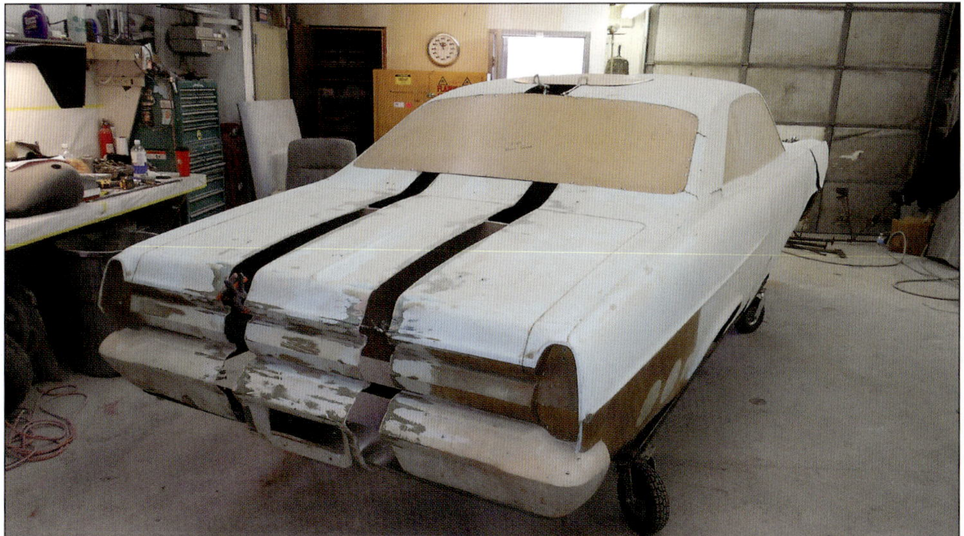
Ken Godsey took on the task that few would have dared. (Photo Courtesy Ken Godsey)

everything from the Pikes Peak Hill Climb to the Bonneville Salt Flats. Their 1966 Comet is said to be the first Funny Car based in Colorado. It was a great season for the pair, as they also campaigned a Top Fuel dragster. They entered several eliminations programs with the two cars and rarely lost at home. At the NHRA World Finals, Ron would qualify the Comet number one, but an ensuing on-track accident ended his weekend and all but destroyed the Comet. Their season-long success ensured that a new car would come from Mercury in 1967.

The new Comet featured several upgrades. For starters, the Logghe chassis featured a four-point roll cage as opposed to last year's roll bar, which made it a safer ride. In addition, the engine was located 5 inches farther rearward to improve traction. The body, which was reported to be 50 pounds lighter in 1967, sat lower on the chassis, and the drip-rail moldings were removed to improve stability at increased speeds. Kenz & Leslie stayed closer to home in 1967, where they equaled their previous season's success.

Mercury produced seven Comet Funny Cars in 1967. Today, only four of them survive. Out of the four, only two have been restored: Jack Chrisman's *GT1*, and the *Kenz & Leslie* car that is featured here. Ken Godsey is responsible for restoring the car, which was made easier by the involvement of Roy Leslie, who shared priceless information and donated numerous original parts.

The story of this restoration began years ago when Godsey purchased

Although the shade of gold that initially covered the car was long forgotten, Godsey was lucky to locate a spot that was seemingly untouched by time. Bob Skidmore matched it up and did a magnificent job of painting the car. (Photo Courtesy Ken Godsey)

With the body finally on the Logghe chassis, Godsey couldn't resist taking a photo of the car lined up with the John Petrie* BP Experimental *Comet. The Petrie Comet is in the process of being restored in Canada. (Photo Courtesy Ken Godsey)

This restoration of the 777 car was completed with the help of the original owner, Roy Leslie. Of the seven Mercury Funny Cars that were produced in 1967, four remain today: Jack Chrisman's* GT1, *Howard Neal's* Stripteaser 4, *the John Petrie car, and this one. (Photo Courtesy Ken Godsey)

the John Petrie 1967 Comet body shell from Roy Leslie. Roy figured that Godsey could restore the shell and build the car as the *Kenz & Leslie* Comet. After discovering the history of the Petrie car, Mercury's lone Canadian Comet Funny Car, Godsey couldn't bring himself to do it. Thankfully, he had a friend in Earl Wade, who was "Dyno" Don Nicholson's old crew chief. By chance, Wade informed Godsey that he knew where the *Kenz & Leslie* body was. So, Godsey scooped it up. Wade really came through when he put Godsey in touch with the Nicholson family, who was doing a bit of cleaning house after "Dyno" Don passed. They also happened to have an original 1967 Logghe chassis for the car.

The restoration really took off in 2014, and the aim was to complete the car by 2016 in time for the NHRA's 50th anniversary celebration of the birth of the flip-top Funny Car. Yes, Godsey had his work cut out for him. At some point in the car's past, a previous owner had narrowed the shell by cutting nearly a foot out of the middle of it. The idea was to narrow the car and build it to compete in AA/FC, but that was as far as that dream went. Thankfully, Godsey still had the John Petrie shell to pull all the measurements from.

With a date to keep, Ken and the Godsey family got busy. Once the body was straightened, Bob Skidmore was called on to duplicate the paint. That was a chore because no one knew what the original color was. Godsey got

Although the Cammer was not completed at this point, it is back right where it belongs. Roy Leslie was invaluable when it came to restoring the car, donating the Cammer, and providing numerous original parts. (Photo Courtesy Ken Godsey)

The tow wagon and trailer give the impression that it's 1967 all over again. One would be hard pressed to find a restoration as exact as this one. (Photo Courtesy Ken Godsey)

lucky and found a spot of original, untouched paint that remained under the headlight covers. Once the paint was dry, John Pugh pulled out the brush and applied the lettering. As the inside tin was long gone and all of the tin in the Mercurys was identical, Godsey pulled the Petrie tinwork and had Jerry Fitz duplicate it.

When it came to the SOHC 427, Roy Leslie, who was just as eager to see the project through, donated the fresh engine. Included in the package was an ultra-rare set (only five sets were made) of aluminum heads. Leslie supplied plenty of original parts he had tucked away, including the unique shifter, B&M transmission, steering wheel, and several other goodies.

Godsey buttoned up the Comet and met his self-imposed deadline. At the 50th-anniversary show, the *Kenz & Leslie* Comet was a hit.

A Pair from Larry Coleman

In 1966, Larry Coleman took over the long-nose Mustang of Ford drag racing boss Dick Brannan. Later, Hubert Platt successfully raced it. (Photo Courtesy Jim Wright/Dean Kirsten Collection)

The Memphis area had a nickname in drag-racing circles that referred to the local racing scene. The "Memphis Mafia" nickname was fitting for guys such as cam guru Joe Lunati and engineer Larry Coleman, who started Coleman-Taylor Transmission with his brother-in-law Bill Taylor.

In 1961, Coleman and Taylor opened their first shop. In 1969, the business split when Taylor began running the converter side of the business, which was called Torque Converters Inc. (TCI).

Coleman had been campaigning a 1965 Plymouth before purchasing a long-nose Mustang from Ford's head of drag racing, Dick Brannan. Brannan previously crashed an experimental altered-wheelbase Mustang, and the Ford brass wanted him out from behind the wheel. The long-nose Mustang was one of six that were built for Ford by Holman-Moody, specifically for drag racing. The cars featured a 2x3 chromoly chassis that extended the front by 14 inches—hence, the long-nose moniker. Each car was fitted with a unique, twisted-leaf front suspension. The rear suspension was moved 10 inches forward and consisted of a 9-inch rear end supported by leaf springs and adjustable traction arms. To help the 11-inch slicks grip the track, the Cammer was set back in the chassis.

Brannan put Hubert Platt in the Mustang before selling the car to Coleman. Platt continued to drive the car into the spring of 1967 earning wins at the 1966 AHRA Nationals, the 1967 NHRA Winternationals (A/XS), and the NASCAR Summernationals. Others who drove the Mustang for Coleman include Sidney Foster and Del Heinelt.

The Mustang was raced 52 weeks out of the year and up to 3 times a week. With pay-outs for these matches being an easy $500 to $800 per event, there was money to be made. This went on through mid-1968, with the biggest win coming at a 23-car show at Lakeland International Raceway. On the program were the nation's best flip-top Funny Cars. Driver Del Heinelt beat them all to win the $1,200 payout. Coleman could see the writing on the wall for the aging Mustang, and at that same race, he bought the flip-top 1967 Mustang of Steve McKesson. Tragically, Heinelt lost his life in the car at the NHRA Nationals on his first qualifying pass. Having lost

The long-nose Mustang weighs 2,400 pounds, which was approximately 1,000 pounds less than the 1965 A/FX Mustang. In the future, plans are for the Mustang to make some easy quarter-mile passes. (Photo Courtesy Nick Coleman)

The most exotic engine ever produced by an American automobile manufacture was the SOHC 427. The engine propelled the Mustang to mid-8-second ETs. Brent Hajek had this one built. (Photo Courtesy Nick Coleman)

The Mustang features a steel shell with fiberglass panels. Larry Coleman Enterprises lives on today as Coleman-Taylor Transmission. (Photo Courtesy Nick Coleman)

his desire to race after the incident, Coleman sold the long-nose Mustang to Clester Andrews.

With some convincing from Larry Reyes, and support from Ford, Coleman built himself a new 1969 Torino Funny Car and put Sidney Foster behind the wheel. It was a very unique car, as there were only three of these bodies produced by Fiberglass Ltd., and just two of them were raced. Phil Bonner campaigned the other one.

Coleman's Torino featured an SOHC 427 engine, Logghe chassis, and tin by Al Bergler. Like the long-nose Mustang before it, the Torino saw a lot of action, with Foster (and occasionally Larry Reyes) racing up to 50 weeks out of the year. The Torino is reported to be the first Ford Funny Car to crack 200 mph.

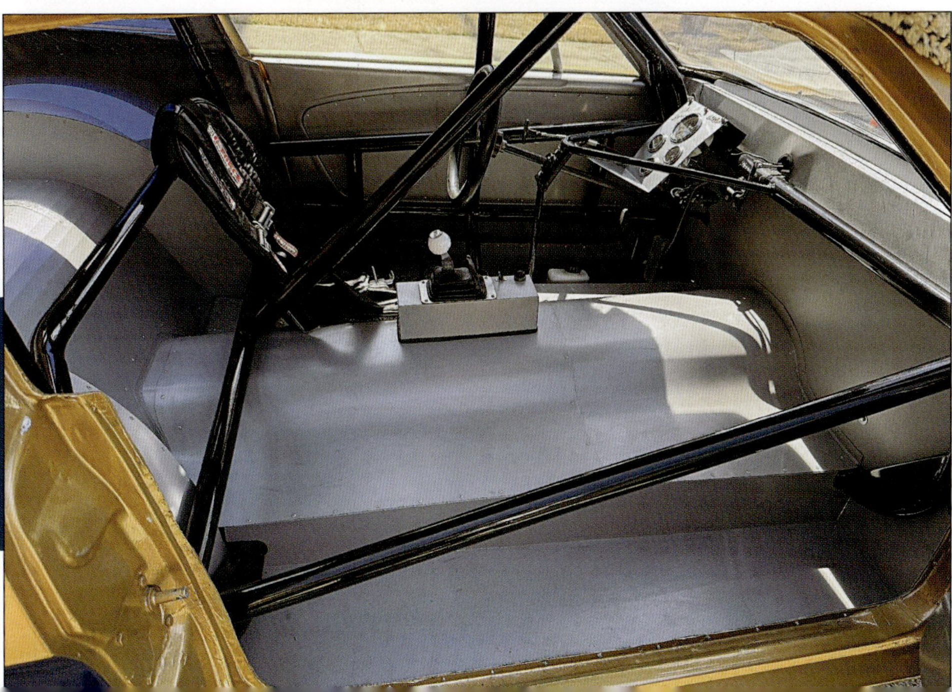

The interior appears as it did when it was assembled by Holman-Moody in 1966. The aluminum floor has been powder coated to prevent corrosion. (Photo Courtesy Nick Coleman)

These Larry Coleman cars have survived the ravages of time. (Photo Courtesy Nick Coleman)

Prioritizing family and business, Coleman finally retired from racing. The Torino went on the market and was quickly scooped up (minus the engine) by Bill Campbell. Campbell campaigned the car with a big-block Chevy for power.

It's understood that the Torino changed hands a few times. Billy Holt, who campaigned the *Alabamian* Funny Car, bought the Torino and later sold it to a gentleman

The original Logghe chassis for the Torino was rescued from being used in a roadster with a Chevy engine. (Photo Courtesy Ronald McDonald/Nick Coleman Collection)

When Nick Coleman purchased the Torino through Sotheby's auctions, it carried the correct Larry Coleman paint and lettering. The body was created by Fiberglass Ltd by using a Hertz rental car. (Photo Courtesy Nick Coleman)

The Logghe chassis has been beautifully restored. Larry and Nick Coleman built the period-correct, aluminum-head SOHC 427 engine. Enderle injection feeds the fuel. (Photo Courtesy Nick Coleman)

in Ohio. After that, the wherabouts of the car get fuzzy, but the chassis eventually turned up in 2009 on an online auction site. Larry Coleman's son Nick discovered the advertisement and had former crewman Larry Grace bid on it.

The Torino was in need of a fresh drivetrain and a complete restoration. The body itself was in great shape and had previously been repainted in the Coleman likeness.

Having the Torino in his possession, Nick went looking for the long-nose Mustang. Coming up short, he planned on building a tribute—one that he could race. Then, word reached him that collector, Brent Hajek, owned his dad's old Mustang. Clester Andrews had retained the car since buying it from Coleman all of those years ago. Andrews had started on the restoration before falling ill. That's when Hajek entered the picture with plans to finish what Andrews had started.

Hajek generally doesn't sell cars that are in his collection, but he knew Larry Coleman and was willing to make a deal with Nick, just to see the car back in the Coleman family. The car was a roller and had most of its original parts with it when Hajek received it. Hajek had completed the restoration long before Nick purchased the car in 2023. Nick went through the Mustang once more, focusing on the finer details. Credit for the restoration goes out to Walter Tate, Jeffery Ferguson, and Jasper Motte.

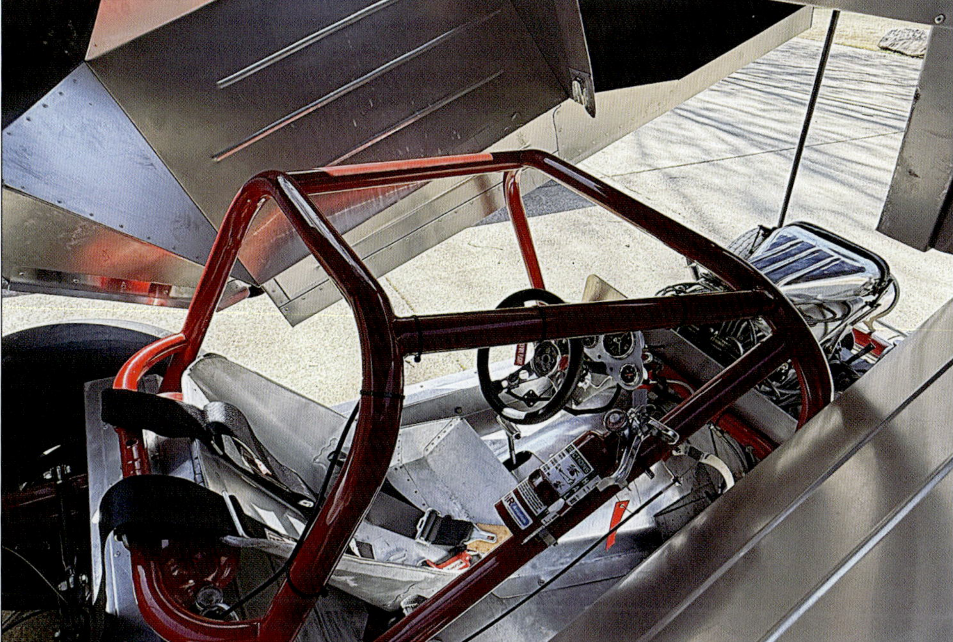

The aluminum seat held Sidney Foster in place. The aftermarket gauges and wheel are correct for the period. Note the location of the C-6 shifter. (Photo Courtesy Nick Coleman)

Twin Simpson chutes are mounted on the rear. The Fiberglass Ltd. molded body included the taillights, which still have the Ford part number. (Photo Courtesy Nick Coleman)

Durachrome Bug

Warren Gunter's fiberglass Volkswagen Beetle shell was extended 14 inches ahead of the windshield. The chromoly chassis was built by Mike Kase.

The *Durachrome Bug*, which is widely regarded as drag racing's most significant Funny Car, was influenced by Disney's *Love Bug* movie. Warren Gunter had been campaigning an Altered T when he made the decision to step up to race in the Funny Car category. He stated that the *Love Bug* was the influence for the Volkswagen body.

Gunter was an engineer who worked on the Apollo 11 program, and for someone with his mental prowess, the *Durachrome Bug* would be unlike any Funny Car before it—in more ways than one.

Mike Kase built the chromoly chassis, and Bill Temple formed the fiberglass shell, which was extended 14 inches in the front. While Temple was at it, he added a fiberglass support to the body before applying the candy red paint. Nestled in the chassis was a blown 427-ci Chevy that was running on a reported 85-percent load of nitro. Behind the engine was a B&M-built 2-speed transmission and a Dana 60 rear end.

Being a NASA engineer, Gunter had access to some things that many of his fellow competitors weren't able to access, such as a wind tunnel. The *Durachrome Bug* benefitted from time at NASA, as Gunter mentioned, the car hugged the track. Further, Gunter installed an onboard computer. This was believed to be a first in drag racing. The computer measured G-forces and acceleration as the car tore down the track at 200 mph.

Gunter found a sponsor in Durachrome, which was a company that made accessories for the Volkswagen Beetle and Don Burns Volkswagen in Garden Grove, California. There were two *Durachrome Beetles*, and the first one had a chassis from an Altered car. This one was wrecked early on and replaced with the car that is pictured on this page. Gunter raced the Beetle through 1972 before parting with it.

The car continued to be raced by its new owner around Southern California into the late 1970s.

At some point, Oregon-based AA/GS racer Mike Molea owned the Beetle, racing it with a blown big-block Chevy. Reportedly, for a time he also ran it on the street

Warren Gunter and his Volkswagen Beetle are shown at the 1971 AHRA Winter Nationals at Bee Line Dragway. Gunter fell to the 'Cuda of "Slammin'" Sam Miller in the first round. (Photo Courtesy J. R. Bloom)

This is how the old Durachrome Bug *appeared when it was discovered by Dru Jaxon. Most restorers would not have taken on this project. (Photo Courtesy Dru Jaxon/Randy Winkle Collection)*

Dru Jaxon performed the initial steps of the Durachrome Bug's *restoration. Body repairs and replacing the glass were done by Stormy Byrd and Randy Winkle. (Photo Courtesy Stormy Byrd)*

All of the interior aluminum is gold anodized, which is how it appeared when it was raced by Warren Gunter. The roll cage was brought up to today's specifications by Rick Henderson. (Photo Courtesy Randy Winkle)

Durachrome Bug *owner Randy Winkle puts the Chevy engine to work and lifts the front wheels. (Photo Courtesy Stormy Byrd)*

The Durachrome Bug*'s paint was applied by Rocky Castro and Randy Winkle. The lettering was by Bob Coslett. (Photo Courtesy Stormy Byrd)*

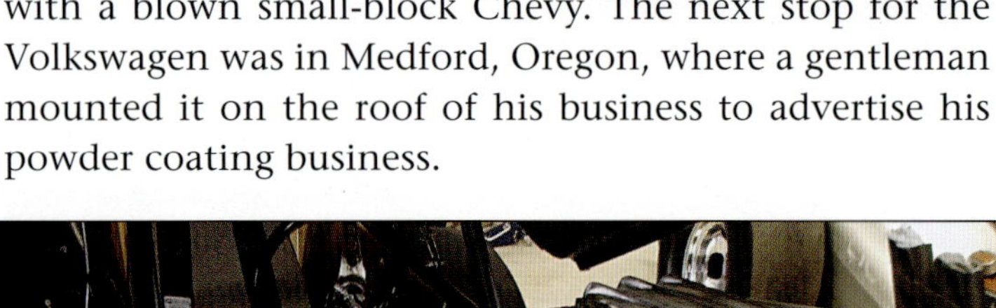
with a blown small-block Chevy. The next stop for the Volkswagen was in Medford, Oregon, where a gentleman mounted it on the roof of his business to advertise his powder coating business.

Years later, when the fourth owner, Dru Jaxon, came along, the car was in pieces beside a barn. It's supposed usefulness had come to an end. Jaxon began the restoration of the Beetle before priorities changed. The current owner, Randy Winkle remembers the *Durachrome Bug* from his youth, and from the time that he heard Jaxon had the car, he bugged him to buy it. It took 8 or 9 years of pestering before he could finally claim ownership.

Jaxon had made significant progress regarding the Beetle's restoration. The body was in decent shape but needed paint. The original Mike Kase chassis was in excellent condition. With plans to race the car, Winkle was required to upgrade the roll cage to meet NHRA requirements. Winkle expects to take the Bug to 8.0 ETs with the 496-ci Chevy and Powerglide that now reside in the car.

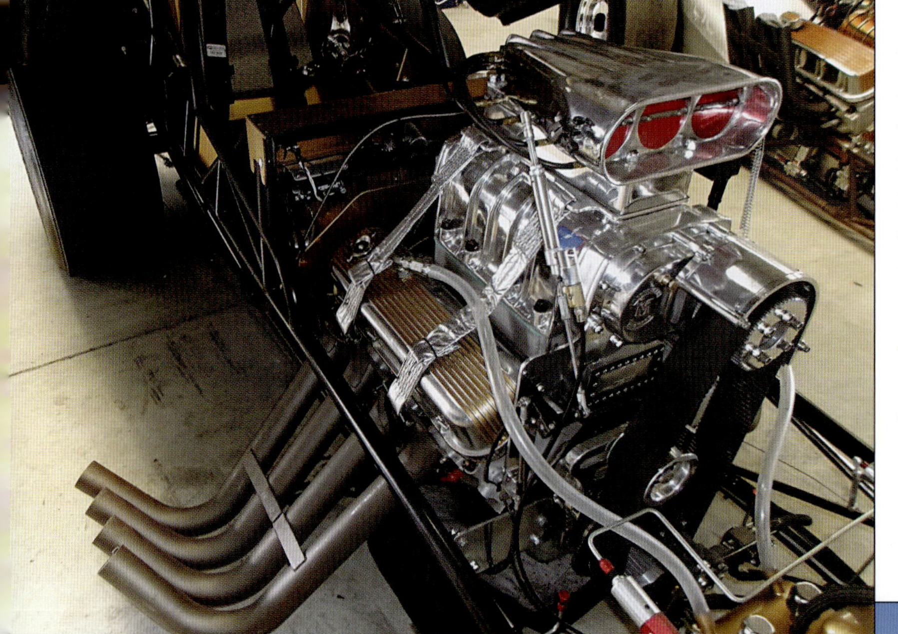

A 6-71 blower and Enderle bug catcher are mounted on the 496 Chevy engine. Internals include a Schneider roller camshaft. The transmission is a Powerglide. (Photo Courtesy Stormy Byrd)

M&H slicks transfer the power of the Chevy engine to the track. The rear end is a Dana 60 with 3.60 gears. Initial light passes were 150 mph. (Photo Courtesy Stormy Byrd)

"Jungle" Jim Liberman Camaro

"Jungle" Jim Liberman and his string of fine Chevys drew crowds. This Camaro, which is shown at Niagara, is being driven by Pete Williams. (Photo Courtesy Dean Johnson)

For many fans, the topic of Funny Cars begins and ends with "Jungle" Jim Liberman. The man was a show in and of himself, and many track owners benefited immensely by having Liberman on the program. Liberman's days in Funny Car date back to 1965, when he hopped behind the wheel of Lew Arrington's *Brutus*, which was a Pontiac GTO match racer.

For Liberman, it was a steady uphill climb from there. He won his first national event in 1966 (the AHRA World Championship) at Lions Drag Strip. Then, in 1967, he fielded a pair of Chevy IIs. In 1968, he campaigned two Novas, with Clare Sanders driving one to a win at the NHRA Winternationals. Following the Novas was a string of Camaros, beginning with two cars in 1970.

Also in 1970, Liberman made the switch from blue cars to red cars, painting the Camaros a dark, candy red. Both cars were nearly identical in appearance. Pete Williams, who was Liberman's longtime crew chief, drove one, which had a big-block Chevy in a Dick Fletcher chassis, while Jim campaigned the other with a Chrysler Hemi nestled in a Logghe chassis. Both cars ran modified Chrysler TorqueFlite transmissions. Liberman campaigned Camaros as late as 1973 before making the switch to a Vega. The Williams car did receive a Hemi at some point, and was driven by Liberman occasionally as well as Larry Arnold and Lew Arrington.

In 1971, the Williams Camaro was sold to the team of Santmyer & Fenner, and it was driven by A. J. Lynch. The history of the car is unclear after that. It is known that the Camaro was being bracket raced in the 1980s. Around 1984, the body and chassis went separate ways.

Santmyer and Fenner, with A. J. Lynch driving, took ownership of the Williams Camaro in 1971. Powering the car was a House of Speed–built big-block Chevy. (Photo Courtesy John Gallant Sr.)

In 2021, current owner, James Hardman purchased the body from Ken Chase. Chase had owned it for about 20 years. Through Shane Saylor, Hardman was able to locate and purchase the original Fletcher chassis. Brothers Gerald and Mark Schultz had used the chassis to build an Altered. In doing so, they had cut a section off the rear and moved the engine forward about 10 inches. Hardman made the deal to buy the chassis just in time, as a week later, Gerald Schultz, who owned the car, passed away.

Hardman had his work cut out for him. With the chassis having been modified, he had to determine how the body sat, where it sat, how high it was, and the angle

Due to modifications over time, owner James Hardman had to determine the engine location before repairs could begin to be made to the body. (Photo Courtesy James Hardman)

It took the owner 3 years to track down the chassis before the restoration could begin. Ricky Neal matched the Camaro's original paint. (Photo Courtesy Chris Graves)

The cast-iron 454 engine features a Cragar intake and the 6-71 blower that was used on Bill Maverick's Hemi-powered Little Red Wagon. *Safety modifications have been made. (Photo Courtesy James Hardman)*

From the rear, the Camaro shows its twin drag chutes and Dana rear end. Those taillights are Chevrolet parts. (Photo Courtesy Howdy Hoffman Jr.)

Its 1970 all over again. This photo was captured at the Camaro's debut in Bowling Green, Kentucky. Bruce Larson's restored Camaro in the far lane was featured in Drag Racing's Quarter Mile Warriors: Then & Now, *which was published in 2014. (Photo Courtesy Howdy Hoffman Jr.)*

at which the engine was positioned. This was determined by gathering every photo he could come across of the car. The chassis did retain the original suspension, and most of the tin work was still present, including the magnesium front and rear bulkheads. A bonus was that the car still had the original Jungle Jim seat and steering wheel. Hardman discovered in the process that at some point, maybe early in 1971, that Liberman had lowered the engine at least a few inches within the chassis.

Hardman had set a goal for having the Camaro ready for the Bowling Green event in June 2024, so that gave him approximately eight weeks to finish the restoration. The body was received in May and handed to Ricky Neal, who did a fantastic job duplicating the original appearance. While Neal was busy on the body, Hardman completed the chassis and driveline. To the delight of everyone involved, the Camaro was completed in time for the Bowling Green event with little time to spare.

Hurri-Cain 'Cuda

Drag racing legend, Butch "the California Flash" Leal campaigned this Barracuda in 1967 with significant success. No one knows what became of the fiberglass body, but the chassis found its way under the Hurri-Cain. *(Photo Courtesy Wayne Langford)*

Drag cars are always being repurposed, and Funny Cars are no exception to the rule. The *Hurri-Cain* 'Cuda is a prime example, having debuted in 1967 as the Logghe Chassis–equipped *California Flash* Barracuda of Butch Leal. Powered by an H. L. Shahan–built injected Hemi, the Barracuda was the quickest and fastest Funny Car in the nation for a time. On a full load of nitro, Leal hammered out a best ET of 7.82 at 181.90 mph.

Funny Cars peaked in popularity during the 1970s. Bob Cain and his 'Cuda were a popular East Coast draw. (Photo Courtesy Todd Wingerter)

In 1968, Leal moved into a Super Stock Plymouth and sold the Funny Car to the East Coast team of Earl "Buckeye" Phillips and Vern Rowley. The pair campaigned the Barracuda, which was injected on gas, as the *Baltimore Bandit* through 1968. In 1969, the team debuted a new Barracuda and sold the ex-Leal car to Fred F. Cain. Fred and his sons campaigned it through 1969, running the same injected Hemi on gas. In 1970, a new 'Cuda body found its way onto the Logghe chassis.

Along with a switch to the new body, the injection and gas gave way to a 6-71 blower huffing on a copious amount of nitromethane. The 'Cuda became a one-brother show at this point, with Bob Cain driving and performing the general maintenance. Dick Perrault, who joined the Cain team in 1965, turned wrenches. Fred's Chrysler dealership sponsored the 'Cuda and provided a trailer and tow rig.

In 1971, with the introduction of new, larger slicks, the rear wheel openings were enlarged, and custom paint by Wayne "Woody" Wood was applied. At the end of the 1971 season, the 'Cuda was sold to John and Rodalyn Knox, who campaigned the car in A/FC as the *Country*

Girl (with Rodalyn driving). After one season, the 'Cuda was sold again. Over the next decade or so, it passed through several hands, running various combinations and in various classes. Eventually, anyone with an interest in the car lost track of it.

In 2015, Blair Smith got wind of the car. It had been owned by a Texan and was being sold through a broker. The distinct side body latch, which was unique to the Leal chassis, was one of the key things about the car that helped identify it as the ex-Leal, ex-*Hurri-Cain* car. When the 'Cuda was received by Blair, it was setup to run in bracket racing. Powering the car was a single 4-barrel 440 engine and TorqueFlite transmission. The body, although it was complete, was a little rough. It had a door cut in the side that was secured by a rope and gate hinges.

It takes dedicated people with a true love of drag racing's history to undertake restoration of this extent. It's time consuming and expensive, but the payoff is satisfying. (Photo Courtesy Blair Smith)

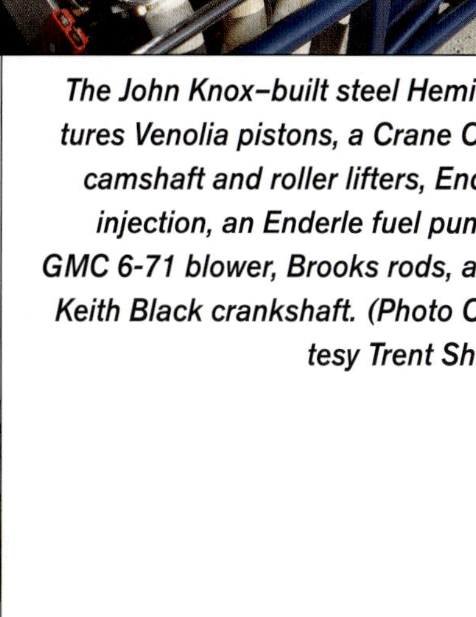

The John Knox–built steel Hemi features Venolia pistons, a Crane Cams camshaft and roller lifters, Enderle injection, an Enderle fuel pump, a GMC 6-71 blower, Brooks rods, and a Keith Black crankshaft. (Photo Courtesy Trent Sherill)

The payoff for restorer Blair Smith is that he saved a piece of history. The fuel tank is original to the car. (Photo Courtesy Trent Sherill)

At Deluxe Auto Restoration, a painter known as "Krazy Flake" replicated the work that was performed by Woody's in 1971. (Photo Courtesy Trent Sherill)

The chassis was still in great original condition with virtually no work needed other than cleaning and repainting. Although the original all-steel Hemi was long gone, Blair had John Knox build a new iron-block, aluminum-headed Hemi as a replacement. "Krazy Flake" at Deluxe Auto Restoration restored the body and duplicated the paint. In 2020, Chuck Fisher became the *Hurri-Cain*'s new caretaker.

The instrumentation was and remains minimal. Correct Stewart-Warner fuel and oil gauges surround the tachometer. The push-knob on the right side triggers the fire suppression. (Photo Courtesy Trent Sherill)

The* Hurri-Cain *sits on aluminum Rebel rear wheels and Halibrand spindle-mounted "kidney bean" wheels in the front. The 'Cuda body survived the years in remarkable shape. (Photo Courtesy Trent Sherill)

Mickey Thompson's Grand Am

Mickey Thompon's Grand Ams were some of the more unique Funny Cars of the 1970s. Butch Maas is shown here at the 1973 AHRA Winter Nationals driving Thompson's first Grand Am. (Photo Courtesy J. R. Bloom)

Mickey Thompson pursued almost every form of motorsport during his 60 years here on earth. He left us too soon. His legacy lives onward thanks to his racing exploits, as well as the fine line of performance tires that are offered by the company he started in 1963.

When it came to drag racing, Thompson campaigned several unique cars, all in an attempt to advance the sport. He is given credit for creating the slingshot dragster in 1955, when he debuted a car that placed the driver behind the rear axle as a means of placing a greater amount of weight where it was needed. In 1970, his venture into Funny Car racing saw him toying with a monocoque Mustang, a car that borrowed heavily from his IndyCar experience. In 1971, there was a titanium chassis Pinto Funny Car. In 1973, when everyone else in the category leaned toward Vegas, Mustangs, or Duster bodies, Thompson chose a Pontiac Grand Am.

His first Grand Am featured a Ron Pellegrini fiberglass body and a 118-inch, John Buttera chassis. Most Funny Cars of the day were running about a 115-inch wheelbase and hanging the front wheels in the air when the light turned green. Thompson reasoned that a longer wheelbase would prevent needing to hang extra weight on the front to keep the wheels on the ground.

In December 1972, the Grand Am made its debut at Lions Drag Strip with Dale Pulde as the driver. By the time that the NHRA Winternationals rolled around in February, Butch Maas was behind the wheel. Maas qualified number one with a 7.18 ET, but fell in the first round after the engine stalled. At the Gatornationals, a fire destroyed the body and sidelined Maas with some serious burns. Although it was felt that the chassis could be salvaged, Thompson chose instead to have Buttera build a new one.

The new car was painted black and featured a controversial laid-back windshield. The NHRA allowed a 2-inch top chop, but Pulde skirted the issue by laying back the windshield, giving the roof an exaggerated chopped look.

In 1974 at Great Lakes Dragaway, Pulde had a blower explosion and ran off the track, damaging the front

At the 1974 NHRA World Finals, driver Dale Pulde set the class record in a new Grand Am, running a 6.16 ET to defeat Don Prudhomme. (Photo Courtesy Rich Carlson/Grant Bittner Collection)

In 1975, the Grand Am had three different drivers behind the wheel. Bobby Pickett took over driving by the time that the NHRA Springnationals came around, and he remained in the seat through 1976. (Photo Courtesy Rich Carlson/Grant Bittner)

suspension. The car was hauled to Romeo Palamides, where the chassis damage was repaired and a new straight axle installed. The Grand Am then reappeared in time for Indy, carrying a new red paint job. At the World Finals, Pulde played spoiler by defeating Don Prudhomme in the second round with a record 6.16 ET at 233.76 mph, thus locking up the world title for Shirl Greer.

As purchased, the body of the Grand Am was down to its gel coat. It was confirmed to be Thompon's Grand Am after stickers and paint were discovered under the spoiler and hood trim. Driver Bob Pickett later verified the car. (Photo Courtesy James Hardman)

The restored Grand Am sits on polished Cragar wheels with M&H tires on the front and Goodyear slicks on the rear. (Photo Courtesy Pam Conrad)

To start the 1975 season, Larry Arnold took over the Grand Am. With the new season came the U.S. Marines sponsorship, which helped to relieve some of the financial strain of maintaining the car. A photoshoot prior to the Winternationals saw the Grand Am go up in flames, which resulted in the car being sent for repairs and Arnold being sent to the hospital with burns.

Charlie Therwanger drove the Grand Am at the Winternationals, where he reached the semifinals, giving the car its best showing of the season. By the time that the Springnationals took place, Therwanger was replaced by Bob Pickett, who remained the driver through the rest of Thompson's ownership.

For the 1976 season, the Grand Am received a new J&E body that was made from the previous shell with a few modifications. At the same time, the chassis was updated with a Jamie Sarte straight axle. Pickett had a decent year with the Grand Am, making the semifinal rounds at the Gatornationals and World Finals and winning class at the Super Stock Nationals. By the end of the season the Grand Am was worn out. The car was sold, and Thompson and Pickett debuted a new Oldsmobile *Starfire* for the 1977 season.

The trail of the Grand Am after Thompson's ownership is unclear. In 2013, the current owner, James Hardman discovered the car for sale on racejunk.com. Apparently, it had been sitting for several years in a

Bobby Pickett takes his place on the seat of the restored Grand Am. (Photo Courtesy James Hardman)

The Grand Am's Keith Black Hemi features a Mooneyham 8-71 blower that is topped with a Crower eight-port injector. An MSD ignition ignites the mixture. (Photo Courtesy Niel Barber)

Kentucky field. At one time, someone had thoughts of racing the car, as it was reported to house a carbureted 454-ci Chevy. A gentleman named Dino Powell discovered the Grand Am and did little with the car before selling it to Guy James, the man who placed the racejunk advertisement.

The restoration of the Grand Am was made easier by the fact that it still carried many of the original parts, including the seat, steering wheel, chassis, wheels, tin work, and even the titanium body pole. As the majority of the chassis remained the original John Buttera parts, some of the parts were carried over from when the car carried the second yellow body.

The drivetrain remains pretty much as was run by Pickett in 1976. It carries the hard-to-find Crower 8-port, and equally hard-to-find Mickey Thompson rocker covers. Just like in the days of old, it has a 2-speed Lenco transmission and a Ford 9-inch rear end. James did a magnificent job in restoring the chassis, but the icing on the cake was the paint, which Jeff Tackett replicated to perfection.

The restored Grand Am looks great from any angle. Thompson picked up the U.S. Marines sponsorship in 1975. Revell, no doubt, sold plenty of kits. (Photo Courtesy Pam Conrad)

The *Underdog*

The only part of the Monza build that Ric Deschner farmed out was the paint. New Jersey's, Rick Gerdes (also known as "Circus") was called upon to complete that task. (Photo Courtesy Gary Walker/Rob Potter Collection)

The *Underdog* was an appropriate name for the Chevy Monza that "Tricky" Ric Deschner campaigned between the years 1975 and 1981. Deschner was a self-made man who did it all—from building to maintaining and driving the car.

As a trained draftsman, Deschner fabricated the chassis of his Monza, working off a 1:1 scale blueprint that he had drawn on the wall of his Lindenhurst, New York, shop that was named RCD Machine. Powering the Monza was an iron-block Chevy with iron heads and a steel crank. Backing the Chevy was a Lenco twin-disc-clutch, 2-speed transmission and a rear end that consisted of Strange full-floating axles and 4.10 gears.

By the mid-1970s, campaigning a AA/Funny Car had become a major drain on the pocketbook. Without the support of a major sponsor, even big-name racers were finding it difficult to compete at the levels they once did. The number of competitors was shrinking, but the diehards carried onward—thanks in large part to the abundance of match races that were available.

The car was very competitive. Deschner managed best ETs of 6.50, running on a 50-percent load of nitro. Why only 50 percent? Well, through blowing things up, Deschner discovered that 50 percent was all that the parts and his budget could take. Through the Monza's long career, Deschner was a Division 1 top-five competitor and was in the top 10 in IHRA competition.

Restoration of the Monza was an on-and-off project that took about four years. The big-block Chevy now runs on alcohol. It is shown and fired when the desire strikes. (Photo Courtesy Dave Hommel)

The last time that Deschner ran the car was around the year 2000. Sadly, he developed Alzheimer's and passed away in 2022. The Monza was sold to a friend who lived on Long Island. The gentleman initially had no real interest in the car. However, a change of heart led to him reaching out to chassis builder Nickey Montana, who cleaned things up. A mutual friend of Deschner, Dave Hommel, then got engine builder Dennis Quintoni involved. Dave Hommel, who is a perfectionist at heart, spent a year restoring the body. It took approximately 4 years to complete the restoration.

CHAPTER THREE

PRO STOCKS

PRO STOCKERS EVOLVED FROM THE MATCH-RACING CARS OF THE EARLY 1960s.

Just like Funny Cars, Pro Stockers evolved from the match-racing cars of the early 1960s. In 1967, the United Drag Racers Association became the first organization to create a heads-up, minimal-rule class for these cars. In 1968, the AHRA followed suit with a heads-up Super Stock class. This was followed by NHRA and IHRA Pro Stock classes in 1970 and 1971, respectively.

For the NHRA, the initial rules stated that to compete in the class, cars could be no older than 1967 models. A minimum weight of 2,700 pounds was set. It was pretty straight forward. Initially, the class was ruled by big-block-powered cars ('Cudas, Camaros, and Mavericks), with Chrysler's Hemi dominating.

Late in 1971, the NHRA crafted weight breaks that allowed small-block-equipped subcompact cars to compete. The weight breaks hampered big-block-powered cars through the decade and allowed Ford Clevelands and small-block Chevys to dominate. The weight breaks fluctuated through 1982 before the NHRA went to a minimum 2,350-pound weight limit, and a 500-ci maximum-engine-size rule.

Above: The Rat Pack 1 *Camaro was campaigned successfully by Wally Booth, first as a S/S Camaro in 1968, then as a NHRA Pro Stocker with 1969 Camaro body panels. Booth would campaign the Camaro into 1971 before parting with the car. Today Neil Zimbaldi owns the Camaro and regularly puts it through its paces.*

1969 Dick Harrell Camaro

Dick Harrell set up ZL-1 number one, and Herb Fox drove the car at its 1969 AHRA Winter Nationals debut. After its debut and through the remainder of the season, Ray Sullins drove the car. Harrell never drove the Camaro in competition. (Photo Courtesy J. R. Bloom)

In early 1969, Dick Harrell took one of Fred Gibb Chevrolet's ZL-1 Camaros (a ZL-1 engine is an all-aluminum, high-performance 427) and prepared the car to run in AHRA heads-up Super Stock. In 1969, at the urging of Fred Gibb, Chevrolet built a limited run of 69 Camaros with this engine. They were definitely not intended for street use. Harrell tested his Mist Blue ZL-1 Camaro, the first one produced, for the February 1969 issue of *Super Stock & Drag Illustrated*. With slicks and headers, the Camaro unleashed a best ET of 10.41 at 128 mph.

The Camaro debuted at the AHRA Winter Nationals in 1969, driven by Fred Gibb employee Herb Fox, who took the car to the semifinals before losing to eventual winner Arlen Vanke. Ray Sullins drove the Camaro through the remainder of the 1969 season. Sullins's best national event showing came in the form of a runner-up finish to Gary Kimball at the AHRA World Championship drags at Green Valley. In the spring of 1970, Sullins went back to work for fellow racer Kelly Chadwick, and Fred Gibb had a few different drivers in the Camaro for 1970.

Propelling the Camaro to low-10-second ETs was the ZL-1, which was punched out to 430 ci. Aftermarket parts included Holley carburetors, a Weiand tunnel ram, and compression that ran as high as 13.8:1. The see-through hood scoop was adopted to showcase the Carter Thermoquad carburetors that were being trialled for the sponsor. Backing the engine was a B&M turbo-clutch transmission and Dana rear end. Sullins recalls switching back and forth between the turbo-clutch transmission and a 4-speed.

In 1971, Jim Hayter and partner Chuck Wright took over the Camaro. The pair campaigned the car with great success, running a Diamond Racing Engines built, steel-block 427. ETs in the 9.60s (with a class record 9.63 ET at 143 mph) became the norm, as Hayter earned national event wins and the AHRA's Pro Super Stock (Pro Stock) season Championship.

With Pro Stock evolving quickly, by 1972, the Camaro was outdated. Bill "Grumpy" Jenkins made chromoly, small-block-powered subcompacts the only way to go in the class, and Hayter moved into a Don Hardy–built Pro Stock Vega. The Camaro was regulated to history, disappearing into the growing world of bracket racing.

The Camaro ended up in the hands of Illinois resident Ross Taylor, who campaigned it as the *Gin Mill*. In 1983, he listed the car for sale in *National Dragster* magazine. Michael Curce was the next owner, and he sold the car to Bill Porterfield in 1988.

In 1971, Jim Hayter took the reins of the ZL-1 Camaro and won the AHRA World Championship with it. The Camaro ran 9.60 ETs. The Motown Missile in the far lane has also been restored. (Photo Courtesy Michael Pottie)

Bill Porterfield gets credit for resurrecting ZL-1 number one—not only once but twice. As it appears today, the Camaro is ready to race. (Photo Courtesy Mecum Auctions)

The ZL-1 engine that now resides in the Camaro is the car's original engine. Modern goods include the Holley Dominator carburetors, braided lines, and ceramic-coated headers. (Photo Courtesy Mecum Auctions)

The all-business interior looks similar to any other well-built drag car that you can see at the track today. It was done without losing the feel of the car's drag racing heritage. (Photo Courtesy Mecum Auctions)

The Fred Gibb/Dick Harrell Camaro features lace paint and steamroller tires. With no front brakes, the parachute was mandatory for AHRA heads-up Super Stock. (Photo Courtesy Mecum Auctions)

The Camaro features a two-piece fiberglass front end and a transparent scoop that were installed in 1969. The see-through scoop was used to showcase the then-new Carter Thermoquad carburetors. (Photo Courtesy Mecum Auctions)

Porterfield researched the car's history and completed the bare-bones restoration. In 1990, a trailer fire damaged the Camaro, requiring Porterfield to once more go through the car. Darryl and Diana Pakka did the paint and lacing after Porterfield performed an extensive search to find the proper material. Once that phase of the painting was complete, Mike McCloud added the lettering and gold leaf.

From Day 1, the Camaro was built for speed, with rear wheel tubs added at some point in its life to make way for larger tires. The 4-speed disappeared long time ago, and the Camaro now runs a Chevrolet Turbo Hydra-Matic transmission. The Camaro retained its fiberglass front end, scooped hood, and inner fenders but lacks the front brakes, which Harrell removed back in 1969. AHRA Pro Stock rules allowed entries to have no front brakes as long as a parachute was used.

In 2012, the Camaro was sold through Mecum Auctions and resides on the West Coast in the Brothers Collection Museum today.

Schartman Cougar

In 1970, Ed Schartman moved into a heads-up Cougar after racing Funny Cars the previous four seasons. The Boss 429, which was one of four that were built by Mercury, never produced the results for which Schartman was hoping. (Photo Courtesy J. R. Bloom)

The Cougar lives again—for the most part. Owner Doug Herzog has history with the car and used all of the available parts from the original to build this one. (Photo Courtesy Doug Herzog)

Doug Herzog's Boss produces close to 800 hp and carries Kaase heads, a Sig Erson camshaft, and twin 850 Holley carburetors. Power is transmitted to the Dana 4.88 rear and a Toploader transmission. (Photo Courtesy Doug Herzog)

Although it was dismissed as a tribute car, this Ed Schartman Cougar is a tip of the hat to those who have built (or are building) tributes using parts from the original car. There were only four Boss 429 Cougars built: two mule cars and two that went to contracted Mercury racers "Dyno" Don Nicholson and Schartman.

The Schartman Cougar was built by Doug Herzog with a helping hand from many people, including Herzog's close friend Steve Comstock, who was the third owner of the car in 1973. Comstock raced the Cougar through 1975 before retiring it, worn and broken. It had been raced for five years with a Boss 429 and had no chassis connectors and no roll cage to tie the car together.

Twisted beyond use, Comstock eventually cut the car into pieces. In 2006, he called Herzog and told him that if he wanted the remains, he should come and pick them up because it was going to be scrapped. Herzog used all of the remaining parts that were salvageable to restore the car. For historical reasons, it's great to see the Schartman Cougar again—even if little remains of the original car.

Dick Landy's 1971 Challenger

In 1971, Dick Landy campaigned two Pro Stock Dodge Challengers. This photo was captured at the NHRA Summernationals at Englishtown, New Jersey, and shows Landy (near lane) facing Mike Fons. (Photo Courtesy Steve Reyes)

Cigar-chomping "Dandy" Dick Landy began his relationship with Chrysler after taking his first ride in a Max Wedge–powered Plymouth in 1962. With factory backing, his star rose quickly. His nitromethane-fed, altered-wheelbase 1965 Dodge was one of the nation's most feared cars. Preferring the new, and safer Super Stock category that was introduced in 1967, Landy campaigned a string of A-Body and B-Body cars.

With the advent of NHRA Pro Stock in 1970, Chrysler jumped in with both feet. Leading the charge were Landy's Dodges on the West Coast, and Sox & Martin's Plymouths in the East Coast. Landy proved to be nothing short of a genius. He remained as a top performer in the category due to his ability to pull unheard-of power from the Hemi engine. With a string of memorable cars through his 25-year racing career, his 1971 Challenger was one of his most innovative.

Beautifully restored in 2005, Dick Landy's Challenger optimizes what the early days of Pro Stock were all about. A big-inch Hemi was near impossible to beat. (Photo Courtesy Mecum Auctions)

Dick Landy's Challenger cheats the wind with a nose-down stance. The narrowed Dana rear kept the Goodyear slicks within the stretched fender lines. (Photo Courtesy Mecum Auctions)

Landy's Hemi propelled the Challenger to best ETs in the 9.50s. The modifications include twin Holley Dominator carburetors, an independent-runner intake manifold, twin-plug Hemi heads, and Hooker headers. (Photo Courtesy Mecum Auctions)

If you compare this Challenger's interior to one of today's Pro Stocks, it looks pretty plush. A Hurst Super Shifter controls the Hemi 4-speed transmission. Note the stout roll-cage bars. (Photo Courtesy Mecum Auctions)

If you installed an exhaust on Dick Landy's Challenger, the car would make a pretty stout street-and-strip performer today. Those spun-aluminum Cragar wheels on the front are some of the first that were ever produced. This car never had wheelie bars. (Photo Courtesy Mecum Auctions)

Landy campaigned two Challengers in 1971. He updated his 1970 car and hired Ken Dondero to drive while driving the new 1971 car himself. The new car was built with Pro Stock's first rack-and-pinion steering, which was an item that Landy lifted from a subcompact Cricket. The new steering allowed for better front-end geometry and additional room for primary header tubing. Late in the season, Landy tested one of Pro Stock's first dry-sump oil systems. The benefits of a dry-sump system are threefold: it allows for better oiling, frees up horsepower (oil is not stored in the pan), and without a deep pan, the front end can be brought down out of the airstream.

Landy added a dual-plug distributor and twin-plug heads to his Hemi. These items were said to be first used by Landy. Atop the Hemi was an independent-runner intake manifold and twin Holley Dominator carburetors. The result was ETs in the 9.50 range. Although national-event wins eluded Landy (and just about everyone else, as Sox & Martin dominated), regional wins and match-race victories came with a fair amount of ease.

Landy updated the Challenger for 1972, adding some fresh body panels and new paint. Performance upgrades saw the best ETs in the 9.30s by the end of the season. It was a new age in Pro Stock, though, with the NHRA adjusting its rules to allow short-wheelbase compacts to compete. The season belonged the radical Vega of Bill "Grumpy" Jenkins, which pretty much rendered all other cars obsolete. Landy's best showings were runner-up finishes at the NHRA Summernationals and the AHRA World Championship at Fremont.

Landy sold the Challenger to fellow racer Art Leong at the end of the season and debuted a Ron Butler–prepared Dart for 1973. The Challenger went on to spend time as a bracket racer before being purchased in 2005 by Erik Lindberg and restored.

Ed Schartman's Maverick

Eddie Schartman was one of the few to see success with the Boss 429. His Maverick, shown here in Minnesota in the summer of 1972, ran ETs in the 9.40s. (Photo Courtesy Dan Williams)

"Fast" Eddie Schartman's success in drag racing can be traced back to the early 1960s. He worked as a line mechanic at Jackshaw Chevrolet in Ohio and campaigned several cars that carried the dealership's name. At Jackshaw Chevrolet, he met "Dyno" Don Nicholson, who stopped by occasionally to pick up parts for his Factory Experimental and match-race Chevys. Nicholson would convince Schartman to come and work for him in Atlanta.

In 1963, when Chevy pulled out of racing, Nicholson was signed by Mercury to run a Comet in 1964, and shortly after that, Schartman received a deal of his own.

As part of Schartman's deal, he initially drove a Factory Experimental Comet for Nicholson. However, when Mercury introduced its flip-top Comets in 1966, Schartman was given one of his own. He was one of the very few who could keep pace with Nicholson and followed close behind, as Nicholson and his Comet Funny Car were the first into the 7s. Schartman continued to campaign Funny Cars through 1969. That year, he added a stablemate in the form of a Lakewood Industries–built SOHC Maverick. Eddie ran the Maverick in Modified Eliminator as well as in weekly match races. A move into Pro Stock followed in 1970.

Schartman started the 1970 season with a Boss 429–powered Cougar but soon unveiled a lighter Boss-powered Maverick. A second Maverick was built in 1970, which was also powered by a Boss 429. As relayed by Schartman to the car's current owner, Frank Druse Jr., Schartman

Brad "Shaggy" Dierup removed the previous burgundy and blue paint before applying the yellow. The right rear quarter panel needed massaging after previously being damage when Schartman had lost a wheel. (Photo Courtesy Frank Druse Jr.)

Ford Maverick Grabber Yellow and Grabber Blue paint were used to mimic the colors that were applied in 1972. Reportedly, Schartman had first campaigned this car with gold paint. (Photo Courtesy Frank Druse Jr.)

The Boss engine that currently resides in the Maverick is 514 ci. Wayne Jefferies built the engine, which incorporates a set of "Dyno" Don Nicholson heads. (Photo Courtesy Frank Druse Jr.)

preferred the Boss 429 over the Cammer, which he called too exotic. Ford had given both Schartman and Nicholson 10 Cammers and 10 Boss 429 engines. The pair made a trade, and Schartman ended up with 20 Boss engines and Nicholson ended up with 20 Cammers.

Schartman's new Maverick was received as a bare-bones body-in-white. He hauled the car to his father's wrecking yard, where, with the help of crewmate John Ciacchi, the Maverick was prepared for its life on the strip. A wrecked Maverick donated its trim and interior. Since removing weight is like adding horsepower, everything about this car was lightweight. The door hinges were titanium, as were nearly all of the bolts in the car. Fiberglass panels were added (where rules allowed), and lightweight bucket seats were installed.

To fit the Holman-Moody-supplied Boss 429 within the tight confines of the engine bay, the shock towers were removed with the help of a reciprocating saw. It sounds messy—and it was. When Ford withdrew from racing partway through the 1970 season, Schartman, who was more aligned with Mercury, converted the car to a Comet by swapping the front clip and taillights.

The Comet recorded 9.40 ETs, and Schartman became known as the "Match Race King," as he won a reported 93 percent of his matches. He campaigned the Maverick through most of the 1972 season before replacing it with a newly built, coilover-front-suspension Maverick.

In national event competition, the Maverick's best showing was at the 1972 NHRA Gatornationals,

The restored Maverick retains the original Schartman interior and roll bar. These early Pro Stockers were basic and functional. (Photo Courtesy Frank Druse Jr.)

where Schartman was forced to run the car in B/Gas (as opposed to Pro Stock). It seems that the tech inspectors had an issue with the fact that the Maverick retained the Comet taillights. The ridiculous technicality paid off for Schartman, as he won class and then was runner-up in Modified Eliminator.

Schartman was one of the very few racers to run the Boss 429 engine in drag racing and win with it. His secret was to run 780 Holleys, as opposed to the new-at-the-time Dominator carburetors. Schartman saw the Dominators as pumping too much fuel, killing the bottom end, and most races are won or lost in the first 600 feet.

The Maverick was sold late in 1972 to Belvin Cooper in North Carolina. Cooper had previously bought the Pro Stock Maverick of Gene Cromer, and used the Schartman car as a parts donor. Little was done with the Schartman Maverick until Stephen Thompson bought the car in 1987. Thompson placed a 302 in the car and raced it for a few years as the *Midnight Express*. In 1991, the car was traded to Frank Druse Jr.

Although the Maverick was surprisingly complete, retaining a good majority of parts from 1972, Druse Jr. had a lot of work to do. When it came to the body, the tailpanel needed work after previously being cut open for Comet taillights. In addition, the right quarter panel needed a little massaging, as at one time, Schartman busted an axle and lost a wheel. After the body was prepped, Brad "Shaggy" Dierup applied the correct yellow and blue paint. Completing the body was lettering by Dick Shypaki.

Jack Dineen pieced together the new 514-ci Boss engine, which houses period-correct parts. A Toploader 4-speed transmission and a 9-inch rear end with 28-spline axles were installed. Schartman used the same axles in the car because he figured that the car was light enough that he wouldn't have problems with breakage. A pinion snubber of Schartman's own design prevented wheel hop.

The restoration was completed in 2005, and Schartman was really taken aback upon laying eyes on it. This is possibly the best-known Boss 429 race car in existence, and is completely documented. Druse Jr. gives credit to his wife, Meribeth, who was a driving force behind the restoration.

Before the restoration of the Maverick was initiated, the current owner had Ed Schartman confirm that this was his old car. Many competitors saw the writing on the tailpanel. (Photo Courtesy Frank Druse Jr.)

Tennessee Thunder Demon

Everything that the team of Sox & Martin touched turned to gold, including this 1971 Demon that was built for Freeman "Lee" Crowder. The "S/S" refers to AHRA Pro Stock. (Photo Courtesy Tommy Lee Byrd)

Sox & Martin built a 1971 Dodge Demon for Freeman "Lee" Crowder to replace the factory Hemi Barracuda that he had been campaigning. To drive and maintain the car, Crowder hired the more-than-competent Nashville-based brothers John and Gerald Livingston.

Now, coming out of the shop of Sox & Martin, the car would be built correctly and with the best parts. The Hemi has twin Holley 1050 carburetors perched on a Weiand intake, a Mallory magneto, and Doug Thorley headers. Behind the Hemi is an A833 transmission that is controlled by a Hurst vertical-gate shifter and a Dana rear end. During the 1971 season, John recorded 9.80 ETs, with a best class-legal ET of 9.82. The *Tennessee Thunder* would be match raced extensively by John throughout the year with favorable results.

The Demon spent time in the 1980s running as a bracket car. Although it was fairly complete, rust required both quarter panels and one door skin to be replaced. (Photo Courtesy Charley Miller)

Larry Ferrell was responsible for the restoration aside from the glass and interior. (Photo Courtesy Tommy Lee Byrd)

Holley Dominator carburetors on a Weiand intake top the period-correct Hemi that was assembled by David Meers. Just like in the days of old, the car uses a Mallory ignition. (Photo Courtesy Tommy Lee Byrd)

Outside of the updated roll cage, the interior of the Demon appears just as it did 50-plus years ago. Owner Lee Crowder III has plans to take the car down the track again. (Photo Courtesy Tommy Lee Byrd)

Sox & Martin dominated NHRA Pro Stock for nearly two full seasons. Those with an affinity for Mopars beat a path to their door to have the team build them a car. (Photo Courtesy Tommy Lee Byrd)

The Demon, which reportedly started life as a 6-cylinder-equipped Duster, had a fairly short lifespan. However, such was life in the quickly evolving early days of Pro Stock. Crowder retired the car at the end of the season when the opportunity to purchase the *Mopar Missile* Dodge Challenger presented itself. John and Gerald were retained to maintain the new *Tennessee Thunder* Dodge.

The Demon was stored away by Crowder and was joined by the Challenger a year later when it was retired. The two remained in storage into the mid-1980s, when Crowder put them up for sale. The Challenger ended up in the hands of Clark Rand and was restored back to its *Mopar Missile* likeness. The Demon went to a new owner in Kentucky, who bracket raced the car with a Wedge engine under the name *Mountain Mopar*. Lee Crowder III, the grandson of the original owner, went looking for the car, and he tracked it to Florida in 2010. It took some convincing, but Crowder III was finally able to procure the car.

A year later, Crowder III (with the helping hands of Larry Ferrell, Charley Miller, and David Meers) completed an extensive rotisserie restoration. Meers built the Hemi, which went together using a new 1971 block and is 472 ci. Internals include an Eagle crank and rods and 14:1-compression Ross pistons. The horsepower is estimated to be 700, and the torque is estimated to be 600 ft-lbs. This car was restored for speed, not just for show.

Keystone Klassic wheels were a common component on the Sox & Martin–built cars. The tires on this car are Phoenix F/Xs. (Photo Courtesy Tommy Lee Byrd)

Gilbert & Maskin 1972 Gremlin

Through the 1977 season, Dick Maskin continued to be a Pro Stock threat—first with the AMC Gremlin and then with a Hornet. (Photo Courtesy Todd Wingerter)

Before being restored, Al Wick of Wisconsin campaigned the ex-Gilbert & Maskin Gremlin as a bracket car. At this point, the Gremlin was powered by a big-block Chevy. (Photo Courtesy Michael Pottie)

In 1971, Bob Swaim, the head of racing at American Motors Corporation (AMC), was given the green light to expand the manufacturer's drag racing presence. Looking to field several Pro Stock Gremlins, Swaim sought a big-name driver to race for AMC. Swaim had recently come over from Ford, and he set his sights on "Dyno" Don Nicholson. By the end of the season, rumors were flying that Nicholson would race for AMC. Well, at the last minute, Nicholson decided to continue running with his Maverick.

At the recommendation of Dick Maskin, a Michigan-based Modified Production racer, Swaim spoke with Wally Booth. Booth liked the idea of racing on someone else's dime and saw potential in the AMC engine. A contract was signed late in 1971.

Later, Dick Maskin and Rich LaMont joined Booth under the AMC umbrella. Swaim said that LaMont was "a political move" because he was connected through Roger Penske. Penske had been under contract with AMC since 1970, and in 1972, Penske campaigned a Matador in NASCAR for the manufacturer.

The three Pro Stock teams had a good starting point, as 1972 NHRA weight breaks favored Wedge-powered compacts, and the AMC engine was designed with an ideal large-bore and short-stroke combination. It was just a matter of trial and error before AMC became a genuine Pro Stock threat.

Dick Maskin and his partner Jim Gilbert ran out of Oak Park, Michigan, and had previously campaigned the

Ron Fournier was called upon by Dick Maskin to prepare the chassis for the AMC-provided body-in-white. As was common practice, the body was acid dipped to reduce weight. (Photo Courtesy Mecum Auctions)

Wally Booth and Dick Arons provided the engine for the Gilbert & Maskin *Gremlin. Considering the lack of racing experience and poor-flowing heads, the engine performed well. (Photo Courtesy Mecum Auctions)*

The Gremlin showed many competitors its taillights. The Fournier-built car did not have a tube chassis but was built similar in fashion to Grumpy Jenkins's innovative Vega, with a 360-degree roll cage. (Photo Courtesy Mecum Auctions)

Mouse Pack 1 Camaro in C/Modified Production. Although the Gremlin did well locally, it (along with the other three AMC-backed cars) failed to make a dent at the national level. It seemed that development still had a ways to go. The biggest performance hindrance was the restrictive cylinder heads.

The Wally Booth/Dick Arons–built 354-ci engine, which was derived from a 0.080 overbore and Moldex stroker crankshaft, was making some power. Helping to produce consistent 9.50 ETs were parts from Mickey Thompson, JE Pistons, Edelbrock, Holley, and General Kinetics. Ron Fourier was responsible for the chassis, which carried a ladder-bar Dana rear end and a BorgWarner transmission.

The Gremlin was sold to LeRoy Roeder in 1973, when Gilbert & Maskin debuted an aerodynamically superior Hornet fastback—a car that was said to be worth a few tenths of a second quicker and was capable of a top speed of 2 mph more than the Gremlin in the quarter mile. The Gremlin was last raced as a big-block Chevy-powered bracket car before AAA Restorations returned it to its former Gilbert & Maskin glory in 2015.

The dash of the Gremlin houses oil-pressure and water-temperature gauges. A Hurst Line-Loc Super Shifter pokes through the floor and mounts a Hurst Line-Loc. In 1972, the rules required two seats. (Photo Courtesy Mecum Auctions)

The clean lines of the restored Gilbert & Maskin *Gremlin are broken by the unorthodox air scoop. That little AMC mill likely gulped more than enough air. (Photo Courtesy Mecum Auctions)*

MacEwen & Williams Pinto

The MacEwen & Williams Pinto was a tough competitor. Driven by Floyd Williams, ETs were in the 8.80s. This photo was taken at Ohio's Dragway 42 in the summer of 1975. (Photo Courtesy Todd Wingerter)

By 1974, it seemed that the only way to win in NHRA Pro Stock was with a Cleveland-powered Ford. A Ford appeared in every national-event final round, and Bob Glidden, in his Cleveland-powered Pinto, won the season championship.

The team of Ernie MacEwen and Floyd Williams debuted their Wolverine-chassis Pinto in the early summer of 1974. MacEwen worked in Ford's experimental garage and had ties to the manufacturer dating back to the development of the 1964 Thunderbolt Fairlane. He built the stock-sized cubic-inch Cleveland that propelled the Pinto to consistent 8.80 ETs. Although national event wins eluded the pair, they could boast that they beat Bob Glidden, the world champ, at Indy during a Division 3 meet.

The pair campaigned the Pinto through the summer of 1976 before selling it off to legendary Northwest racer, Jim Van

West Coast racer Jim Van Cleve had his own success with the Pinto. Van Cleve updated the nose and the tail while running the car through 1984. (Photo Courtesy Rich Carlson/ Grant Bittner Collection)

Pro Stock Restorations and Recreation completed the Pinto's meticulous restoration. The paint is a Candy Metallic Dark Blue and a lighter 1969 Mustang Winter Blue Metallic. Pearl White divides the two paint colors. (Photo Courtesy Ron Berges)

The two restored Pintos harken back to the golden age of Pro Stock. It was a time when the cars were recognizable and brand loyalty meant a lot more than it does today. (Photo Courtesy Ron Berges)

Cleve. Van Cleve campaigned the Pinto in Pro Stock and B/FX and coaxed a best ET of 8.39 out of his combination.

In the summer of 1984, he sold the car as a roller to Monte Green.

Green raced the car for about 5 years in Super Gas, using a single-4-barrel-equipped 351 and Powerglide transmission. From there, the Pinto was sold to Bob Yoak of West Virginia.

In 1995, the Pinto was sold again, this time to Steve McGinnis. McGinnis raced the car briefly between 1996 and 1998 at West Virginia's Kanawha Valley Raceway. In 2011, McGinnis put the Pinto up for sale.

With the nostalgia Pro Stock craze catching fire, Ron Berges wanted the car. In 2013, he worked out a deal with McGinnis and purchased it as a rolling chassis.

Doug Schmitt, along his father, at Pro Stock Restorations and Recreations, were called upon to restore the car back to its *MacEwen & Williams* likeness.

The Dale Shafer Cleveland engine reportedly produces 775 hp. After the bugs have been worked out, 8-second ETs will once again be attainable. (Photo Courtesy Ron Berges)

The restoration started slowly but was finally completed in 2023. Powering the Pinto today is a Dave Shafer Cleveland. If the Shafer name rings a bell, it's because he was a standout in AHRA Pro Stock competition for several years.

As part of the restoration, Schmitt replaced the roll cage with a modern (legal) copy of the Wolverine-designed cage, which featured a larger tubing diameter and thickness. Berges's future plans call for making some full-on passes in the car.

The interior appears just as it did when it was produced by Wolverine Chassis in 1972. The updates, including a certified roll cage, all relate to safety. (Photo Courtesy Ron Berges)

The Pinto originally had the hatchback with a big back window. However, since the car has about 100 hp more today than it did in the 1980s, owner Ron Berges elected to keep the later, large wing with a small back window. It adds stability at speeds of 160 mph and beyond. (Photo Courtesy Ron Berges)

Gapp & Roush Pinto

The Cleveland-powered Fords ruled NHRA Pro Stock in the 1970s, and few could compete with the team of Gapp & Roush. The Gapp & Roush *Pinto bent the rules and was lightweight. (Photo Courtesy Bob Stire/Rob Potter Collection)*

For the most part, Ford had a stranglehold on the 1970s NHRA Pro Stock category. In total, Ford cars (that were all powered by various-displacement Cleveland engines) won five season championships during the decade. The team of Wayne Gapp and Jack Roush won the title in 1973 and remained a threat through the 1977 season.

In 1976, Gapp & Roush hired Wolverine Chassis of Romulus, Michigan, to build a Pinto as a stablemate to their *Juana Taxi*, which was a 4-door Maverick. While they focused the Maverick on NHRA events, the Pinto competed at AHRA meets. It was a tough nut to crack, though, as Bill "Grumpy" Jenkins's Monzas had a stranglehold on AHRA Pro Stock, winning world titles in 1975, 1976, and 1977.

The *Gapp & Roush* Pinto was lightweight, and before being retired in early 1977, it ran Cleveland engines up to 430 ci. Its match-race ETs were in the 8.50s. As the current owners of the car, Al and Doug Schmitt discovered during the restoration that the body had been acid dipped to reduce weight. Once the body was mated to the chassis, the car was again dipped. They didn't do a thorough job of rinsing it because when Doug cut into the chassis, water flowed out.

Other weight reduction came in the form of chassis and roll-cage tubing that was small in diameter. Aluminum bolts were used throughout the car, and the front-wheel lug nuts, which were supposed to stick out so far past the wheel nuts were actually short. The end of the lug nuts had set screws so that it looks like a long stud was used. With the driver and no ballast, the Pinto weighed in at 2,000 pounds.

Gordon Frank bought the Pinto from Leroy Roeder in 1979 and had his own success through 1982 while racing at United Drag Racing Association (UDRA) events. In 1980, he was the UDRA's Rookie of the Year. (Photo Courtesy Gordon Frank)

In 1977, the Pinto was sold to UDRA Champion Leroy Roeder. He continued to run the Pinto in Pro Stock, competing at UDRA and IHRA events. In 1978, he updated the Pinto with a newer model slant nose and a large rear bumper. Prior to new yellow paint being applied, damage to the left quarter panel from contact with a retaining wall was repaired.

Drag racing historian Bret Kepner said, "[Leroy] took delivery of this car and immediately ran it with nitrous oxide in the UDRA's "no rules" Pro Stock. He won his first race out with it—the UDRA Spring Nationals."

It took a significant amount of work to restore the **Gapp & Roush** *Pinto to this point. All of the effort was well worth it, and it is evident in the final result. (Photo Courtesy Doug Schmitt).*

In 1979, Gordy Frank became the next owner. He campaigned the Pinto in UDRA Pro Stock, winning titles of his own through 1982. According to Frank, the Pinto ran a best ET of 8.48 at 163 mph with a 377-ci, Gapp & Roush Cleveland. In 1980, Frank won the UDRA Rookie of the Year honors as well as the Best Appearing Car and Crew award. Circumstances saw Frank selling the Pinto to Al Schmitt as a rolling chassis in 1983 after damaging the Cleveland. Al, who was crew chief for Pro Stock's "Animal" Jim Feurer, dropped a 302 and Toploader transmission into the Pinto and went bracket racing. This lasted a few years before he retired the car, parking it until 2015, when the nostalgia racing bug bit.

In 2015, Al and Doug decided to breathe life back into the car. The plan from the beginning was to restore the Pinto to *Gapp & Roush* livery while ensuring that it would be safe and capable of making full-on passes.

Al and Doug operate Pro Stock Restoration and Recreations in Illinois, and between the work that was performed for customers, they worked on the

When viewing the **Gapp & Roush** *Pinto's interior, all eyes are attracted to the 4-speed Lenco shift handles. This Pinto is built for speed, and driver safety is paramount. (Photo Courtesy Doug Schmitt)*

The plan from the beginning of the restoration was to be able to make safe, full-on passes in the Pinto. As this photo shows, that mission was accomplished. (Photo Courtesy Doug Schmitt)

"Animal" Jim Feurer built the Cleveland that currently powers the Pinto. Where possible, period-correct parts were used. (Photo Courtesy Doug Schmitt)

Pinto. The car was stripped to its bare bones, and the non-original parts were tossed to the side. The thin-tube roll cage was cut out, and a certified cage was installed. This necessitated replacing some of the original tin work. Before the Kia blue, pearl white, and orange paint went on, the rotted doors were replaced with fiberglass units, and a new 1976-style front clip was obtained. The large rear bumper was removed, which was hiding the small original fiberglass bumper behind it.

Between the frame rails went a Jim Feurer–built 412-ci Cleveland engine. Period-correct parts were complemented by the addition of an MSD ignition and rocker shafts. Just like in 1976, a Lenco 4-speed transmission and ladder bar supported a 9-inch rear end to complete the driveline. Early quarter-mile outings produced 8.60 ETs, and more is to come.

Doug Schmitt proves that history repeats itself as he heats the hides prior to making another pass with an 8.60 ET. (Photo Courtesy Mike Sopko Jr.)

More Gapp & Roush

The Gapp & Roush Mustang II (pictured here in 2024) debuted in 1974 at the NHRA Gatornationals. At the race, Jack Roush qualified the car in the number-two position with a 9.03 ET, and he finished right behind his partner, Wayne Gapp, in the team's Pinto.

The Mustang II was campaigned by Gapp & Roush through the 1974 season before being sold to Vicente Lugo in Puerto Rico. The Mustang II later was sold to Luis Forteza, who saw great success with the car before it was sold back to the United States in the mid-1980s.

In the mid-1990s, Roush discovered that the Mustang II was located in Miami, Florida, and bought it. The car was in rough shape but went through a thorough restoration that was completed in 2024. A period-correct 351 Cleveland engine is being built before any full-on passes are made.

From their first Pro Stock Maverick in 1971 to their last Pinto in 1977, the team of Gapp & Roush remained in the top echelon of the Pro Stock category. Restoration of the Don Hardy-chassis-equipped car was completed in 2024. (Photo Courtesy Tyler Wolfe)

Dyno Don: World Champion

In 1977, "Dyno" Don Nicholson set his sights on winning the NHRA Pro Stock crown, driving his Cleveland-powered Mustang II. He dominated the season and won the title in convincing fashion. (Photo Courtesy Michael Pottie).

"Dyno" Don Nicholson was Ford's go-to driver when the NHRA debuted its Pro Stock category in 1970. At the 1971 Summernationals, Nicholson accomplished what no one else could: he broke Chrysler's stranglehold on the category by defeating 1970 Pro Stock World Champion Mike Fons and his Dodge Challenger in the final round. In 1972, Nicholson won the AHRA Pro Stock Championship with a Cleveland-powered Pinto. In 1975, he won the IHRA Pro Stock championship driving a Don Hardy–built Mustang II.

A new Hardy Mustang II was built for 1976, and by 1977, everything clicked for Nicholson. Jon Kaase, a master technician who had previously campaigned a Cleveland-powered Pinto with Larry Ford, joined Nicholson's camp in 1977. The pair set its sights on winning the season's NHRA championship. Although the Cleveland-powered Fords had to carry more weight than other brands, the season got off to a good start, with Nicholson finishing as the runner-up to Larry Lombardo at the Winternationals. Things improved as the season progressed, due to Nicholson's wins at the Gatornationals, Springnationals, and U.S. Nationals. At the U.S. Nationals, he ran a low ET of 8.61 and defeated Bob Glidden in the final. Nicholson held off a late-season rush by Glidden to win the championship with 14,589 points to Glidden's 14,000.

In class-legal competition, the Mustang ran a 340-ci (4.08-inch bore and 3.25-inch stroke) Cleveland engine. When it came to running cash-friendly match-race dates, the 340 was pulled and replaced with a rare aluminum 392-ci Cleveland.

Nicholson campaigned the Mustang II in 1978, and, although class wins were elusive, the match race wins continued. With a 516-ci engine (thanks to a stretched-out aluminum 429/460 block), Nicholson recorded what many say was Pro Stock's first 7-second time. The historic moment came during a match race at Englishtown's "Crazy Eddie's Night of Thrills," when, on a run against Grumpy Jenkins, Nicholson recorded a 7.97 ET at 175 mph. The Mustang II weighed 1,900 pounds and featured lightweight, windowless doors and a humongous Formula 5000–style hood scoop.

Late in 1978, the Mustang II was sold to Johnny Dowey to help finance a new Don Hardy Mustang II. Dowey's best showing came when he qualified number eight at the 1979 Gatornationals in March. A month later, Nicholson bought the Mustang II back after crashing his new car. Nicholson raced the Mustang II into the

The Mustang II made "Dyno" Don Nicholson a fortune when he was matching racing competitors such as Bill "Grumpy" Jenkins. An aluminum 516 propelled the Mustang II to record ETs. (Photo Courtesy Mike Sopko Sr.)

The Mustang II is shown as it appeared while it was being driven by Vernon Summer. Thankfully, the majority of "Dyno" Don Nicholson parts remained with the car. Where possible, original parts were retained. Parts that were useable were cleaned and, if necessary, repainted. (Photo Courtesy Don Nicholson)

Here, a bare Cleveland is hoisted into place to help with fitment and fabrication. The doors and glass from a donor car were used. (Photo Courtesy Don Nicholson)

1980 season before parking it at his Orange, California, home.

In 1983, the Mustang II was dusted off and raced by South Carolina's Vernon Summer. Summer campaigned it mainly in IHRA competition with a Nicholson-built, big-inch Boss engine. When Summer moved on to another car, the Mustang went into storage and sat until January 2023. At that time, Cindy Nicholson ("Dyno" Don's daughter) and Don Nicholson ("Dyno" Don's great-nephew and namesake) decided that it was time to restore the car and let fans enjoy it. Don brought the car to his home near Phoenix, Arizona, to begin the restoration.

Although a good majority of the Mustang's components were still intact from the days when "Dyno" Don campaigned the car, several key components were missing and needed to be sourced or fabricated. Master fabricator and builder Bryon Pryde of Queen Creek, Arizona, was hired, and he focused on the build for several months straight. Challenges presented themselves, and Pryde found solutions. Kaase specified that 2.25-inch header primaries went into a 4-inch collector, and Pryde came through.

"That's what we ran back then," said Kaase.

From plumbing the fuel and brake lines to reworking a bellhousing (there's no off-the-shelf bellhousing to mate a Lenco transmission to a Cleveland engine) and making brackets, Pryde got the job done.

Jon Kaase, now a world-renowned engine builder, was tasked with building a period-correct Cleveland engine. During the build, Kaase called Don and said, "The camshaft is bent in two different directions. This engine was blown up bad. I have another cam on the shelf, but it wouldn't have sounded nearly as good as the bent cam. So, I straightened the cam, cleaned it up, and reinstalled it."

The World Champion Mustang II nears completion at this stage. The Nicholsons were careful to not over-restore the Mustang II. (Photo Courtesy Don Nicholson)

Kaase dynoed the Cleveland (mainly just to break it in) and spun it up to 7,500 rpm. Kaase said that it made more than 700 hp and was still climbing sharply.

"Man, if I had just a few hours with the knowledge and equipment that I have now, back then, we could have really put a beating on the competition with this engine," Kaase said.

Pro Street car builder Matt Hay assisted in sourcing parts and rebuilding the Hurst/Airheart calipers. Buster Baglieri flew in for a day and wired the entire car after ripping out yards of bare copper wires that were cooked. The transmission was rebuilt by Lenco. The entire rear axle was dropped off at Currie, and Ray Currie oversaw the rebuild.

The Mustang had been repainted by Summer, so period-correct paint was in order. The car had two rather similar paint schemes during its time with "Dyno" Don: its original 1976 paint and a refresh in 1977. The Nicholsons chose to go the 1977-championship-season route. The decal arrangement was based on how the car appeared at that season's U.S. Nationals event.

Prior to bodywork and paint, a donor Mustang II gave up its doors and glass to the cause. Fellow Arizona resident and drag racer Darin Dolezal prepped the body and applied the paint and stripes. However, first, repairs were required to the old fiberglass panels. The pressure was on

The "1 Pro" on the glass recognizes "Dyno" Don Nicholson's 1977 NHRA Pro Stock World Championship win. The effort that was put into this car paid off, as the Mustang II won its class at the 75th-annual Grand National Roadster Show. (Photo Courtesy Matt DeYoung)

John Kaase, who partnered with "Dyno" Don Nicholson in 1977, was asked to build the Cleveland engine for the restored Mustang II. The engine makes more than 700 hp using mostly period-correct parts. (Photo Courtesy Matt DeYoung)

The interior of the Mustang II was cleaned but left as it was. The Nicholsons felt that this was "Dyno" Don's office and that it should remain as he raced it. (Photo Courtesy Matt DeYoung)

to debut the car at the 2024 SEMA Show, and Dolezal delivered, completing the work in just 10 days. Tim Sieger replicated all of the period-correct sponsor decals along with the prismatic "DYNO DON" for the doors, creating them in vinyl for Don to apply.

The number of contributors to the restoration is large, and both Cindy and Don are quick to give thanks. Without the helping hands, the Mustang II never would have made its scheduled debut. No doubt, SEMA attendees were thankful as well.

Removing the fiberglass hatch reveals the more of Don Hardy's handywork. Straps support the parachute. Expandable spray foam was applied to the inside of the acid-dipped body. (Photo Courtesy Matt DeYoung)

Even though this car was restored and is shown in memory of "Dyno" Don Nicholson, it can still lay down tracks. (Photo Courtesy Matt DeYoung)

The clock tells the story. Darin Dolezal and his Auto Image Paint & Body company in Chandler, Arizona, matched the Mustang II's 1977 paint. (Photo Courtesy Matt DeYoung)

Bob Glidden's Plymouth

Bob Glidden debuted his Plymouth Arrow at the NHRA Winternationals in fine fashion. In the category final, he defeated the Camaro of Joe Satmary. (Photo Courtesy Rich Carlson/ Grant Bittner)

After nearly a decade of success driving Cleveland-powered Fords, Bob Glidden surprised the masses when he jumped ship and debuted a Plymouth Arrow at the 1979 NHRA Winternationals.

The switch to Chrysler came when Dave Koffel, a staff engineer for the manufacturer, approached Glidden at the IHRA Northern Nationals in July 1978. Koffel, knowing that Glidden was getting no support from Ford, flat-out asked him if he'd like to come race for Chrysler. The company offered an enticing deal that covered a car, parts, and a trailer. Glidden took some time to consider the offer before signing with Chrysler at the NHRA Fallnationals—an event that he won.

Don Hardy was called upon to build the chassis for the Arrow, while Glidden studied the LA-series Chrysler engine. His work began with a high-nickel "X" block and proceeded from there. The W-2 heads received a lot of welding, filling, and reshaping, as did the Holley Pro Dominator intake manifold. As was expected of any good racer, Glidden kept the extent of his modifications a closely guarded secret. As expected, Glidden counted on the best of parts: twin 1150 Holley carburetors, Venolia gas-ported pistons, Brooks rods, and a Comp Cams camshaft. He tested engines of various sizes, including 339 ci and 342 ci. Power was transferred through a 3.10-first-gear Lenco transmission to a 5.57-geared 9-inch Ford rear end.

The fact that Glidden switched from Ford to Chrysler remained under wraps until 1979. One can just imagine the reaction of his peers when he showed up in Southern California driving a Plymouth. At the Winternationals, Glidden defeated the Camaro of Joe Satmary in the final

In 1981, Paul Gentilozzi, in Bob Glidden's old Plymouth Arrow, faces Bob Glidden, in his Ford Fairmont, at Martin, Michigan. Gentilozzi ended up on the short end. (Photo Courtesy Steve Reyes)

By the mid-1980s, Bob Glidden's Plymouth Arrow was owned by Jerry Hurley and being driven by Sonny Ray in Comp Eliminator. (Photo Courtesy Buddy Houts/Wayne Tonia Holland Collection)

The Plymouth Arrow was disassembled to its bare bones during its restoration. The restoration began in 2020 and was completed by Carl Arciprete by himself in his home garage. (Photo Courtesy Carl Arciprete)

round for his seventh consecutive national-event win, giving Chrysler its first NHRA Pro Stock victory since 1973. Of the 10 NHRA national events in 1979, Glidden lost only three—and two of those were red-light losses.

Glidden set the class record with an 8.48 ET at the Gatornationals, and soon after, the NHRA hit him (and the other short-wheelbase, small-block cars) with more weight. After seeing the beating that the Hemi took from the NHRA, I'm sure that the Chrysler fraternity must have felt that it would never catch a break from the sanctioning body. Initially, the small cars ran at 6.70 lbs/ci, but this was bumped to 6.80 lbs/ci. Most other combinations saw a drop in weight—anywhere from 0.05 pounds to 0.10 pounds for the Hemi cars. However, Glidden kept marching onward.

In 1979, Glidden won the Pro Stock world championship. It was an amazing feat, considering that it was a whole new car and combination to start the season. However, Chrysler was in financial trouble and on the verge of bankruptcy. It cut its paid drivers loose, as its involvement in racing activities all but came to an end. Glidden, who had a new Don Hardy Volare being built, got stuck with the bill for the car and sold it before it was completed. A new Hardy Fairmont was commissioned, and Glidden sold the Arrow to Don Campanello.

Campanello campaigned the car for a year in Pro Stock before selling it to Paul Gentilozzi. From Gentilozzi, the Arrow made a quick stop with Pat Musi before being sold to Jerry Hurley. Hurley campaigned it in the Comp category with various drivers behind the wheel, including

Carl Arciprete prepped the body and laid down the Ford colors himself. Arciprete leaned on his experience as a painter of Pro Stock trucks. (Photo Courtesy Carl Arciprete)

Bob Glidden ran 340-ci engines in the Arrow. This one, which was built by the current owner, is slightly smaller. Glidden's parts that were sold with the car were used throughout. (Photo Courtesy Carl Arciprete)

Welcome to Bob Glidden's office. Waiting on hard-to-find Lenco parts, Carl Arciprete installed a Liberty 5-speed transmission in the Arrow for the time being. (Photo Courtesy Carl Arciprete)

The intake ports of the heads show some of the reworking that was performed by Bob Glidden. There was no rest for drag racing's "Mad Dog," who put in long hours to stay on top. (Photo Courtesy Carl Arciprete)

Dempsey Hardy, who would become the next owner of the car. Hardy, a resident of Fort Lauderdale, campaigned the Arrow in the Gas category into the mid-1980s before retiring the car. He stored it in an old box hauler for the next 15 years.

Carl Arciprete, a native New Yorker, moved to Fort Lauderdale, Florida, in the early 1980s and opened a shop. The shop was named South Florida Frame, and it was where he built chassis for Pro Stock Trucks. He quickly befriended Hardy. Arciprete became aware of the Arrow, and, like Hardy, he never thought much of it. In 1997, Hardy offered the car to Arciprete, who dragged the car from its storage to his own shop.

The Arrow collected dust for several years and made the move to New York when Arciprete decided to go home about a decade later. When business slowed in 2020 due to the COVID-19 pandemic, Arciprete got busy on the restoration. A serial tag on the roll cage confirmed that it was a Don Hardy car, and a quick call to Hardy in Floydada, Texas, confirmed that it was indeed Glidden's old ride.

Arciprete figures he spent at least 3,000 hours on the restoration, which was made easier by the fact that the majority of parts Glidden used remained on the car. The restored Arrow made its debut at the Chrysler show at Carlsbad in 2023.

Approximately 3,000 hours were spent restoring the Plymouth. It was only raced for five seasons before being put into storage. (Photo Courtesy Carl Arciprete)

Supporting the rear of the Arrow is a ladder bar–suspended Ford 9-inch rear end that houses 5.57 gears. The restoration was completed in 2023. (Photo Courtesy Carl Arciprete)

The restored Arrow surprised many when it debuted at the Chrysler show at Carlsbad in 2023. Sadly, Bob Glidden had died 5 years prior. (Photo Courtesy Carl Arciprete)

Woodall-Nicholson Oldsmobile

"Dyno" Don Nicholson painted the Oldsmobile at his Orange, California, shop, retaining the same colors and the design that he used on his earlier Mustangs. (Photo Courtesy Ray Cunningham)

Ralph Woodall, who is from the state of Washington, landed himself an Oldsmobile Pro Stock deal for 1983. Woodall, a well-known West Coast Super Stock racer, landed the deal when he called Oldsmobile's Tom Erb. It seems Woodall was on GM's radar, due in large part to his experience with the big-block Chevy. Erb stated that he'd be interested in having Woodall join Oldsmobile, and Erb flew to Washington the next night to sign Woodall to a contract.

"Dyno" Don Nicholson had been hoping to land a deal with Oldsmobile, but Woodall was at the top of Oldsmobile's list. Nicholson, an acquaintance of Woodall, called shortly after the deal was signed and inquired as to how he landed the Oldsmobile deal. At the time, Woodall was still asking himself that same question. Knowing that Nicholson had sold his Ford mount, Woodall took the opportunity to ask Nicholson if he wanted to be a partner in running the Oldsmobile. Nicholson needed no coaxing and agreed.

Woodall immediately requested Ciera body panels from Oldsmobile (a roof, doors, and quarter panels) so that he could start building. After a comedy of errors, which included Oldsmobile sending him a total of three complete Cieras, a body-in-white, and a semitruck, he finally received the panels that he originally requested. Ray Cunningham was called upon to build the chassis.

Oldsmobile provided the 500-ci cast block, aluminum heads, and nitrite crankshaft, which would be pieced together by Woodall. Sonny Bryant in Anaheim performed a good part of the machine work. Filling the block were 14:1-compression Brooks pistons and Holley 1,150-cfm carburetors (reworked to 1,230 cfm) to feed the fuel. Horsepower was near the 1,100 mark. For IHRA and match racing, the two relied upon a 560-ci mill.

Records show that on the car's first full pass, Nicholson recorded a 7.88 ET at 174 mph. The first national showing for the car was the NHRA World Finals in 1983. Nicholson qualified the car but fell in the first round. At the 1984 Winternationals, he ran a 7.83 ET to qualify, but, on a subsequent run, the clutch went south. He broke a rod on another run and was not able to make eliminations. Nicholson and the Oldsmobile ran 8

In the 2000s, Paul Wiechmann ran the Oldsmobile Ciera in the Pro Gas class. With a Chevy engine and Powerglide transmission, the car ran best ETs in the 8.40s. (Photo Courtesy Dave Kommel)

M&L Painting matched the yellow to a chip of paint that came from the car. Old photos were used to determine the location of the stripes. (Photo Courtesy Bruce Pederson)

national events through 1984 and qualified at five of them. His best showing was a number-8 qualifying position at the Cajun Nationals in Baton Rouge. Reflecting, Woodall felt that they could have gone higher in the season standings if the parts would have held up.

Late in 1984, Nicholson and his racing buddy Dick Estevez made the decision to shorten the car by removing 4 inches of it forward of the firewall. The reasoning behind the idea was to take advantage of the NHRA rules, which okay the move as long as the number-one cylinder remains aligned

The Oldsmobile Ciera rides on period-correct, polished centerline wheels. The original Lamb struts, shocks, and brakes were rebuilt by Lamb Components. (Photo Courtesy Bruce Pederson)

The 500-ci engine mounts ultra-rare rocker covers courtesy of Ralph Woodall as well as a just-as-rare magnesium intake from Warren Johnson. The heads were modified by Johnson and used on one of his earlier Oldsmobiles. (Photo Courtesy Bruce Pederson)

An Autometer Pro-Comp II tachometer is front and center in the restored interior. A well-designed Ray Cunningham roll cage protected the driver. (Photo Courtesy Bruce Pederson)

with the front spindle. The reason behind the modification was to move the weight of the engine and transmission closer to the rear wheels.

According to Woodall, a big-inch Chevy nitrous motor finally wore out the Ciera. In 1985, he gave the whole program (truck, trailer, and race car) to Nicholson. All accounts show that Nicholson did nothing with the Ciera before selling it to Bud Treadway in 1986. Treadway painted the car red, dropped in a 468-ci Chevy engine, and went Super Gas racing. Treadway raced the car for about 4 years before selling it. The car eventually ended up in the hands of Paul Wiechmann. Wiechmann raced the car for several years in Super Gas with a big-block Chevy and Powerglide transmission. He won several races with the car, recording ETs in the 8.40s.

The body panels on the Oldsmobile Ciera are original to the Woodall-Nicholson car. The front clip is comprised of two-piece of fiberglass. The trunk lid is also fiberglass. (Photo Courtesy Bruce Pederson)

The Oldsmobile Ciera spent about three decades running in the Super Gas category in Southern California before being purchased by Bruce Pederson and restored. (Photo Courtesy Bruce Pederson)

With his hands full with two drag cars, Wiechmann sold the Oldsmobile to Bruce Pederson in 2021 (without the engine or transmission). Pederson had considered campaigning the car himself with a big-block Chevy and Powerglide transmission before he made the decision to restore the car to its "Dyno" Don likeness.

Being a builder and fabricator, Pederson did the majority of the restoration himself. He procured the correct Drag Race Competition Engine (DRCE) block, crankshaft, and heads from former Pro Stock racer Warren Johnson and then had Top Dragster racer Andy Spiegel assemble it. The engine is 500 ci and makes 914 hp at 7,500 rpm. On the dyno, the engine continued to make power through 8,400 rpm.

The correct Lenco CS1 4-speed transmission and Hurst Lightning Rods were purchased from a gentleman in Indiana. The car retains its correct 9-inch Ford rear end and 4-link suspension.

Years of use and modifications required most of the tin work to be replaced. Pederson did most of the forming but left it to Ron Williams at Victory Race Cars to create the new tubs and transmission tunnel. Before reassembly, the chassis was powder coated. When it came to the body, the dents and dings were pulled before M&L Painting in Corona, California, applied the yellow paint. Pederson said that the car shows better than ever.

"Race cars never looked this good back then, as this amount of effort was never put into body and paint," Pederson said.

It does look good.

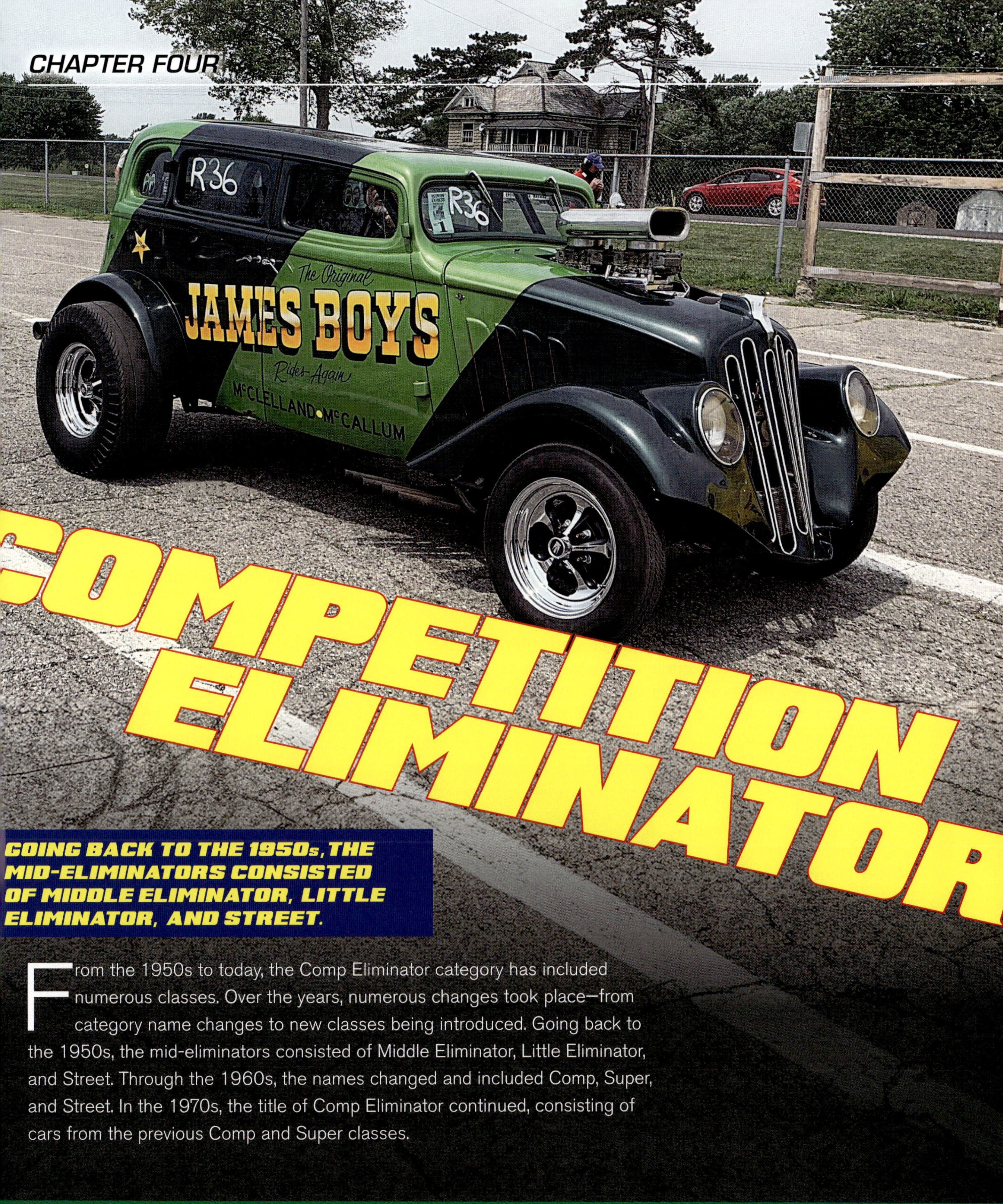

CHAPTER FOUR

COMPETITION ELIMINATOR

GOING BACK TO THE 1950s, THE MID-ELIMINATORS CONSISTED OF MIDDLE ELIMINATOR, LITTLE ELIMINATOR, AND STREET.

From the 1950s to today, the Comp Eliminator category has included numerous classes. Over the years, numerous changes took place—from category name changes to new classes being introduced. Going back to the 1950s, the mid-eliminators consisted of Middle Eliminator, Little Eliminator, and Street. Through the 1960s, the names changed and included Comp, Super, and Street. In the 1970s, the title of Comp Eliminator continued, consisting of cars from the previous Comp and Super classes.

Above: The James Boys 1933 Willys from Ontario, Canada, was built in 1967 by Jim McCallum and Jim McClelland. Today, the restored Willys is owned by Canadian George Watson and appears just as it did in the late 1960s. In its day, the big-block Chevy ran injectors. Today, it uses a 6-71 blower. (Photo Courtesy Tim Sykes)

Rebel Rouser

Shirley Rader, the original driver of this Plymouth, poses proudly with a sampling of the hardware that was earned while racing the car. (Photo Courtesy Dwayne Rader)

The 1958 song "Rebel Rouser" by Duane Eddy was an instrumental arrangement that became a smash hit. In a way, it was similar to Denzil Rader's 1932 Plymouth. Rader built the car in 1959, and the sound of its twin 4-barrel-equipped 361 engine (like Duane Eddy's guitar) was music to the ears of automotive enthusiasts. Based in Winchester, Kentucky, Rader named the car *Rebel Rouser*, as he thought that it was a fitting name for the Plymouth.

Rader completed the build right around 1960 with help from his brother Shirley, who did most of the driving. As with most drag cars, the Plymouth was continuously evolving, and in 1962, the 361 had been replaced by a three 2-barrel-equipped 390 that had been plucked from a Thunderbird. Throughout its lifetime on the track, the Plymouth ran in the B/Altered, and B/Coupe classes.

Big changes came in 1964. Under the body was a new 120-inch tube chassis that was fitted with a Holman-Moody 427 High Riser. Backing up the 427 was an Art Carr–prepped 3-speed transmission. It was around the same time that "Rebel Rouser" was painted in bold letters on each door. Giving the car its nose-up stance was a 1946 Ford axle. The Plymouth had a great season. In August, the guys won opening day at Bluegrass Dragway in Lexington, Kentucky, taking B/Altered. In addition, they received some ink in *National Dragster* magazine. At the time, the car ran a best ET of 11.20.

By 1967, the cost to stay competitive was soaring, so Rader sold the Plymouth to Tommy Bradley, who then sold it to Melvin "Snookie" Taylor. Taylor beefed up the chassis and installed an SOHC 427. He squeezed 9.30 ETs at 144 mph out of it before he retired the car and parted it out. In 1971, he sold the rolling chassis to Larry Cummings. Cummings did some metalwork to the car but little else before selling it to Lonnie Dillingham in 1999. Dillingham intended to put the car on the street, but his plans fell through. Fortunately, the car sat. This is

Resurrecting the barn-fresh Plymouth was a chore that was happily performed by Dwayne Rader. It was surprising how complete the car was when it was discovered. Photo Courtesy Dwayne Rader)

The Rebel Rouser *features Habanero red paint. Dwayne Rader spent three years restoring the car, and he debuted in 2015 on Father's Day at the Hot Rod Reunion in Bowling Green, Ohio. Sadly, his father passed away before the car was completed. (Photo Courtesy Tommy Lee Byrd)*

The Plymouth was powered by 427 Ford side-oiler engine that was stroked to 460 ci. Twin Holley 660 carburetors are shown on top of the Dove aluminum heads. (Photo Courtesy Tommy Lee Byrd)

The bank of dash-mounted gauges allowed the driver to monitor the mill. Power was transmitted through a Ford Toploader transmission. The gas pedal was made by Eelco. (Photo Courtesy Tommy Lee Byrd)

The pie-crust slicks are bolted to an Ford 8.8-inch rear end. A period-correct Oldsmobile 9.3-inch rear has since taken its place. (Photo Courtesy Tommy Lee Byrd)

The owner said that he has never made a full pass in the Rebel Rouser. *"It's been usually just a burnout and launch, and then I let off because I'm afraid to wreck it. (Photo Courtesy Dwayne Rader)*

where Rader's son, Dwayne entered the picture.

In 2012, Dwayne went looking for the old Plymouth, tracked down the car, and purchased it. Although the car was rough, all of the key pieces were there. The front suspension, the rear ladder-bar setup, and even the metallic Covico steering wheel remained.

Dwayne restored the car to its 1964 appearance, with upgrades so that he could make some passes at the track. A 460-ci Ford now resides where so many engines once rode. Dove aluminum heads and twin Holley 660 carburetors mounted on a Mickey Thompson cross-ram intake were also used.

Though Dwayne did most of the work (with his dad chipping in), he credits Raymond Borders for a fantastic job of restoring the body, Mitch Lewis for applying the paint, and Kirby Stafford, for the lettering.

Orange Crate

Today, original 1963 Revell Orange Crate *'32 Ford Sedan model kits are sold for about $100. Due to its popularity, this model kit was reissued a few times. (Photo Courtesy Dan Podobinkski)*

What is the world's most famous '32 Ford—aside from Milner's *American Graffiti* five-window? It has to be Bob Tindle's *Orange Crate*. The beautiful "show-and-go" Naples Orange sedan won the Best Competition Coupe award at the Oakland Roadster Show in 1961, 1962, and 1963. In 1962, it graced the cover of *Hot Rod* magazine, and in 1963, Revell produced a 1/25-scale kit.

In 1959, when Tindle bought the sedan, it was without an engine, but it was in primer and already had a 5-inch chopped top and molded rear fenders. A six-Stromberg-equipped Oldsmobile engine and a LaSalle transmission were installed. Tindle opted for a lemon-yellow paint to cover the primered body. He raced the car at area tracks in his home state of Oregon and entered the car in the 1960 edition of the Oakland Roadster Show.

Catching the show bug, Tindle decided to take the Ford to the next level, and it was Keith Randol who took Tindle's ideas and made them a reality. Randol was a machinist by trade and a Sprint racer at heart, and a lot of his ideas helped make the *Orange Crate* what it was.

Randol formed a Sprint Car–style chassis out of 3-inch seamless tubing, onto which he hung a dropped front axle and a Halibrand quick-change rear end. Mounted on each corner were ancient Halibrand wheels.

Dick Maris rebuilt the Oldsmobile engine, opening it up to 417 ci, and he added the front-mounted, polished Potvin blower. A B&M Hydro replaced the LaSalle transmission. The cherry on top was the Funny Car–style, flip-top body that was designed to show off the masterful work. Bracing and numerous body supports were added to make the feat possible. Sure, the added weight slowed the car, but the jaw-dropping reactions made the trade-off worth it in Tindle's eyes.

The Orange Crate *features a 6-inch top chop and 5-inch channeled body. The paint was applied in 1961 and still looks great. (Photo Courtesy Trent Sherill)*

A person can be forgiven for thinking that the flip-up body was first applied to a drag car in 1966. The innovative Orange Crate *influenced how show and go cars were built for years to come. (Photo Courtesy Trent Sherill)*

Those individual header tubes off the Oldsmobile mill look great. The Orange Crate *was built with heavy Sprint car influence. (Photo Courtesy Trent Sherill)*

Dee Westcott, of fiberglass boat fame, made a panel to fill the roof before Von's Body Shop completed the prep and applied the paint. All of the work paid off, as the *Orange Crate* won America's Best Competition Car honors at its first showing, the 1961 Oakland Roadster Show. On the track, the A/Altered recorded low-11-second ETs at 130 mph.

In 1963, the *Orange Crate* was retired from touring, as Tindle and his brother Terry opened up a Chrysler-Plymouth dealership that ate up their time. In 1965, the *Orange Crate* was sold. Then, the car swapped hands a few times before being bought in 1975 by Washington state resident Ted Gord.

In 1961, a three-point roll bar and a lap belt were the only pieces of safety equipment required for a low 11-second, 130-mph Altered. Note the transverse-style rear suspension spring. (Photo Courtesy Trent Sherill)

The Oldsmobile engine is 417 ci. Power is enhanced by a front-mounted Potvin blower, Hilborn injection, and Joe Hunt magneto. Everything is chrome plated, including the tube chassis. (Photo Courtesy Trent Sherill)

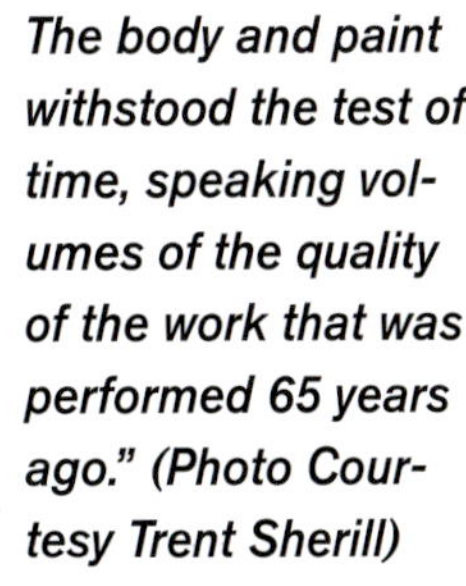

The body and paint withstood the test of time, speaking volumes of the quality of the work that was performed 65 years ago." (Photo Courtesy Trent Sherill)

In 2012, Steve Gilligan bought the Crate from Gord. Although the car wasn't in running condition when Gilligan purchased it, everything on it was and is original to how it last appeared in 1963. Gilligan rebuilt the engine and transmission, and he found it necessary to replace the engine block itself during the process. Upon completion, Gilligan delighted the crowd at Santa Barbara when he took the *Orange Crate* on a few easy passes.

The 15x9-inch M&H Racemasters are mounted to a Halibrand quick-change rear end. The gear ratio varied, but 3.78 was common. The devil is in the details, note the orange-letter tires and the spinner caps. (Photo Courtesy Trent Sherill)

Silver Bullet

Owner Stan Johnson took this, his initial drawing of the Silver Bullet, to Chrysler with a hope and a dream. Johnson's self-promotion paid off. (Photo Courtesy Stan Johnson)

Drag racing's golden age is so loved because of the variety of cars and classes that it featured. One prime example from the period is the *Silver Bullet*, a Modified Roadster belonging to Stan Johnson. The story of the *Silver Bullet*, a car that was designed by Johnson himself, began in 1962.

In 1962, Johnson graduated from Illinois Institute of Technology and had been campaigning a crudely assembled Buick-powered 1930s Roadster. He built the car from junkyard parts in 1956 to compete at the newly opened Union Grove Dragstrip. Graduating with a degree in industrial design, Johnson set his sights on building the ultimate Modified Roadster to replace his existing Roadster.

Starting with conceptual illustrations, Johnson's initial drawings morphed into a Roadster that incorporated a canopy that covered the driver's compartment, enclosed slicks, and a long wheelbase with a dragster body forward of the firewall. Class rules dictated that a grille was required. He called the car the *Silver Bullet*, which was a name that he pulled from the *The Lone Ranger* television series.

In 1964, Johnson took the chance and cold called Chrysler, hoping to land a sponsorship deal for the yet unbuilt car. In a surprise to Johnson, Chrysler gave him 15 minutes to sell them on his idea. Although Johnson was looking for a deal that included a Hemi engine, he was more than happy to walk away having been asked to run one of the manufacturer's newly designed LA-series 273-ci engines. With an agreement in hand, Johnson, along with his brother Tom and good friend Connie

Not only was the Silver Bullet *a great drag car but it was also a winning show car. The headlights were a late addition that were added when the car was shown. (Photo Courtesy Stan Johnson)*

It took years to gather the original parts of the **Silver Bullet**, *as they were scattered around southern Ontario, Canada. (Photo Courtesy Stan Johnson)*

With the body hammered and straightened, trial fitment took place. The owner had retained all of the original blueprints, which made the restoration easier. (Photo Courtesy Stan Johnson)

Friedhofer, headed out to his two-car garage to begin work.

Outside of the 127-inch Schubeck dragster chassis and turtle deck, everything else had to be fabricated or modified. The one-off body was sculpted in clay and wood. Then, along with the canopy and wheel covers, it was made using hand-laid fiberglass. When completed, Johnson sprayed on Cadillac Fire Mist Silver paint.

Stan's intentions were to run fuel injection on the 273, but being an all-new engine, nothing was available. This forced him to design his own. He utilized Algon adjustable fuel nozzles, a camshaft pump drive, and wild-looking, curved ram tubes. Wrapping up the 273 was a fabricated 7-quart oil pan and exhaust headers. A Dodge truck transmission (using second and third gear only) and rear end completed the driveline.

The build took approximately a year and a half to complete, and it was well worth the effort. The *Silver Bullet* looked as good as it performed and picked up numerous trophies, including Best Engineered honors. On the track, the car held the *Drag News* 1,320 quarter-mile record in 1966 with a 10.37 ET at 142.85 mph. The class required the *Silver Bullet* to run gasoline, but Johnson couldn't resist trying nitro through the 273. On a 95-percent load, the car reached 165 mph.

Johnson raced the car through 1969 before putting it up for sale to raise cash to start his own design business. A buyer was found in Canada, and, according to Stan, he "really messed up the car. He painted it in rose-colored fish scales."

The new owner took it to Europe, where he showed it for about 5 years. On its return trip to Canada, the car was damaged. Reportedly, at one point it was raced at Cayuga Dragway with a small-block Chevy engine. The car was eventually disassembled and the remains were lost.

Around 1999, enthusiast Rick Proctor was searching for old drag cars and was contacted by Gerry Nemz. Nemz, who owned a scrapyard, had an old dragster that he was looking to part with. Proctor took a look, liked what he saw, and the pair swung a deal. Proctor had no idea what he had bought until he began making inquiries online. The telltale body, with its formed wheel openings and the peek-a-boo rear window made it clear that he had the *Silver Bullet*. A little sanding on the car revealed the Cadillac Fire Mist Silver.

For Proctor, the next step was to look up Johnson, who still lived in Wisconsin. Searching the remaining history of the car, Proctor discovered that it was Nemz who bought the car from Johnson. Shortly after, Proctor

The restored Silver Bullet *now resides at the Museum of American Speed in Lincoln, Nebraska. On occasion, it is taken from the display for local events. (Photo Courtesy Stan Johnson)*

Among other accolades, the Silver Bullet *won the Best of Show award at the 2015 Grand National Roadster Show in Pomona and the Best of Show award at the 2022 NHRA Nationals Hot Rod Junction in Indianapolis. (Photo Courtesy Marc Gewertz)*

received a call from Nemz, telling Proctor that he had found the clutch pedal for the car. A few months later, Nemz called again to say he found the original slicks for the car. Over the course of time, Nemz found the original 273 engine with the complete fuel injection still intact and stashed away in a storage container.

"In 2007, he received a call from an owner of a scrap yard saying he had bought all of Gerry's [Nemz's] stuff, and I had better come take a look," Proctor said. "To my surprise, he had a container where Gerry had put all of his cars when he showed them in Europe. It was like showing me the mother lode of memorabilia—not only of my dragster but also of several other famous show cars. Many of the parts that I recognized were from the *Silver Bullet*, including the

Being a newly released engine when the car was built, everything had to be fabricated. The fuel injection is a work of art. (Photo Courtesy Marc Gewertz)

one-piece sheet metal, the grille, fiberglass wheel covers, and headers. That was a huge find at no cost. Thanks go out to this generous donor for helping me to gather original parts."

By 2011, the chassis was hanging on Proctor's shop wall collecting dust. It was at the enticement of a terminally ill friend, who thought that he would never see the car assembled, that Proctor set out to prove him wrong. Proctor used the pieces he had and assembled the car. A photo was sent to Johnson, who always had dreams of getting the car back. It took until 2012 for Johnson to finally convince Proctor to give it up.

The restoration, which took approximately a year to complete, was made easier by the fact that Johnson had retained everything from the car's past. In his files, he had the original drawings, construction photos, magazine articles, and even old time slips. Johnson had about 80 percent of the car when he began the restoration, and the remaining parts were either fabricated or purchased. Like the original build, all of the restoration work was completed in Johnson's own shop. Sadly, his partners Tom and Connie are no longer with us. However, there's no denying that they would be proud of what Johnson accomplished.

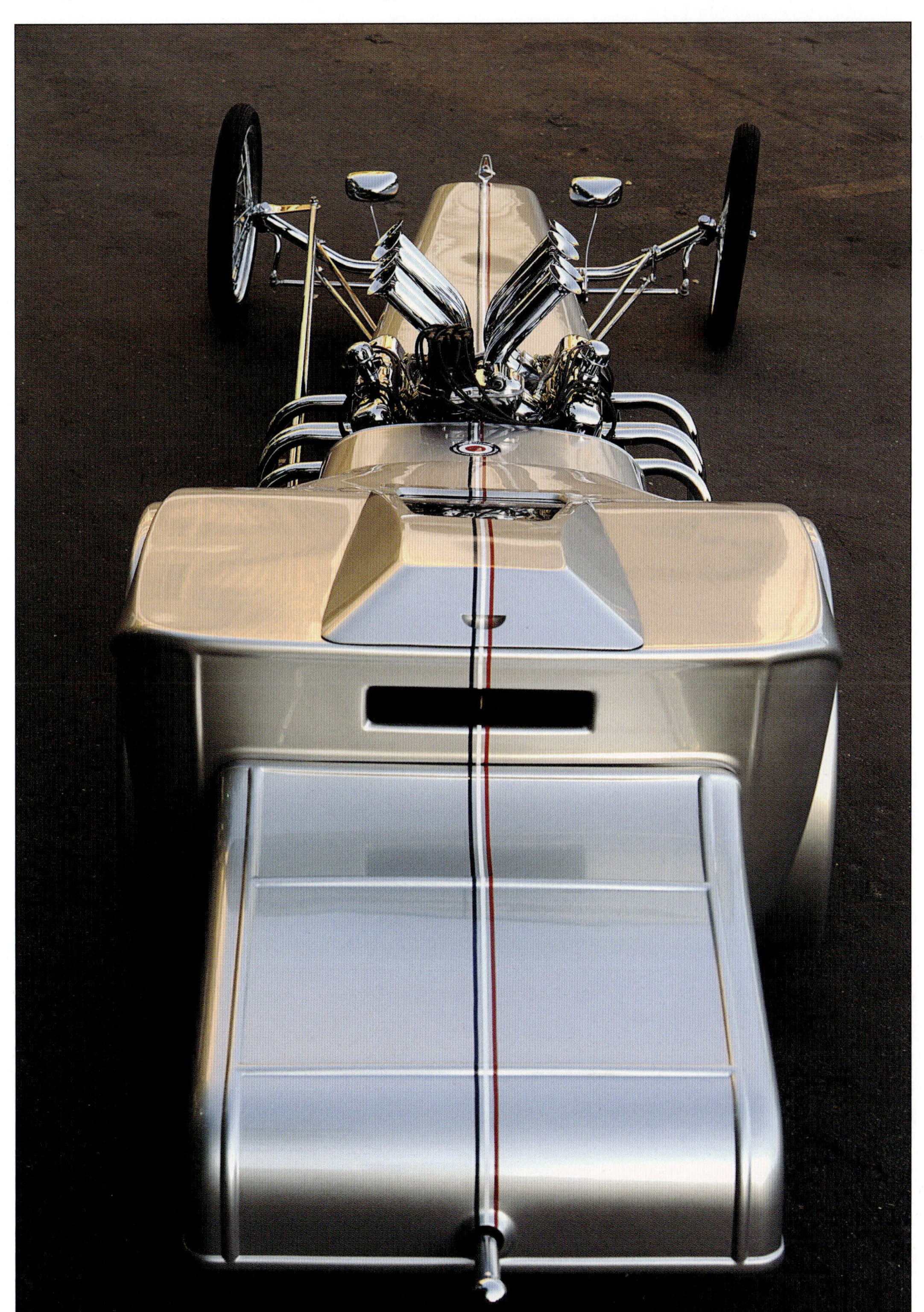

The only part that was not fabricated by the owner was the turtle deck. The rear window, which was installed to signal the push vehicle, helped identify the body when it was found. (Photo Courtesy Marc Gewertz)

Hamberis & Mitchell Willys

The team of Hamberis & Mitchell debuted this Willys in June 1965 at Half Moon Bay. The car was prepped by Chuck Finders and Ted Brown. From the beginning, this car was competitive.

The *Hamberis & Mitchell* (Al Hamberis and Mike Mitchell) 1933 Willys began life as a Gasser project that legendary builder Chuck Finders had initiated for Jon Edmonds. Finders had found the barn-fresh Willys for Edmonds, whose intentions were to campaign the car as a supercharged Gasser. Edmonds had Finders install a rear coilover suspension, front tube axle, roll bar, floorboards, and fiberglass front-end, doors, and fenders. Edmonds intended to run the car with a small-block Chevy and a B&M Hydro transmission. Finders had completed his work on the Willys in early 1964.

However, like many best-laid plans, this one went awry. Uncle Sam came calling on Edmonds in June 1964, with plans to ship him off to Southeast Asia.

"I called Chuck and told him that because my parents were retiring and moving to Northern California, I had to sell the car," Edmonds said.

Enter San Francisco–based Al Hamberis and Mike Mitchell. The two purchased the rolling Willys for less than half of the $2,500 that Edmonds had invested.

With the help of Finders's sideman, Ted Brown, Hamberis, and Mitchell completed the build. They applied burnt orange paint and stuffed the Willys with a blown small-block Chevy and a B&M Hydro transmission. With Mitchell at the wheel, the pair frequented the tracks at Fremont and Half Moon Bay through 1965. Tracks in Southern California, and tracks as far east as Indy weren't immune to the Willys winning ways. Running in A/GS, ETs in the 10-second bracket quickly became common. If they ran into stiff Hemi competition in class, they would drop down to B/GS by adding weight in the form of lead that was hidden inside the rear tube bumper. By the end of the season, the Willys was cranking out record ETs of 9.89 at 145 mph.

The year 1966 was the start of a new chapter for the Willys. With the small-block Chevy slowly falling

In 1966, the Willys was reborn with the name Wild Mouse II, *a sectioned body, new paint, a new chassis, and a Hemi engine. (Photo Courtesy J. R. Bloom)*

With the Hamberis & Mitchell partnership coming to an end, the Willys received new psychedelic paint and a new name. Here, in 1969, the Willys is being campaigned by its new owner, Mike Vincz. (Photo Courtesy Bob Martin)

With a new owner, the psychedelic paint of the Willys was replaced with crimson. Power now came from a 565-hp big-block Chevy. (Photo Courtesy Paul Kennedy)

behind the Hemis, the pair decided to step up with a Ted Brown–built 450-inch Hemi that rode on mounts that allowed for the engine to be shifted up to 4 inches from front to back. The original chassis, which had been twisted, straightened, cracked, and welded was replaced with a rectangular unit that was fabricated by Fletcher and Brown Race Cars. To wrap up the overhaul, the all-steel body was sectioned 4 inches and painted green by Don Kirby. The fabricated chassis took the Willys out of the Gas category, as the rules required original manufactured frames. This left the Willys to run BB/Altered and the ever popular, money-making match races.

By 1968, the partnership began to wane, as Mitchell looked to take to the road more and Hamberis wanted to stay closer to home in California. On the road, Mitchell counted on Doc Arnold to keep the Willys in tune. By the end of the season, Hamberis was through. He looked to travel and left the Willys for Mitchell to campaign. Mitchell laid a multicolored paint job on the car and labeled it with his now-famous moniker "the World's Fastest Hippie."

In 1969, Mitchell moved up to Funny Car and sold the Willys, complete, to Mike Vincz of Ohio. Vincz raced and showed the car through 1979, gathering his share of "show-and-go" trophies before selling it to John Lambert (without the engine and transmission). Lambert teamed with Sam Patrick, and the pair campaigned the car through the 1980s with a big-block Chevy under the hood. The next move for the Willys brought it home, in a sense.

Lambert contacted Chuck Finders, who now ran his business in

After sitting for far too long, the stalled project was picked up and completed by the current owner, Paul Kennedy. (Photo Courtesy Paul Kennedy)

Today, the Willys calls Liverpool, England, home. It is now a licensed street rod but still retains the flavor of yesterday. (Photo Courtesy Paul Kennedy)

The fresh 392 Hemi barely fits in the engine bay of the Willys. The BDS blower and an automatic transmission make the combination streetable. (Photo Courtesy Paul Kennedy)

The interior of the Willys has a ready-to-race look due to the fiberglass buckets, row of gauges, and B&M shifter. The only item that's missing is the roll bar. (Photo Courtesy Paul Kennedy)

Living on the streets is much easier with a "down to earth" stance, as opposed to the mile-high look of a drag car. It's tough to beat the look, though. (Photo Courtesy Paul Kennedy)

Elyria, Ohio. Finders recognized the old Willys and immediately bought the car on sight. Finders's plans were to put the Willys on the street. He got as far as replacing the Chevy mill with a 392 Hemi and putting a coat of primer on the car. It would languish in the back of his shop for the next few years before he decided to part with it. Ian Dawes, an Englishman who was in love with all things Willys, contacted Finders after spotting the advertisement. Sight unseen, Dawes bought the Willys and flew to the United States to have the Willys and assorted parts gathered and shipped across the ocean.

With intentions of turning the Willys into a street rod, Dawes came to the quick realization that the car wasn't going to fill his needs of transporting his family of four. In 1989, Dawes put the Willys up for sale and went searching for a more suitable Willys sedan.

Then, the *Hamberis & Mitchell* Willys passed to Phil Bowen. Bowen fixed several ills with the car, including swapping the front suspension with an independent suspension that was more suitable for street use. Bowen had put a phenomenal amount of work into the Willys and even managed to get the Chuck Finders Hemi running. However, in 2000, financial hardship fell upon him and the Willys once again moved to a new owner.

The buyer was current owner Paul Kennedy. The car still needed a lot of work before it could be driven legally on the street. The first task was to rebuild the blower and gearbox. Kennedy then took on the upholstery. When it came time to paint the Willys, Kennedy was thinking of doing it in the "Hippie" colors, but since it was going to be a street car, he felt that may have been over the top.

Kennedy completed most of the body work himself before turning the car over to Tracy Chantrey for final prep and paint. The colors chosen were emerald green with green metalflake and mint green with silver metalflake to give it a bit of a Mitchell vibe. The artwork on the doors was applied by Chris "Froggy" Froggett. In 2025, the Willys was completed and is ready for the streets of England.

Burkholder Brothers Altered

Pete and Harry Burkholder's first Altered was this Oldsmobile-powered 1934 Ford that was built in 1959. Here, Burkholder climbs through the hatch. (Photo Courtesy Harry Burkholder)

Hailing from Sacramento, California, Pete and Harry Burkholder grew to be one of the nations most feared Fuel Altered teams. The pair gives thanks to their cousin Bob Zetz for instilling the racing bug in them at an early age. The brothers learned through hands-on experience, with Pete leaning toward body and paint, and Harry building the power.

In 1959, the Burkholder Brothers built their first Altered coupe. It was a red 1934 Ford on Model A rails and was powered by a bored, stroked, and blown Oldsmobile engine. That car met its demise at Vaca Valley after the chute failed on Pete's first attempt as the driver. The car was destroyed after running off the end of the track at close to 150 mph. Pete was okay, but that was the end of his driving days.

In late 1961, the brothers debuted a AA/A Fiat that was initially powered by the same Oldsmobile engine that took their Ford to 9.30 ETs. In late 1962, they teamed with fellow Sacramento racers Don Argee and Lawrence Brocchini and plugged the pair's Chrysler Hemi into the *Burkholder Brothers* Fiat. Harry then proceeded to set the standard 1,320 record for Fuel Altered when he ran 170.77 mph in December 1962.

In 1964, the team disbanded with Agree and Brocchini taking the Hemi when they parted. Shortly after that, Pete was drafted by the U.S. Army. Harry continued to campaign the Fiat, which now had the big-inch Oldsmobile mill. In Pete's absence, Harry set a new AA/Gas Altered record at Fremont with a top speed of 157 mph.

Upon Pete's return, the brothers marched onward. A fiberglass Bantam body replaced the Fiat, and on occasion, the boys would run a dose of nitromethane through the 470-ci Oldsmobile to run in the Fuel Altered category. The best run was an 8.71 ET at 175.43 mph.

The year 1967 saw great change. Pete built a 100-inch -wheelbase chromoly chassis, on which the pair mounted a much-modified 1923 T aluminum body. In 1969, the Oldsmobile mill gave way to a bored and stroked 392 Hemi that lived on a large dose of nitro. The new engine, like the old, featured the best of parts: a Crane Cam camshaft, Howards rods, a Hampton blower, and Hilborn four-port injection.

For 1969, the car had a new chassis and body but the same blown Oldsmobile engine. Later that year, the brothers switched to a Hemi on nitro. (Photo Courtesy Steve Reyes)

By 1972, the Fiat was lower to the ground, thanks to the adaption of the dropped front axle. Topping the tank is crew man Ron Buzdas. Pete Burkholder is at the rear slick. (Photo Courtesy Steve Reyes)

Jack Beleinski is credited with restoring the Fiat. Rick Evens from Oregon did the beautiful job of matching the original paint, which was applied in 1970 by Pete Burkholder. (Photo Courtesy Harry Burkholder)

Through 1970, the pair enjoyed great success, running the increasing number of Fuel Altered programs that were offered up by California strips. Their biggest win was probably taking Fuel Altered over the Fiat of Mike Sullivan at the March Meet at Bakersfield. In 1971, the T body was switched out for the fiberglass Fiat shell that we see today.

In 1973, the brothers parted with the Fiat when they decided to give Funny Car a shot. The Altered passed through a few hands and ran brackets for a time with a big-block Chevy in Northern California. Eventually, it ended up in Idaho, being raced with a big-block Chevy under the name *Willin' Villian*.

In 1996, Jack Beleinski discovered the Fiat for sale in *National Dragster* magazine and quickly scooped it up. It is Beleinski who gets the credit for restoring the car back to the Burkholder Brothers likeness.

It took many hands to ensure that the restoration was period-correct, including Harry himself, who provided history, details and images. Jerry Ruth helped find many rare pieces. Rick Evens, who is from Oregon, recreated the paint, and Performance Coatings did all of the chrome plating and powder coating. In 2005, Beleinski sold the Fiat to Harry, and today, with his cousin Robert Reel, the Fiat shows and cackles in memory of Pete.

Inside, there is very little to distract the driver. The butterfly wheel and gas pedal kept Harry Burkholder busy enough, as these Fuel Altereds were a handful. (Photo Courtesy Harry Burkholder)

The Burkholder Brothers *Fiat is a thing of beauty. The lower rear states, "In Memory of Pete Burkholder," who passed away in 1999. (Photo Courtesy Harry Burkholder)*

Nothing beats nighttime drags. Nitro flames, which are unseen in the daylight, look great in the evening. (Photo Courtesy Jeff Burkholder)

Hemi-Healy

Bob Ida is set to make his first pass in the Healey. It's amazing that the Hemi didn't tear this car apart, considering the lack of chassis ties. (Photo Courtesy Bob Ida)

New Jersey resident Bob Ida learned from campaigning a BB/GS Willys that if he wanted to go faster, he'd have to move into a smaller car that was lower to the ground and pushed less air. In 1965, Ida's hunt for the Willys replacement led him to a scrapyard in Brooklyn, New York, where he found the *Hemi-Healy*—a 1956 Austin Healey.

With plans to stuff the Healey with the 354-ci Hemi and the remainder of the driveline from the Willys, the Healey was going to need a few modifications. Surprisingly, the Hemi fit the engine bay nicely, and it was far enough back in the chassis that the front suspension didn't need any modifying. The firewall needed a little work, and the transmission tunnel was opened up to make room for the Clutchflite transmission. The 4.88-gear-equipped Ford 9-inch was installed, and fabricated rectangular ladder bars that extended just behind the seat helped to hold it in place. There were no chassis ties installed. Only a simple roll bar was added for safety.

When it came to the all-steel body, few modifications were made. To help with maintenance, the fenders were cut from the main shell just ahead of the windshield so that it could be lifted off and out of the way. Since a scoop was going to be needed for the Detroit Diesel 6-71 blower, Ida headed to the local hardware store, where he purchased a wheelbarrow. It's true—that scoop on the hood was fashioned from a wheelbarrow! The only other modifications were enlarging the rear wheel openings for tire clearance.

Once the bodywork was complete, Ida applied a few coats of a dark, eye-popping purple paint. However, the paint was later changed to a more familiar copper color after a hair-raising experience at Ida's home track of Englishtown. A dowel pin fell lose inside the bellhousing and knocked the drain plug out of the converter. Transmission fluid blew everywhere, including onto the headers and tires, which caused a lot of smoke and for the car to spin out. It came to a stop facing back toward the starting line. The incident left Ida shaken, and he painted the Healey that night.

In 2016, the restored Hemi-Healy *debuted sans lettering, which was later added by Alan Johnson and Anthony Diliberto. The paint is a special blend. (Photo Courtesy Bob Ida)*

In July 2016, the Hemi-Healy was a hit at the Digs Summer Blast at Raceway Park in July 2016. M&H slicks fill the wheel wells. (Photo Courtesy Yanna Trance)

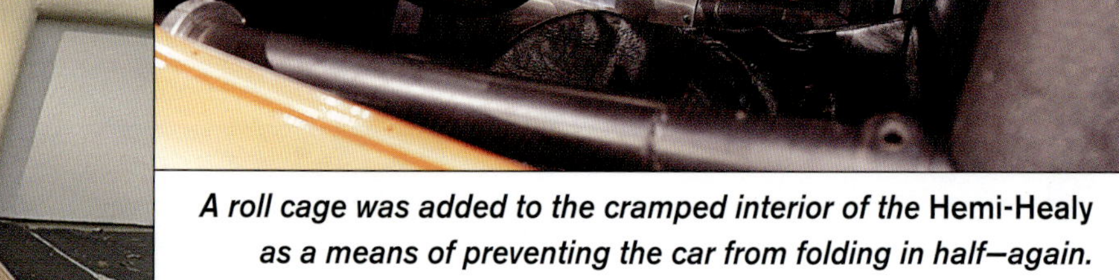

A roll cage was added to the cramped interior of the Hemi-Healy as a means of preventing the car from folding in half—again. (Photo Courtesy Al Mach)

The Hemi-Healy is powered by a 354 that was bored 0.030-over. A 6-71 blower was mounted on top of a tall Roto-Faze intake manifold. (Photo Courtesy Bob Ida)

The blower surround on the hood was fashioned from a wheelbarrow. How's that for using your imagination? (Photo Courtesy Marcia Baker)

The best ET turned for the *Hemi-Healy* was a 9.20 at Englishtown. The class record in 1969 (the last year that Ida competed with the *Hemi-Healy*) was 9.76. A promising trip to Indy went south when the tow rig blew the transmission, and then the starter went. When they finally made it to Indy, Ida drew a red-light on his only pass in class.

The final pass came at Englishtown. It was to be another great run, but the Healey, which had a habit of lifting the front wheels, took off sky high on another wheel-stand. However, this time it kept going up, and when it came back to earth, the impact buckled the car. Ida had to literally fight to open the door. As far as Ida was concerned, the *Hemi-Healy* was done. The car was stripped, and all of the parts went into his next project, a Mustang Gasser. The Healey went back to its former home—the scrapyard.

However, little did Ida know, the owner of the scrapyard felt that the Healey was too nice to scrap, and he sold it to a gentleman in Connecticut. From there, it was sold to another person in Indianapolis. In 2013, Ida family friend Shawn Tucker knew that Rob and Bob Ida were looking to build a clone of the *Hemi-Healy*, and he contacted them when he found what he thought was the perfect candidate. Rob bought the car and towed it back to their shop in New Jersey. Although the car had black primer for paint, the large rear-wheel openings and the body cut across the windshield helped to distinguish it as the *Hemi-Healy*. It was confirmed to be the car after Bob scratched below the primer and revealed the original paint.

In restoring the car, Rob, Bob, and their Ida Automotive team straightened out the bent car and tied the chassis to prevent any future damage. Bob built a fresh 0.030-over, 354-ci Hemi, and installed a TorqueFlite transmission. In 2016, the restoration was completed.

Prock & Howell *F Troop*

In 1968, the F Troop *Willys was built using a Logghe Funny Car–style chassis. The chassis and one-piece flip-up body made the car ineligible to compete in the Gas classes. (Photo Courtesy Tom Carter)*

In 1967, the Gas category was evolving. The aging 1930s and 1940s Anglias and Willys cars were slowly disappearing, giving way to the aerodynamic-superior bodystyles of the day. Some blame (or credit) "Ohio" George Montgomery for the change. In June 1967, Montgomery replaced his dominant AA/G 1933 Willys with a Ford-sponsored 1967 Mustang. Montgomery immediately went out and beat his own class record, taking it from a 9.34 ET at 155.97 mph to an 8.93 ET at 162.16 mph. With that, the floodgates to new iron opened.

In 1969, the F Troop *Willys joined the outlaw gasser circuit. Those "ears" on the rear fenders stabilized the car at speeds approaching 180 mph. (Photo Courtesy Carl Rubrecht)*

In 1969, Pete and Ben Hill looked to revitalize the old bodies by creating a short-lived Blown Fuel Gasser circuit. The circuit consisted of four non-class-legal "Outlawed Gassers." This included the Hill brothers' own 100-inch wheelbase, 488-inch Chrysler flip-top 1933 Willys; the Shores & Hess 98-inch-wheelbase flip-top 1949 Anglia, which was running a 460-inch Chevy; Chuck Finders's 98-inch-wheelbase flip-top 1949 Anglia that was powered by a 461-ci Chrysler; and the Prock & Howell 100-inch wheelbase flip-top 1933 Willys that was powered by a 488-inch Hemi.

With a combination of a short wheelbase and hordes of torque, Finders said, "The cars were a bit squirrelly. When we cleared the top end (that is to say, after crossing the lanes a few times, back pedaling, and basically steering clear of each other and the wall), we usually ran in the mid to upper 8s."

Tom Prock and Jay Howell formed one of the most successful drag racing partnerships of the late 1960s. At the time, Howell was working at the famed Logghe

The F Troop *Willys found its way to Hawaii, where it was raced as a bracket car. (Photo Courtesy John T. Francis)*

Stamping Company, overseeing their chassis-building shop. Together, the two campaigned the *F Troop* 1933 Willys in AA/G.

In 1968, the Willys was rebuilt, and instead of going the standard, class-legal route of using an OEM or box chassis, the guys put a modified Logghe round-tube Funny Car chassis under the B&N Fiberglass body. Al Bergler completed the tin work. The pair match raced the car in 1968 with a big-block Chevy and then mothballed it at the end of the season.

"We ran the car some in 1968 and put it in the attic at Logghe that winter," Howell said. "Then, the Hill brothers called in early 1969 with their Outlaw Gassers idea."

Joining the Outlaw Gassers circuit, the Chevy mill gave way to a nitro-fed late-model Hemi that was backed by a TorqueFlite transmission and a Ford 9-inch rear end. The pair repainted the Willys, and today, the car carries matching paint.

Mimicking what Finders said, Howell said, "At 165 mph, the fun really began as the Willys would skate around. The Logghes came up with the solution, [which was] mounting a pair of small wings on the rear fenders. When Tom and I showed up out East for a race, we rolled the Willys out of the trailer and the Hill brothers and group cracked up. Pointing and laughing, they referred to the wings as Mickey Mouse ears. The first pass I laid down was a 178 mph! The next week, they all had the wings! The *F Troop* pretty much dominated the circuit, running consistent 8.0 [ETs] at 185-plus mph."

The F Troop *body flips up like a Funny Car for ease of maintenance. Halibrand magnesium wheels are bolted to a chrome-plated Ford 9-inch that is equipped with a spool and 4.30 gears. (Photo Courtesy John T. Francis)*

The F Troop *sits outside of the Hilton University of Florida Conference Center. No expenses were spared, ensuring that this car was built the right way. (Photo Courtesy John T. Francis)*

Original tin work by Al Bergler surrounds the lone fiberglass bucket seat. For the sake of ease, a Powerglide with all of the good internals was used. (Photo Courtesy John T. Francis)

In 1970, Prock and Howell parked the Willys and moved into a Logghe-sponsored AA/FC Mustang. The Willys was sold and ended up in Florida. Then, it went to Hawaii. In the early 2000s, the Willys showed up for sale in *National Dragster* magazine. Dan Hix bought the car and had it restored. Scott Palmer gets credit for doing an amazing job duplicating the paint.

In 2006, Stephen Timoszyk purchased the Willys and owned it until 2023, when it was sold to John Francis. Francis swapped out the 427 Chevy for a correct Hemi and stuffed it with parts from Venolia, Ross, and Herbert.

***The F Troop** Hemi was assembled by Larry and Amber Shepard at Hemi's Only. The Bowers 6-71 blower with a Hilborn 4-port was set up to run on 80-percent nitro. (Photo Courtesy John T. Francis)*

The paint on the Willys was applied by the talented Scott Palmer. Extensive chrome plating helps to make this car a show-stopper. (Photo Courtesy John T. Francis)

Hart Automotive Willys

Seen here in April 1969, this Hart Automotive fiberglass body is believed to be the second one that was produced by the manufacturer. Note the dropped nose and flush Lexan windows. (Photo Courtesy John T. Francis)

The memories of Cleveland's Hart Automotive live on, thanks to the engine-building prowess that was established years ago by its proprietor, Mike Hart. Hart started Hart Automotive in his parents' Cleveland garage in the early 1960s. It wasn't long before his reputation grew, forcing him to move into his own shop and then into a larger shop. On any given weekend, cars prepared by Hart were sitting pretty in the winner's circle of Ohio's tracks. On the street, the results were similar.

The *Hart Automotive* 1933 Willys was Hart's own car—a match racer that he assembled with his more-than-competent crew of Chuck Finders, Larry Sikora, and Willy Barath. Starting with a Cal Automotive fiberglass body, Barath dropped the fenders and lowered the hood line to improve the aerodynamics. Going a step further, the windows were flush mounted and the decklid was drilled with ducting to utilize airflow to improve stability.

The rectangle-tube chassis and components went on a diet, with holes being drilled throughout. The desire to reduce weight turned absurd, as the roll bar was bent from exhaust tubing. Nestled in the chassis was a big-block Chevy. In 1969, this was replaced with a blown Hemi. A straight axle supports the front of the car, while an 8.75 Chrysler rear and Corvair coils support the back. In 1971, the initial black paint was replaced with the colorful paint that is seen today. At the same time, the chassis was tweaked to help prevent the violet twisting that takes place upon launch.

Sadly, Hart's driver, "Wild" Bill Levic, lost his life while wheeling another person's car at Ohio's Thompson Raceway in 1972. Losing his close friend took the wind out of Hart's sails, and he lost interest in racing. In 1973, the Willys was sold (without the engine) to Ohio resident Larry Covert. Hart eventually closed the shop and moved to Colorado to retire.

Covert campaigned the Willys with an injected big-block Chevy. He was a regular at Ohio's Dragway 42 and Thompson Raceway for the next few years before retiring the car. For several years, it sat in his garage, collecting dust. Sadly, Covert passed away in the late 1990s, which left it to his widow to find a new home for the Willys.

In 2009, Ron Wilson purchased the car and turned it into a street rod. The fancy paint went away, as did the race engine and related parts. Under the hood went a tunnel-ram-equipped 454-ci Chevy engine that was backed by a Muncie 4-speed transmission. Wilson enjoyed the Willys until his untimely passing in 2010. Then, the car was purchased by Don Moyer. He drove

In 1971, the Willys received the show-quality paint, which is mimicked on the restored car. On occasion, the Willys was known to appear at the street races on Cleveland's famed Quigley Road. (Photo Courtesy John T. Francis)

The Willys sat for several years, as it was garaged after being retired. This is how the Willys appeared when it was purchased by Ron Wilson in 2009. (Photo Courtesy Don Moyer)

Gellner Engineering built the Willys tall-deck 427 Chevy engine. A period-correct Vertex magneto and vintage four-port Hilborn injection were used.

The Willys spent a brief time on the street before Don Moyer returned it to its 1971 appearance. (Photo Courtesy Don Moyer)

it for a year before embarking on a three-year restoration that returned the Willys to how it looked and ran back in 1971.

The Willys is certified to run 8.50 quarter-mile ETs. Propelling the car is a tall-deck 427 Chevy with a Littlefield 6-71 blower. The rest of the driveline consists of a Powerglide transmission, and just like days of old, a 35-spline Chrysler 8.75 rear end and Corvair coils in the rear.

The Willys now resides with John T. Francis and looks just as good as it did 50-plus years ago, due to Mark Swartzlander, who matched the paint scheme that was applied in 1971 by Jerry Shieve.

The restoration was underway when this photo was taken. E&J Precision Welding replaced the butchered floorboards and roll cage. During the restoration process, the frame rails were strengthened. (Photo Courtesy Don Moyer)

Most parts on the Willys are original to the car, including all of the plastic windows and rear wings. The wheelie bars are original with adjustment modifications. All of the safety equipment is new. (Photo Courtesy John T. Francis)

The restored Willys has run a best ET of 8.32 at 156 mph. The windshield has been replaced with mar-resistant Lexan, and the brakes are Wilwood. The wheelie bars are original to the car. (Photo Courtesy Don Moyer)

Sassy Gremlin

Paul Pittman's* Sassy Gremlin *initially ran Hilborn injection on the early Hemi engine. Its best ETs were in the 8.80s. M&S Welding prepped the chassis. (Photo Courtesy Rich Carlson/Grant Bittner)

By 1970, when it came to the Gas category, modern bodies were overtaking the once-favored Willys and Anglia bodies. Popular Southern California racers K. S. Pittman and his brother Paul were two who made the switch. The brothers had been racing a BB/GS Anglia when a tie-rod broke, destroying the car and leaving Paul with a broken leg. K. S. moved on to a AA/GS Opel, while Paul took the remains of the Anglia and built himself the Sassy Gremlin for BB/GS competition.

Paul hit up Ricker Motors in Whittier, who agreed to sponsor him with a new AMC Gremlin. The car was stripped of all nonessentials right at the dealership, including the drivetrain and interior, before being hauled to George Britting, where the chassis was worked over. A dropped front axle and coilover shocks replaced the Gremlin's control arms and shock towers, while sheet metal replaced the inner fenders and firewall to make room for the 331-ci Hemi. Sheet metal also replaced the dashboard and transmission tunnel, which made room for the Turbo-clutch transmission.

Replacing the weak-link Gremlin rear axle was a mid-1950s Oldsmobile 9.3 unit that was supported by coil springs, ladder bars, and a Panhard bar to keep it all centered. Tying the car together was an 8-point roll cage. The all-steel body itself remained relatively stock, with the only changes being the mini wheel tubs that were added for the wider tires and enlarged wheel-housing openings.

Competing at Southern California tracks, Paul initially ran Hilborn four-port mechanical injection atop the 8-71 blower before switching to eight-port. Around 1972, the blower was ditched altogether, and it was replaced by twin Garrett Research turbochargers. Paul's new combination knocked 2 tenths of a second off the class record, taking it down to a 9.02 ET at 158 mph, and sending the competition into a frenzy. Competitors screamed that the turbos were an unfair advantage, and the NHRA agreed. A new class was designated for Paul's combination BB/GS-T. Eventually, he would run as quick of an ET as 8.87 ET at 162 mph.

Unhappy with the NHRA's decision, Paul retired the Gremlin after racing it at Lions Drag Strip's "Last Drag Race" in December 1972. The turbos were removed, and the Gremlin was eventually sold to local resident Carl Smith. Smith initially ran the car with the Hemi and Hilborn injection. This later gave way to a big-block Chevy and Turbo-400 transmission. The Gremlin competed in Super Gas (9.90 index racing) until around 1987, when it was retired. For the next 30 years, it sat under a tree behind a house in Riverside, California.

In 2006, Smith passed away, leaving the Gremlin to his son. Owing back rent, the owner of the house took possession of the car. It eventually passed through a few owners, including in 2016, a *Hot Rod* magazine employee who had visions of it being a magazine project car. The plan never came to fruition, and in 2020, the Gremlin was sold to current owner George Helmer.

The Gremlin would run as a bracket car through to the mid-1980s using an injected big-block Chevy engine. It won its share of Super Gas races. (Photo Courtesy Dave Kommel)

By the time that George Helmer, the current owner, got a hold of the Gremlin, it was in pretty rough shape. Telltale signs confirmed that this was the Sassy Gremlin. *(Photo Courtesy Phillip Thomas)*

The Fresh Sea Foam Aqua paint matches the car's original color and was sprayed on by Daniel Todd of Pro Collusion Works in Oceanside, California. Larry Fator of Quicksilver Pinstriping matched the original Pittman lettering. (Photo Courtesy George Helmer)

The formed dashboard is complemented by racing buckets and a bank of gauges. A B&M shifter controls the 1958 Chrysler TorqueFlite transmission. (Photo Courtesy George Helmer)

The 331-ci Hemi features components from Weiand, Enderle, Isky, Arias, and Egge. The 3-gallon oval beer keg that doubles as a fuel tank is the same one that was used by Paul Pittman. (Photo Courtesy George Helmer)

Although the Gremlin was complete for the most part, it was rough. The original Hemi and TorqueFlite transmission were long gone. The body was solid, but it needed touch-up repairs, which Helmer attacked himself. He stripped the body of its yellow paint with a razor blade to reveal the factory Seafoam Aqua. Once the body was prepped, fresh Seafoam Aqua was applied.

Under the all-steel body, a new firewall was in order, and the rack-and-pinion steering that had been added by Smith had to go. A proper 1955, 331-ci Hemi and 1958 TorqueFlite transmission were purchased and rebuilt by Helmer. The restoration was helped along by Jim Bridgewater, who knew the car well, having been a crewman for Pittman in the past.

As of this writing, Helmer is wrapping up the final details. Built by Pittman 55 years ago, when rules were more lax, Helmer doesn't ever see the day when the *Sassy Gremlin* ever makes a full pass down the track again. He values life and the significance of the Gremlin too much to chance it.

The body of the Sassy Gremlin *is all metal with the only modifications being the stretched rear wheel openings. Pitman set the BB/GS-T record in 1972, and it still stands today, as the NHRA eliminated the class afterward. (Photo Courtesy George Helmer)*

"Ohio" George's BB/FC Mustang

Although "Ohio" George Montgomery was discouraged by the NHRA, he never gave up on the turbos. This turbo Mustang F/C debuted in 1972. (Photo Courtesy Nick White)

"Ohio" George Montgomery was called the "King of the Gassers" early in his career, thanks in part to a pair of Little Eliminator wins at the NHRA Nationals in 1959 and 1960. Montgomery and his A/GS 1933 Willys always seemed to be one step above the competition.

In 1966, he swapped the Chevy engine for a Ford SOHC 427. In 1966, a class win followed at the Nationals. In 1967, Montgomery won class at the Winternationals and Nationals.

Looking to get the most bang for their sponsored buck, Ford pushed Montgomery into building a Gasser Mustang and provided him with a fiberglass 1968 body to slip over his Willys chassis. Montgomery and his *Malco Gasser* forever changed the category. The new bodystyle was the beginning of the end for the old Willys and Anglia bodystyle.

The Mustang was followed by a fiberglass-bodied 1969 Mustang that was initially powered by the same blown SOHC 427 engine. In 1971, Montgomery swapped the blown Cammer for a twin Schwitzer turbocharged Boss 429.

Although Ford had pulled its racing support by this point, Montgomery enjoyed backdoor assistance from Ford Indy expert Danny Jones. The pair relied heavily on the manufacturer's defunct Indy program for turbo parts and technology.

A highlight of Montgomery's career was using the Mustang to win Comp Eliminator at the NHRA Gatornationals in 1973 and 1974, which didn't seem to make the NHRA to happy.

"They didn't understand turbos and were afraid of them," Montgomery said. "In not so many words, they let me know that the car was no longer welcome."

In a previous interview, Montgomery had stated that it took a few years to work the bugs out of the system. Following the Gasser was the BB/FC Funny Car that is seen here.

The Funny Car featured a Chapman Race Cars chassis and was built in 1972. Nestled between the rails was

The car was a work of art but a tuner's nightmare. The turbochargers scared many competitors away due to their lack of understanding the technology. (Photo Courtesy Nick White)

"Ohio" George Montgomery's final incarnation (shown in 1975) of the Mustang used a supercharged Hemi in place of the turbocharged Boss. (Photo Courtesy Michael Pottie)

The restored twin-turbo **Boss Turbo** *once again resides within the Chapman chassis. Owner Nick White said that he paid more for the parts than he did the car. (Photo Courtesy Nick White)*

The body was close to trash when the car was discovered. The fiberglass had begun to separate. Nick White counted on Alchemy Engineering to bring the car back. (Photo Courtesy Nick White)

a 496-ci Boss that produces 2,000 hp. The Schwitzer turbo setup on the car was an amazing sight to behold. A Bendix fuel-injection system delivered the fuel, and a Mallory ignition lit it.

As turbo technology was lagging (no pun intended) at the time that the car was built, Montgomery had said that the trick was to kill some of the top end and try to compensate for the turbo lag. The fuel nozzles were downsized, and cylinder heads were modified by downsizing the stock 2.28-inch intake valves.

"We killed 400 to 600 top-end hp in an attempt to overcome the initial lag," Montgomery said. "Each turbo

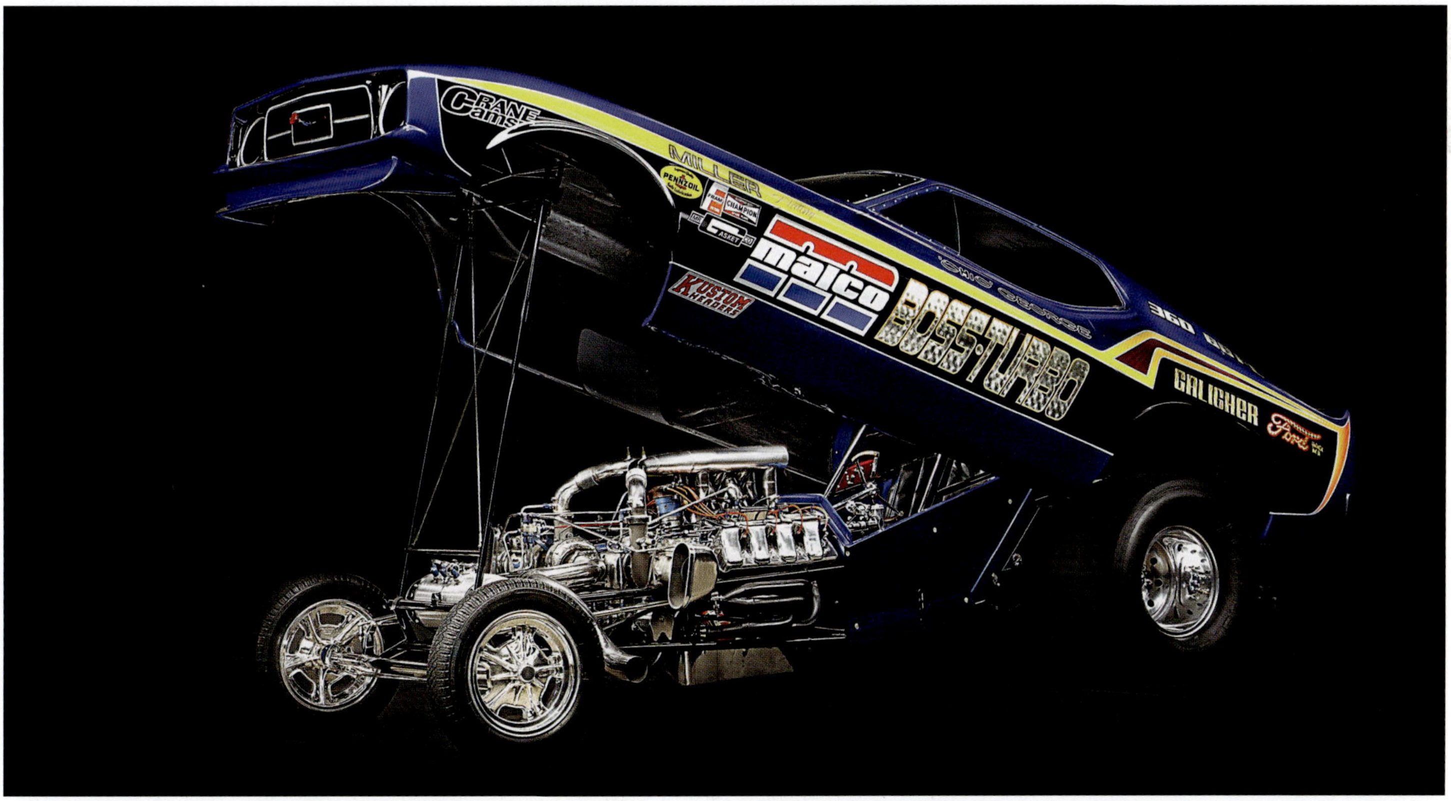

Shawn Dill of Alchemy Engineering completed the majority of the restoration. Steve Dekkenga of SD Enterprises was responsible for the paint. (Photo Courtesy Eileen Cote)

was putting out over 30 pounds of boost."

Due to the car's killer midrange and top-end speed, Montgomery could often drive around cars that were quicker off the line.

Montgomery raced the Mustang as a BB/FC in three incarnations: as the light blue *Malco Boss Turbo*, in dark blue with graphics, and as a blown Cammer, which dubbed the *Super Gasser II*. Montgomery sold the car in 1975 (without the engine and numerous other parts), having put no more than about a dozen runs on it.

Dave Garner was the lucky new owner who campaigned the Mustang well into the 1980s under the name *Speed Fever*. After the car was retired from racing, it sat outdoors, and the ravages of time took its toll until a gentleman named Mike Roth came to the rescue.

Current owner Nick White said, "Mike was visiting my shop and noticed a Boss 429 that I had on an engine stand. He asked if I was into the old Ford stuff and said that he might have a cool project for me. He said that he found an 'Ohio' George car at a swap meet in Springfield, Ohio. It needed help but had all of the documentation to do a restoration."

Dave Garner had retained the car all those years and was the person who Roth purchased it from. When White bought the car, it was in parts: the engine was in Florida and, fortunately, Montgomery still had all the parts he had removed from the car years before. It was a huge effort, but White was able to bring it all together.

Dave Garner ran "Ohio" George Montgomery's Mustang well into the 1980s. Although Ford fans will cringe, Garner ran a Chevy engine in the Mustang. (Photo Courtesy Allen Tracy)

The Mustang retains the majority of its original parts. Each Funny Car you see in the background of this image is a restored car. (Photo Courtesy Nick White)

Veney's Vega #2

NHRA's Pro Comp category debuted at the 1973 Supernationals, where Veney was the number-one qualifier. Veney made Pro Comp's first 6-second pass, doing so at the 1974 NHRA Winternationals. (Photo Courtesy Michael Pottie)

Ken Veney is probably one of drag racing's most recognized names. He had success as a driver, crew chief, designer, builder, and fabricator. As a driver, he won 13 national events, and 9 of those came in Pro Comp alone.

Pro Comp was a new heads-up category that was introduced by the NHRA in 1974 to fill a perceived gap between the Professional and Sportsman classes. Pro Comp was comprised of six classes: A/FD, B/FD, AA/D, BB/FC, A/FC, and AA/Altered. Rules stated that nitro use was allowed in A/FD, B/FD, and A/FC only. In AA/D, only pump gas was allowed. In BB/FC and AA/A, only alcohol was allowed.

Veney's reign of terror predates Pro Comp and began with a dominance of Southern California's injected Funny Car scene in 1972. That year, Veney and close friend Ken Cox debuted an alcohol injected big-block Chevy Vega that went undefeated. This would be the first of four Veney Vegas. The cars that followed were a new injected nitro car in 1973, a Keith Black–powered candy red car in 1975, and a 1976 car that was also powered by Keith Black and was magenta in color.

The 1973 car was updated in 1974 with the new slant nose. The first race for the car was Irwindale's 64 Funny Car Show in March 1973. Its final race was the 1975 edition of the race, which Veney won. The race was also the first race in which Veney ran a Keith Black engine.

This Veney/Cox–built Vega was a unique car for the time, incorporating many aerodynamic design features in a similar fashion as the renowned Don Schumacher/John Buttera *Wonder Bread* Vega. Interestingly enough, both cars debuted around the same time. Veney's Vegas, like Schumacher's, was low slung and required a reclined driver's position. Also built into the chassis was a solid-mounted rear axle, which was one of Funny Car's first.

Powering the Vega was a 481-ci Chevy engine that was built by Veney. Behind it was a Lenco 2-speed transmission, which was one of the first in an Alcohol Funny Car. To start the 1974 season, the Vega received a new slant nose and a blown Donovan Chevy engine. At the season-opening AHRA Winter Nationals in January, Veney became the first Pro Comp racer to break the

The Vega's last trip down the quarter mile was at the 1988 NHRA Winternationals, and it was driven by Greg Daebelliehn. Daebelliehn owned the car from 1986 to 1989. (Photo Courtesy Bob Snyder)

Sanding the body of the Vega revealed the numerous colors that covered the car throughout its history. The hood, which was damaged over time, was repaired. (Photo Courtesy Darrell & Pam Conrad)

The Corvette red paint on the Ken Veney/Ken Cox–formed body makes the Vega stand out.

The chassis was stripped to bare metal before receiving fresh black paint. Few modifications had been made over the years. (Photo Courtesy Darrell & Pam Conrad)

Looking ready to make a pass, everything about this car is period-correct. Darrell and Pam Conrad have many people to thank for bringing the Vega back to life. (Photo Courtesy Darrell & Pam Conrad)

6-second barrier when the Vega ran a 6.98 ET at 194.38 mph to defeat the AA/D of Dave Mack in the final round. Weeks later, he made the NHRA's first Pro Comp 6-second run (6.99) at the Winternationals. Later that season, he made the NHRA's first BB/FC 200-mph pass. Veney qualified the Vega number one at nearly every race he attended. At the end of the season, he was presented with the *Car Craft* magazine award for being the Pro Comp Driver of the Year.

Veney campaigned the 1973 Vega into 1975. In its last incarnation, it had new paint with graphics and a sponsorship from the model kit maker Revell. This was the only BB/FC that Revell made as a plastic kit. Although Veney had the best year of his career in 1976 by winning four NHRA national events, he said that the second Vega was always his favorite.

After Veney sold the Vega, it passed through eight different owners before ending up with current owner Darrell Conrad—and it couldn't have been bought by a better person. Conrad fell in the love with the Vega the first time that he laid eyes on it back in 1973.

Pam Conrad was tasked with tracing out the sticker arrangement. Looking at the completed car, you can see that she nailed it. (Photo Courtesy Darrell & Pam Conrad)

Larry Ofria, who worked at the legendary Valley Head Service, prepped the block, heads, and crank of the 454 engine. What you see here is exactly how it was campaigned by the late, great Ken Veney. (Photo Courtesy Darrell & Pam Conrad)

In August 1991, Conrad had just finished a day of work and was relaxing on the couch with the latest issue of the *National Dragster* magazine. He was casually browsing the classified advertisements, and, lo and behold, he noticed the Vega. The number in the advertisement was local to Conrad, and he called it immediately. Conrad was the first one to call, and upon confirming it was the Veney Vega, he bought the car on sight.

After removing multiple layers of paint, Conrad began undoing years of modifications. This included filling the 18-inch escape hatch that had been cut into the roof and replacing the twin-drag-chute mount with the original single mount. It was a little trickier to remove the taillights that had been installed around 1975 by a proceeding owner. With Conrad's wife, Pam, wanting to get involved, she volunteered to wear her "beehive" suit (to avoid the fiberglass making her itchy) and crawled inside to cut out the taillight mounts from behind.

Conrad found a 1972 Vega body with the proper taillights stored 20 feet above the ground in a friend's shop. Picture Conrad climbing up on a forklift to take a mold of said taillights. He put his newfound forming skills to work and created the four new taillights that he needed. Another repair that was needed was made to the left front, due to when former owner Greg Daebelliehn kissed the wall at Pomona in 1988.

When Conrad purchased the Vega, the car was pretty complete, and little had been changed over the years. The tin work needed cleaning and minor straightening, whereas the chassis itself needed little more than cleaning and paint. With the chassis painted, a 454 Chevy with a 427 crank was installed—just as Veney used in 1974. On top of the engine was an ultra-rare Ed Pink magnesium 8-71 blower.

After the body was prepped, Conrad applied the 1973 Corvette red paint to match the Vega's 1973 appearance. To match the graphics, a photo of the car was enlarged to scale. Then, poster paper was laid on the car, and the image was painstakingly traced by Pam. The final touch was the gold leaf, which was applied by Darrell.

The Vega was completed in 2016, and Carrie Ferguson, Ken Cox's daughter, took the seat for the car's first private fire-up. It was a special moment that left everyone with tears in their eyes. Shortly after that, the Vega was loaded for its public debut at the California Hot Rod Reunion. Todd Veney, Ken Veney's son, saw the car a few days later and was astounded. This was a car that he hadn't seen since his youth. You can imagine how he felt when he was given a chance to take the seat. There were many people to thank for that moment.

CHAPTER FIVE

MODIFIED ELIMINATOR

MODIFIED ELIMINATOR BECAME A CATEGORY THAT WAS DEDICATED TO STREET-WORTHY CARS.

The Modified Eliminator category, which was referred to as Street Eliminator until 1970, served up a hodgepodge of cars and classes. Into the 1970s, you could see a lower-Gas-class Volkswagen racing an injected dragster. As the decade progressed, the dragsters were moved out of the category, and Modified Eliminator became a category that was dedicated to street-worthy cars. By far, the most popular classes were Modified Production and Gas.

It broke a lot of hearts when the NHRA discontinued Modified in 1981, merging the classes into Super Stock and Comp. Although it has been long gone, the popularity of Modified remains intact, and a large number of the cars survive today.

Above: In the early 1970s, Carl Robinson tried his hand at the Modified Eliminator category with his 1968 Camaro. The Camaro went through several iterations, but each one was always powered by a big-block Chevy and a Chrysler transmission. The Camaro was retired in 1991. It then sat for years before being purchased by current owner, Nick Teitsma. Teitsma was able to save the 9.40 ET big-block, which retains all of the original aftermarket parts. (Photo Courtesy Nick Teitsma)

Hemi Hurricane Willys

The Hemi Hurricane *was a star of NASCAR's short-lived drag-racing wing. The Willys ran low-9-second ETs at more than 140 mph.*

No car screams "Gasser" like a decked-out Willys or Anglia from the 1940s or 1950s. A straight axle and a blower or injector stacks poking out from a fiberglass front end were common traits. The Georgia-based *Hemi Hurricane* 1940 Willys that was built by Frank Groves optimizes the look.

Groves bought the Willys in 1964. He teamed with Roger Swanson and built the Willys with all of the fixings of the day. Spacer blocks were added to raise the front end, and a not so commonly used quarter elliptic sprung suspension and ladder bars were incorporated in the back to support the Chrysler 8.75 rear end.

In 1965, Lamar "Bunky" Bobo joined the fray, investing in the project in the form of a brand-new Hemi and TorqueFlite transmission. Bobo bought a lightweight 1965 A990 Hemi Coronet from the famed Grand Spaulding Dodge for the soul purpose of stripping it of its drivetrain. The Hemi was stroked to 484 ci before being placed in the Willys, and the TorqueFlite was prepared by Art Carr. What remained of the A990 car was lost in gambling game to fellow racer Randy Payne. Payne turned around and sold the car to a local racer, who installed a Wedge engine and went racing.

The *Hemi Hurricane*'s first big win came at the 1966 NASCAR Winter Nationals in DeLand, Florida. It won class but hurt the Hemi in doing so. Groves threw in the towel at that point and sold his share in the Willys to Bobo. Bobo freshened the Hemi, and, in 1967, he returned to DeLand, where the Willys once again won its class. This time, he went all the way and won Competition Eliminator.

The Willys is a standout today due to the Larry Abernathy paint. The American wheels provide a nice show quality. (Photo Courtesy Tommy Lee Byrd)

Through 1967, Bobo ran match races with the Willys, recording 10.05 ETs on gas in the low 9s on a dose of nitromethane. With a top speed of 164 mph, those slicks were lacking bite. At the close of the season, Bobo retired the Willys and went Funny Car racing with a Logghe chassis–equipped A/XS Barracuda. He tried to sell the Willys (without the engine and transmission) $350 but found no takers. The Willys sat until 1970, when Groves picked it up and installed a six-pack-equipped 340 that was

The Hemi that currently resides in the Willys is 484 ci. Hilborn injection feeds the fuel. (Photo Courtesy Tommy Lee Byrd)

pulled from a Challenger T/A. The idea was to make it a street car, but it never really panned out. So, back in the garage it went, and it sat until about 2004.

It was Bobo's son, Tony, with pressure from his kids, who talked Bobo into blowing the dust off the Willys and restoring it. The car was stripped and resurrected with a new Hemi. Larry Abernathy prepped the body and applied the red paint. Tommy Bollen lettered the Willys in 1965 and returned to do it all over again. Helping to get things rolling was Bobo's old friend Roger Swanson, who did the wiring and injector work. The restoration took four years to complete.

Inside, the bright tin work is offset by a pair of fiberglass bucket seats. The Chrysler push-buttons control the Art Carr–prepped TorqueFlite transmission. (Photo Courtesy Tommy Lee Byrd)

The car features fiberglass panels, wheelie bars, and a drag chute. Tommy Bollen duplicated the lettering that he had applied more than 60 years ago. (Photo Courtesy Tommy Lee Byrd)

The Hemi Hurricane *looks as if it's all set to make another pass down Paradise Drag Strip in Calhoun, Georgia. The restoration paid off with numerous awards. (Photo Courtesy Tommy Lee Byrd)*

Triad Willys

In 1964, this Willys Gasser debuted, and by the time that this photo was taken in 1969, it was on its third owner. The Triad *name appeared shortly after this photo was taken. (Photo Courtesy Jeff Bloedorn)*

After six decades, it's inevitable that any drag car that survives has passed through numerous owners. In 1964, the *Triad* Willys was initially raced by Leroy and Mary Lou Psyk under the *Big Wheel Auto Parts* name. Al Tschida took over the car in 1965 and teamed with Dave Fure and Gary Farsund. Tschida had campaigned a C/Gas Willys in 1964 and won class at Indy that year. Many parts from that car found their way onto this new Willys. Tschida drove and tuned the new car, and at its NHRA Nationals debut in 1965, it was runner-up in C/Gas. At the 1966 Winternationals, some weight was added to the Willys to fit the more favorable D/Gas class. The change in class paid off, as the Hilborn-injected small-block Chevy moved the car to a class-winning 12.21 ET.

Here, it gets a little fuzzy, but we do know that Farsund left the team shortly after the Winternationals. Farsund, Fure, and Tschida campaigned the Willys through Indy in 1966. There, the car ran in B/Gas and fell early in eliminations. Shortly after that, the Willys was sold to Bill Mitchell.

Tschida stuck around to tune and occasionally drive the car. They took the Willys back to Pomona in 1967, when Tschida was the runner-up in D/Gas. They followed that with a trip to the Nationals, where the Willys ran in C/Gas.

Doug Mosch of Marshall, Minnesota, owned the Willys long enough to put his, "Doug's Used Cars and Speed Parts" logo on it. (Photo Courtesy Jeff Bloedorn)

In 1968, things were quiet for the pair, who moved their operation from Minnesota to Southern California.

For the 1969 season, the Willys was painted the candy green color that remains on it today. Proving that he had a sense of humor, Mitchell added the fictious name "Antelope Valley Speed Center." Mitchell was a part owner in the Triad Land Company, which was located in California's Antelope Valley. Later in the season, the Willys was relabeled with the *Triad* name to promote the Trida Land Conpany. Mitchell entered the Willys at the 1969 Winternationals but bounced the car off the guardrail, damaging one side. Another trip to the Nationals followed, where the Willys was the runner-up in C/Gas.

Aside from the doors being repainted, the Willys has the same paint that was applied in 1969. It features a fiberglass front clip, doors, and fenders. (Photo Courtesy Chadly Johnson)

Shortly after the 1970 Winternationals, Mitchell sold the Willys (without the engine) to Minnesota resident Doug Mosch. Mosch owned the Willys for about 2 years before selling it to Doug Woltjer. Woltjer rechristened the Willys as *Wild Willys* and swapped in a tunnel-ram-equipped big-block Chevy. Woltjer added equipment needed to drive the Willys on the street, and he used the car to go to and from school. Eventually, a tamer small-block Chevy found its way into the car before Woltjer parted with it in 1980.

The Willys passed through a few more owners before Jim Minnichsoffer purchased the car in 1985. Minnichsoffer's plans were to modernize the Willys and make it a fine street rod. He began by stripping the front beam axle out. However, his priorities changed, and that was about as far as he made it before the project was sidelined.

In 2014, John Zechbauer purchased the dormant Willys from Minnichsoffer. Zechbauer's idea was to preserve the Willys and restore it back to its 1960s

For a drag car, this one features a show-quality interior. Aftermarket parts date back to the later 1960s. A Hurst Indy shifter moves the 4-speed transmission through its gears. (Photo Courtesy Chadly Johnson)

Just like it had in the past, an injected small-block Chevy powers the Willys. It features the early, finned rocker covers. (Photo Courtesy Chadly Johnson)

Staggered Cragar wheels provide a nice stance for this Willys. Do you think that there is any lead still hiding in that tube bumper? (Photo Courtesy Chadly Johnson)

appearance. He had the fun task of hunting down the missing pieces, and period-correct parts. Finding the missing front clip was easy, but retrieving it was tough. The parts had gone to Minnichsoffer neighbor, who had passed away. His family had retained the parts all of those years but were reluctant to give them up at first. A deal was finally made, and the parts found their way back onto the Willys.

Just as it was in the 1960s, a Hilborn-injected small-block Chevy resided under the fiberglass front clip. Backing it was a 4-speed transmission, an early Oldsmobile rear end, and a ladder bar suspension.

In 2023, Zechbauer sold the Willys (without the engine) to his friend Jeff Bloedorn of Stillwater, Minnesota. Bloedorn built a period-correct 327 to fill the engine bay.

"John [Zechbauer] had replaced the injected engine with a mild street motor prior to putting the Willys up for sale," Bloedorn said.

Zechbauer had done a great job of returning the Willys to its former glory, leaving Bloedorn little to do but clear up some of the details.

Wompin Wagon

This car transitioned from being a junkyard relic into the Wompin Wagon. *Fiberglass replaced the front clip and doors. The windows are Lexan. (Photo Courtesy Bob Miller)*

In the good old days, you could haul a Chevy Nomad out of the junkyard for less than $100 and think nothing about tearing into it to build a drag car. That pretty much was what Alabama's Bubba Cummins did back in 1962.

Bubba had clear intentions from the start. He planned to build his '55 Nomad into a hair-raising Gasser. Bubba began working in his Mobile garage, stripping the body from the chassis and cutting out the floorboards and firewall. In their place, lightweight aluminum paneling was installed. The heavy glass also went by the wayside, as it was replaced by lightweight Lexan.

Getting to work on the chassis, the A-arm front suspension was dropped and replaced with a 1928 Ford model A axle, 1939 Ford spindles, and Chevy brakes. The rear end was swapped for a beefy Oldsmobile/Pontiac unit. For power, Bubba used a 301-ci Hilborn-injected 283. To help with weight transfer and to take advantage of the rules, the engine was set back 8 inches in the chassis. Behind the potent engine was a BorgWarner 4-speed transmission.

With "Dirty" Danny Cummins manning the stick, the E/Gas Nomad launched with its wheels high in the air and recorded 11.90 ETs. Bubba and Danny raced the Nomad in Florida, Louisiana, and Alabama before retiring from racing in the early 1970s. The Nomad was placed in Bubba's garage, and there it sat for the next 30 years.

Sadly, Danny passed away in 2004. In 2006, longtime friend, "Sneaky" Pete Pearce received the okay from Bubba to restore the car in memory of Danny. The restoration took about 2 years and about 40 friends and family members helped with the project. The Nomad retains all of the original body panels, the Model A straight axle, interior aluminum, Lexan windows, and even the steering wheel.

Since plans were to race the car once again, several upgrades were required, including a roll bar, safety belt, and the lone seat, which initially was a low-back Ford Thunderbird bucket seat.

With the restoration complete, old friends, crewmen, and family gathered as the Nomad was presented to Bubba Cummins. Bubba made the first pass in the restored Nomad. From there, longtime friend Randy

All of the work that was done to the Nomad was completed in Bubba Cummins home garage. "Dirty" Dan Cummins was the lead mechanic and primary driver. (Photo Courtesy Bob Miller)

Like a phoenix rising from the ashes, the **Wompin Wagon** *returned to the track in 2006. (Photo Courtesy Bob Miller)*

Griffis of Mobile, Alabama, became the caretaker and full-time driver. The driveline now consisted of a 355-ci engine, making use of a turbo 350 transmission for reliability and a stout 4.88-gear Dana 60 rear end. The best runs to date with the new combination are a 7.0 ET at 100 mph in the eighth mile.

Time marches onward, and illness takes its toll. In 2019, Pete Pearce, the man who initiated the restoration passed. In 2020, Bubba Blanton joined the team as driver after Griffis became ill. Griffis passed away in 2021.

Ashley Cummins Fleming is now the owner of the *Wompin Wagon*, and it is still in Mobile, Alabama, and still in the family. With Ashley's full support, Bubba is keeping the *Wompin Wagon* competitive and looking good at the track and car shows.

The **Wompin Wagon***, which is now powered by a stout 355-ci Chevy, takes flight. (Photo Courtesy Bob Miller)*

As permitted by the Gas classes, the engine was set back in the chassis 10 percent of the length of the wheelbase. An aluminum radiator and transmission cooler help to keep things in check. (Photo Courtesy Bob Miller)

Aside from modern safety features, the interior of the car changed very little from the car's racing heyday. Gauges to monitor water temperature and oil pressure were installed. (Photo Courtesy Bob Miller)

Restoring the body of the **Wompin Wagon** *fell to the capable hands of Jerold Nichlos. Johnny McDonald applied the Dupont 1967 Marina Blue paint. (Photo Courtesy Bob Miller)*

Mize's Anglia

The starting point for this Anglia Gasser was a rough-but-complete 1950 model. Jim Mize built the car in the garage that is shown in the background. (Photo Courtesy Tommy Lee Byrd)

The Anglia features its original axle. Jim Mize added the Volkswagen brakes. The Anglia sat in the basement for 40 years. Mize's son remembers bouncing ping pong balls off of it. (Photo Courtesy Tommy Lee Byrd)

The current engine in the Anglia should run 6.90 ETs in the eighth mile. The engine has been detuned to the car in case of an incident. (Photo Courtesy Tommy Lee Byrd)

Drag racing has always been about fighting costs. Jim Mize had been racing an injected Gas Dragster with his brother and a friend, but when they wanted to step up to running nitro, Jim chose to go his own route.

In 1969, Jim went looking for an Opel GT to build himself a Gasser but lucked when he came across a 1950 Anglia. He spent the next 18 months building the car in his home basement.

Having experience with the early Chrysler Hemi, I mean real early Hemi, Jim built himself a 1953 Dodge 241-ci Ram. The engine was opened up to 260-ci and it featured Hilborn injection, Roto-Faze ignition, fabricated headers, and an aftermarket cam. Many parts were fabricated by Jim, including the fuel pump and adapter that mated the Chevy Muncie transmission to the Hemi. Jim's handy work can be seen out back as well, where an early Oldsmobile rear end packed 5.86 gears. In short, Jim did it pretty much all himself, aside from applying the Ford Grabber blue paint.

Jim ran in D/Gas and D/Altered with the combination through 1973. He wanted to go faster, so he built a fresh Hemi. On its first pass, it swallowed a valve. That brought an end to Jim's racing days. The cost of drag racing was getting out of hand, and with a growing family, priorities changed. The Anglia went back into the basement, and there it sat until 2012, when Jim's son Scott started pushing Jim to resurrect the car.

Helping to preserve the Anglia all of those years was the fact the basement garage was heated in the winter and air conditioned in the summer. The Anglia was nearly complete but needed help. The first step was to repair the broken engine, which had been sitting partially disassembled since 1973. Next on the list was replacing the brake and fuel lines. It's amazing how many 1950 Anglia parts this car retains. The car still has its original rubber roof and wooden bows, and the body is all original steel.

With Scott's help, the restoration was completed in 2017. Quain Stott of the Southeast Gasser Association invited Jim to be Grand Marshall at one of his races at Chattanooga. There, the Anglia made its first pass (an easy one) in nearly 50 years.

Mize wanted to build a 250-ci Hemi, but when the pistons he ordered arrived, they were 0.125 over. This gave him a shade over 259 ci. The ignition is a Roto-Faze with two coils. Each coil fires four cylinders. (Photo Courtesy Tommy Lee Byrd)

The interior remains as it appeared over 50 years ago. The only change needed was to replace the cover of the driver's seat. (Photo Courtesy Tommy Lee Byrd)

The rear end remains its stock width, and offset Tornado wheels are mounted. The slicks are M&H Racemasters, and Goodyear tires are mounted on the original Anglia rims in the front. (Photo Courtesy Tommy Lee Byrd)

Granny Goose 1961 Corvette

The Granny Goose *Corvette carries its original jewel blue paint in 1967. Running in the C/MP category meant that the car had to carry between 11.00 and 12.99 lbs/ci. (Photo Courtesy Randy Hendricks)*

History shows that when it came to Modified Eliminator Chevys, the Corvette's batting average was unmatched. The car's slippery aerodynamic design and the built-in engine setback contributed to the Corvette winning 20 national events through the 1970s. Being powered by a small-block engine (an engine to which the aftermarket catered) that loved to rev and could be bored and stroked (or destroked) to make it fit in almost any class, it's easy to see why the Corvettes were so prevalent.

The *Granny Goose* 1961 Corvette of Cincinnati's Bruce "Goose" Scott and Dave Lewis is a prime example of a winning Modified Production Corvette. In 1966, the pair teamed up after Bruce purchased the Corvette with a blown engine from a neighbor. Scott turned to Lewis to build him a 315-ci engine, and the pair formed a team.

Scott and Lewis's first season saw them campaigning the Corvette in the old Modified Sports Production category. That lasted for a year before a move to Modified Production was forced on them when the NHRA killed off the Sports Production category.

Scott and Lewis were a first-class act that saw them towing the Corvette to the drags behind Bruce's new triple-black 1969 SS 396 Chevelle. The Corvette was freshened with new, Bill Roell–applied pearl blue paint and lettering by the renown "Dauber. "The Corvette proved to be just as successful at custom shows as it was on its home track of Edgewater, winning four awards the first time that it was shown.

The Corvette, with Lewis behind the wheel, had no problem running under the class record of mid-11 times. Scott recalled that the team's biggest competition was the *Reher, Morrison, & Cross* Chevy-powered Maverick.

"They had a license plate on the Maverick with a big wine glass and a cooked goose laying beside it," Scott said.

Backing the engine was a slick-shifted BorgWarner 2.54-first-gear transmission and an Oldsmobile rear end. The pair hauled the Corvette to Amarillo, Texas, for the 1971 World Finals, where they promptly blew the rear out of the car. They didn't make eliminations but did upset the Pro Stock racers who were in line behind them. Without a spare rear end, their weekend ended even before it started. The two sold the Corvette to sponsor Warren Gross of Competition Mills not long after hauling it home. They replaced the Corvette with what was an equally successful Modified Production Camaro.

In 1969 the Granny Goose *was wearing beautiful, but expensive paint by Bill Roell. Roell incorporated every trick of the day, from lace to webbing, and fade. (Photo Courtesy Bob Martin)*

Fred Logan of Cincinnati, Ohio, purchased the Corvette around 1976. He added red paint and a bulletproof Dana rear end. (Photo Courtesy Bob Martin)

Ray Nash, the car's current owner, purchased the Corvette in 2015 and returned it to Granny Goose *likeness. Nash completed the restoration in his own shop. (Photo Courtesy Ray Nash)*

The 277-ci engine that now fills the bay was built to go and makes use of the combination of "then" and "now" parts. (Photo Courtesy Ray Nash)

The Corvette retains all of its original interior and a few additions: the driver's safety harness, a tachometer, gauges, and a roll bar. (Photo Courtesy Ray Nash)

Gross raced the Corvette for a few years in E/Gas before selling the car to Fred Logan. Logan repainted the Corvette red and continued to run the car at Edgewater in Modified Production and Gas. Sadly, Logan was shot and killed in the prime of life. The Corvette was retired and sat in the family garage until current owner, Ray Nash, came along in 2015 and purchased it.

Nash knew that the Corvette had been parked around 1979, and he had kept his eye on it. When the Corvette was listed for sale, he jumped on it.

Today, the Corvette features a 277-ci engine that is capable of revving to 12,000 rpm and makes enough power to lift the wheels. A BorgWarner 4-speed transmission is back at home in front of the 4-link-equipped Dana rear end. Making the car a stand out is the *Granny Goose* matching paint that Nash applied at his shop, Nash's Corvette Restorations.

DG Custom Chrome took care of the brightwork. Nash prepped the body and applied the candy blue paint over a white base. (Photo Courtesy Ray Nash)

Spunctious Chevy

These old drag cars are still out there–hibernating and waiting for a wake-up call. A prime example is this '55 Chevy owned by Dwayne Malek.

In 1966, Malek bought the Chevy while he was stationed in Ohio, and he has owned it ever since. It had a 265 engine, but in short order, it tossed a rod, and a 283 was installed. The car saw a significant amount of street racing before Malek moved to Spokane, Washington in 1969.

In Washington, he used the Chevy as a street/strip car, frequently competing at the drag strips in Deer Park and Walla Walla. Malek recalled that he was unable to beat one '57 Chevy. Well, that '57 wasn't running a 283. Instead, it was running a 327. It was at that point that Malek decided to get serious about his racing.

Malek built a 301 that was fitted with Jahns pistons, an Edelbrock tunnel ram, and twin Holey carbs. Backing the potent little mill was a wide-ratio Muncie transmission and a Ron Pryor–built 12-bolt rear end that housed 6.17 gears. The '55 ran well under its E/MP class record of 11.54. Malek recalled running well under the record at a points meet but was unable to back it up after wrecking the slick-shifted transmission.

With Deer Park Raceway closing in 1973, Malek raced at Walla Walla, avoiding Spokane due to the politics that surrounded the track's operation. He ran the Chevy one more season before retiring from drag racing. For the next 45 years, the car sat in seclusion.

It took the prying of Malek's granddaughter before the car once again saw the light of day. They dusted off the Chevy and began piecing it back together in 2021. The engine, which was last used in a sand dragster in the late 1970s was freshened and reinstalled. The aluminum slotted rims, which had been sold years before, were bought back when it was discovered that the gentleman to whom they were sold still had them. Now that the Chevy is back together, plans are to show the car on occasion.

The Spunctious '55 Chevy of Dwayne Malek is a fine example of the caliber of car that was found in the Modified Production ranks. This high-winding Chevy was capable of record ETs. (Photo Courtesy Rich Carlson/Grant Bittner Collection)

This is what the '55 Chevy looked like when it was pulled from its slumber in 2021. The Chevy has since received a wash, the proper aluminum slot wheels have been installed, and it is up and running. (Photo Courtesy Rick Dittwiler)

Starship Camaro

When word reached Sal Carbone's young ears that the 396 had been added to the Camaro options list, he spent the money that he saved on this Granada Gold SS/RS. (Photo Courtesy Sal Carbone)

Picture that you're a high-school student working two paper routes and saving your earnings. Then, one day, you have enough in the piggy bank to buy the car of your dreams. Nevermind the fact you don't even have a driver's license yet. Well, that is about how it went for Connecticut's Sal Carbone, who still owns the car to this day.

Carbone walked into Grody Chevrolet in Hartford, Connecticut and dropped his hard-earned cash on a 1967 Camaro. Carbone knew what he wanted and ordered his Camaro with both the SS and RS options. Under the hood, he selected the recently announced 325-hp 396. When it came to the transmission choice, the only option in Carbone's eyes was the Muncie Rock Crusher 4-speed. By the time that Carbone got his driver's license, he was working weekends at Connecticut Dragway, and the Camaro was seeing double duty.

The Camaro remained Carbone's daily driver through the spring of 1970, when he built himself a healthy 402 and dedicated the Camaro to a life on the dragstrip. Carbone campaigned the Camaro in B/MP at Connecticut Dragway and Lebanon Valley Dragway through 1972. It was during the same period that he labelled the Camaro *Starship*. Getting a jump on the whole *Star Wars* theme (the first *Star Wars* movie appeared in 1977), Carbone drew inspiration from the band Jefferson Starship. Applying the paint and graphics (that remain on the car to this day) was Wayne Wood of Woody's Auto Body in New Britain, Connecticut. His worked paid off for Carbone, as the Camaro always showed well at International Show Car Association (ISCA) events.

Within a few years, the Camaro had become a dedicated strip car and was running in the B/Modified Production category with a punched-out 396 engine. (Photo Courtesy Sal Carbone)

The engine retains all its 1970s parts but was freshened up by former Stock/Super Stock racer Ed Elderkin. (Photo Courtesy Sal Carbone)

The factory black interior is complemented by the necessary gauges and a full roll cage. Note the ignition components that are located on the passenger-side floor pan. (Photo Courtesy Sal Carbone)

In 1975, the Camaro moved into E/MP after Carbone went to a 287-ci small-block that was built by New Jersey's, Duffy's Performance. In addition, he called upon SRD Race Cars in Malvern, Pennsylvania, to install a ladder-bar slider leaf-spring-mount setup.

A Jesel brothers' Competition Machine Service (CMS) 287 engine was the next powerplant that was used. The last 287-ci engine in the car, which is still in it to this day, was built by Tony Feil in 1979. Completing the driveline is a Chrysler Hemi 4-speed transmission and a 6.50-gear-equipped Dana. The combination took the Camaro to mid-10-second ETs.

Carbone retired the Camaro in 1980. He parked it in his aunt's garage and forgot about it for the next 20 years. He attempted to sell it at one time, placing an advertisement in *National Dragster* magazine, but had no takers. There's no doubt that he's quite happy about that today. The Camaro remains unchanged from when it was last raced.

The experts at Speed Research and Development Race Cars in Pennsylvania installed the floating rear suspension. This car hooked well. (Photo Courtesy Sal Carbone)

Owner Sal Carbone stated that holding onto the Camaro all these years was a total accident. The appropriate 1970s name on the side of the car was inspired by the rock group Jefferson Starship. (Photo Courtesy Laura SanGiovannia)

Ault & James Corvette

Jerry Ault is shown racing at Iowa's Tri State Raceway during the 1971 season. The injected Corvette set record 11.40 ETs. (Photo Courtesy Bob Martin)

Jerry Ault went from working as an engineer for ACDelco Marine to opening his own speed shop around 1969. Plans were to open the shop with his best friend, James Derringer, but sadly, Derringer died in a car crash before they had the chance to open the business. In honor of his friend, Ault stuck with the name that they had chosen together.

The *Ault & James* Corvette wasn't Ault's first venture into the world of drag racing. He had previously campaigned a successful 1925 Model T. That was followed by a few more cars, including a Shelby Mustang GT500, before he purchased the 1963 Split-Window Corvette in 1970. The car carried a tan-over-tan factory color combination, but that quickly changed to a multicolor paint scheme. The more familiar black paint was applied in 1972 by Bill "Cloud" Sheets. The color remain black as long as Ault campaigned the car.

Unlike the majority of his competition, which used tunnel-ram manifolds with twin Holley carburetors, Ault ran injection from the start—first a Hilborn and then a Crower unit because they were so easy to tune. His engines ranged in size from 277 ci to 292 ci.

During the 1976 season, the driveline in the Corvette consisted of a 287-ci engine, a 3.05-first-gear Doug Nash 5-speed transmission, and a Dana 60 rear end that housed 6.50 gears. According to "crude" chief Dave Thomas, the rear end had to be replaced every dozen runs or so.

The Chevy engines liked to rev. Ault left the line at 8,500 rpm and shifted at 10,000 rpm. Keeping the small-block alive were the best of components, including Brooks rods and 13.1-compression Duffy pistons. The weights on the crank were cut down and came to a dull point to help cut through the oil. Before moving on to a Chevy Monza in 1979, the Corvette ran its best ETs in the 10.20s at 132 mph.

"[Bill 'Grumpy'] Jenkins figured we had the quickest small-block Chevy in the nation and called about the heads and the valvetrain," Dave Thomas said. "We ran a quick-change rear end for about a month for Schiefer. Jenkins wanted to know all about it and crawled under the car to measure it up."

The Corvette was also a test bed for Crane Cams. In 1974, Paul Frost of the Billy Stepp Pro Stock team provided Ault with a Lenco transmission. He ran it for about two weeks before the NHRA clarified its Modified rules by stating that manual-transmission-equipped cars needed to engage the clutch for each gear change. The Nash transmission was installed immediately after.

The Corvette was repainted once: in 1976, and in 1977, Wolverine installed the roll cage and narrowed Ford 9-inch rear end. Along with the car's large number of wins, Ault also won the NHRA Division 3 Modified championship in 1972 and 1973.

Ault sold the Corvette to Jesse Campbell of Louisville, Kentucky. It passed through a few more hands before showing up in Northern Indiana, where it saw some street and bracket action. In 2005, the Corvette was sold to a gentleman in Chicago, Angelo DeCarlo, who gave it a nice red paint job and campaigned the car in SS/HA until 2017. From there, it was sold to a gentleman in Tennessee, who never really utilized the car. He hung onto it for about a year before selling the car to Pro Mod racer Rod Saboury. Saboury's idea was to make it into a Pro Street car, but he had a change of plans. That's when the current owner, Rex Turner, stepped in to purchase the car.

Jerry Ault campaigned this Corvette through 1977 before switching to a C/Gas Chevy Monza. The Corvette set class records numerous times with a variety of different-size, injected small-blocks. (Photo Courtesy Bill Truby)

In 2005, the Ault & James Corvette received new red paint and a new interior, and it was no longer recognizable. The Corvette last raced in 2017 in the SS/HA category with a Jeff Taylor–built 327 engine. (Photo Courtesy Rex Turner)

Ready to be placed in the Corvette is the Jerry Ault built 287-ci engine. Components include Duffy's 13:1 pistons, BRC aluminum rods, a crankshaft with smaller and thinner counterweights, 292 turbo cylinder heads, and, of course, Crower injection. (Photo Courtesy Rex Turner)

In 2019, Turner bought the Corvette as a roller. With the intent to restore the Corvette back to mid-1970s status, the first thing that he did was have a local shop repaint the car black. Next, Turner had to find or build the right engine for the car. Word reached him about a fresh 287 engine that Ault assembled in 1976.

"The engine was built, but the customer never used it," Turner said. "He soaked it in oil, wrapped it, and set it under his bench. It stayed there all of those years."

Behind the engine resides the correct Doug Nash transmission and Dana rear end with 6.50 gears. The restoration was completed in 2022, with the help of many people, including Jerry and Dave Thomas. Many tears flowed upon its reveal.

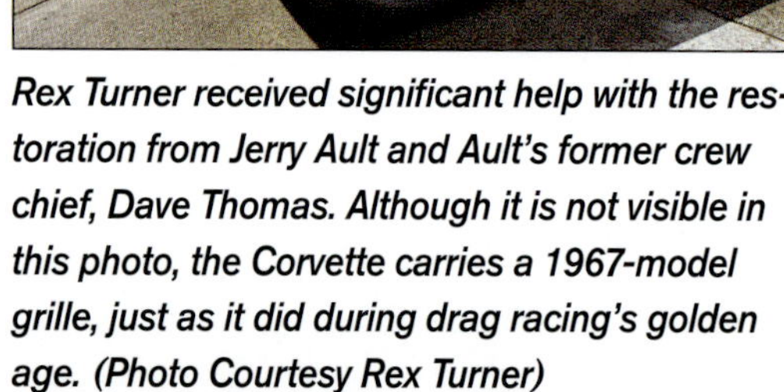

Rex Turner received significant help with the restoration from Jerry Ault and Ault's former crew chief, Dave Thomas. Although it is not visible in this photo, the Corvette carries a 1967-model grille, just as it did during drag racing's golden age. (Photo Courtesy Rex Turner)

The interior color differs today, but the current owner chose to leave it as-is. Jerry Ault loved it, and it goes well with the black exterior. (Photo Courtesy Rex Turner)

The famed "Dauber" (Dan Delaney) brushed on the lettering (including the sponsor "stickers"), gold leaf paint, and stripes. Bill Sheets, who applied the original gold-leaf paint in 1971, had some left over and donated it for the cause. (Photo Courtesy Rex Turner)

It's not common to see a tubbed-out 1963 Split-Window Corvette. Wolverine Chassis narrowed the rear end and installed the linked suspension and roll cage. (Photo Courtesy Rex Turner)

The *Race Shop* VW

Darrell Vittone and the* Race Shop *Beetle were dominant in the Modified Compact category. In this quarterfinal round matchup during the 1975 Winternationals, Vittone lost a close race against Butch Leal. (Photo Courtesy Jere Alhadeff/Dean Kirsten Collection)

In 1973, the NHRA introduced two new classes to its Modified Eliminator category. Designated as A/Modified Compact (A/MC) and B/Modified Compact (B/MC), these classes catered to 4-cylinder-equipped compact cars with an original displacement of no more than 140 ci.

Unlike the Gas classes, Modified Compact rules prevented major modifications and required these cars to be raced closer to their showroom appearance. In both the A/MC and B/MC classes, Volkswagens ruled the lanes, and two of the most famous competitors were Dave Andrews and Darrell Vittone, both of which competed out of Vittone's "The Race Shop" business, which was located in Riverside, California. From 1973 through 1975, these two racers were tough to beat, but with constantly changing weight breaks making it tougher to remain competitive, both Volkswagens were eventually sold.

The two Volkswagens continued to race under their new owners. Dave Andrews' former Beetle soon was heavily modified and stuck with the name *Termite*. Ownership changed more than once, and its whereabouts today are unknown. The Vittone 1967 Volkswagen continued to race—first out of Texas and then Louisiana under the name *White Lightning*. In 1985, after a long history of setting class wins and records, it was stripped of its drivetrain and placed in storage with no plans to return to racing anytime soon.

Fast-forward 35 years, and Modified Eliminator was long gone. With the memory of these former Modified Compact racers fading, the question arose regarding where Vittone's white 1967 Volkswagen Beetle end up? No one seemed to recall—even Vittone had no clue as to what became of the car.

However, Dean Kirsten, the longtime technical editor of *Hot VWs* magazine, knew that Vittone's Volkswagen had been raced under the *White Lightning* name. He tracked down the car to Baton Rouge, Louisiana, where it was discovered being stored in a greenhouse. Several years later, and after numerous letters and persistent phone calls, he convinced the owner to sell it to him with the understanding that it would be restored back to its former glory as the *Race Shop* A/MC sedan.

The Beetle was removed from its long hibernation and shipped to Southern California, where the restoration began. The body and floor pan were separated, and the shell was shipped to Tempe, Arizona, where it was media blasted and placed on a rotisserie. Luckily, the years in that greenhouse had treated it kindly, and

Although it was lost for years, Dean Kirsten hunted the old* Race Shop *Bug and located it in Baton Rouge, Louisiana. Persistence paid off. (Photo Courtesy Dean Kirsten)

When restoring the Race Shop *Beetle, all of the original body panels (including the fenders, doors, hood, and structural panels) were used, which kept the car's true history intact. (Photo Courtesy Dean Kirsten)*

The restored floor pan and suspension turned out so nice that it was almost a shame to cover them up. (Photo Courtesy Dean Kirsten)

no rust holes were present. While the body was being restored by Buddy Hale and Type One Restorations, the floor pan was being restored at Dean Kirsten's shop. Like the body, the floors were still in excellent condition, and once the entire floor plan was blasted, it was restored and powder coated black.

The body was painted using a single-stage Lotus White color on the exterior and Zenith Blue on the interior panels so that it would look identical to how it looked in the mid-1970s. In early 2021, the body and floor pan were once again united. Old photos were used to duplicate the hand-lettering, which was completed by the talented Richard McPeak—the same gentleman who applied the lettering for Vittone 47 years earlier! The interior was completely restored, and original parts were reused,

The Beetle looks great in its Lotus White paint and lettering by Richard McPeak. It features M&H tires and EMPI's 1968 chrome-plated steelies. (Photo Courtesy Dean Kirsten)

The meticulously built engine is 2,090 cc's and uses the best of parts from EMPI, Engle, Joe Hunt, and Mahle. (Photo Courtesy Dean Kirsten)

including the original Chase Morse roll bar, the original factory seats, and the 1973 Simpson safety belts.

The final touch was to re-create the engine by locating a pair of super-rare Fumio Fukaya-ported angle-port cylinder heads, EMPI manifolds, and a Chase Morse merged-collector exhaust. The engine remains 2,090 cc (127.5 ci) and features 89-mm Race Shop Mahle pistons, an 82-mm EMPI crank, Engle FK89 cam, Joe Hunt/Vertex cable-drive magneto, and an EMPI oil sump and high-ratio rocker arms. When placed on the dyno, this modern engine made the same peak horsepower that Vittone made in 1974: 195 hp at 6,800 rpm!

Now completed, the Vittone A/MC sedan still tips the scales at legal race weight and front-to-rear bias 1,650-lbs (742/907). Kirsten has made exhibition passes with the Beetle in California, and at a nostalgic race in Chimay, Belgium. Kirsten still has the five NHRA Wally trophies earned by this car and three of its national record certificates as well. The restoration was completed in 2014. Sadly, Vittone passed away in 2020.

The interior has been restored using as many of the original parts as possible. It carries the original Chase Morse roll cage, seats, and Simpson harness. The Stewart-Warner tachometer is a cable-drive version. Darrell Vittone did not trust "modern" electronic tachometers of the era due to needle float. (Photo Courtesy Dean Kirsten)

Darrell Vittone's best quarter-mile ET was 11.94 at 111 mph, when the Beetle ran under the class record during the 1974 March Meet. Today, the car is limited to 1/8-mile exhibition runs. (Photo Courtesy Dean Kirsten)

The California Flash 1975

Seen here at Sanair in August 1975, Butch "The California Flash" Leal rarely lost in class. The Duster consistently ran 9.60 ETs. (Photo Courtesy Bob Boudreau)

In the 1960s, Butch "the California Flash" Leal built his strong racing reputation campaigning Chevys, Fords, and Mopars. After a deviation in 1969 and 1970, he was back with Chrysler in 1971. That year, he commissioned Ron Butler to build him a Pro Stock Duster that proved to be one of the very few cars that could beat the team of Sox & Martin.

When 1972 rolled around and the NHRA introduced Pro Stock weight breaks that Chrysler felt were unfair to its Hemi cars, the manufacturer took the stance that it wasn't going to race in a category in which it had no hope of winning. Factory-supported racers were instructed not to race in NHRA Pro Stock. Instead, racers competed in AHRA and IHRA events through the 1973 season. For Leal, the protest kept him out of NHRA Pro Stock until 1976, when he campaigned his multipurpose Plymouth Arrow.

In 1974, he ran in Super Stock with a Ron Butler–built A-990 Plymouth, and in 1975, Leal would debut this B/Modified Production Duster. With the success that he had with Butler, he decided to count on his shop once again. While builder Gary Hansen prepped the chassis, Leal was busy building a 396-ci Hemi. The plan was to debut the Duster at the NHRA Winternationals, which was only 10 days away.

Leal passed tech inspection at the Winternationals with hours to spare, and then battled his way to the final in Modified Eliminator. There, he faced the Volkswagen Beetle of Dave Andrews and fell just short, unable to make up the handicap. At the Gatornationals, Leal redeemed himself by defeating Jerry Marquart's Corvette to win Modified with a 9.67 ET at 142 mph.

The season should be considered a success for Leal because he captured class at nearly every national event that he attended. In 1976, he made the move into a Gas class and a heads-up Plymouth Arrow. However, that was not before making up for his 1975 Winternationals loss by defeating Norm Mayerson at the 1976 event.

Leal lost track of the Duster's whereabouts after he sold it, and the car just seemed to have disappeared. That is, until 2016, when it showed up for sale on the internet. Current owner Denny Laube received an email from his brother with the subject line: "Car for You!" he said. The email had a link to an advertisement, offering a Direction Connection, B/MP Duster for sale.

Now, anyone who knows Laube knows that calling him a diehard Mopar enthusiast is an understatement. He loves Mopars, especially the A-Body cars and those of the drag-racing persuasion. After picking up his jaw from the floor, Laube checked the cover of his old Direction Connection catalog, and the April 1975 issue of *Car Craft* magazine, which both feature the Duster on the cover. Convinced that it was the real deal, Laube, with the blessing of his wife, quickly made a deal with the seller.

There's no denying that Laube had his work cut out for him. Though the car retained the Ron Butler, Gary Hansen handiwork, including the narrowed rear frame rails and roll cage, there was still 40 years' worth of modifications to the car that needed to be undone. The biggest corrections were replacing the front clip, part of the firewall, and the front half of the floorboards. The twin-plug 396-ci Hemi that Leal used was long gone, and in its place was a big-inch Wedge engine that was backed

Ohio's Boutwell Customs applied the paint to give the Duster its as-raced appearance. Early A-Body spindles that were swapped side to side moved the front wheel centerline forward by 1 inch. The fenders were modified accordingly. (Photo Courtesy Denny Laube)

These are three surviving California Flash cars. Behind the Duster is the 1965 A-990 Super Stock car that Butch Leal campaigned in 1974. To the Duster's left is the Super Stock Dart Sport that Butch campaigned in 1975. (Photo Courtesy Denny Laube)

The Butch Leal–built de-stroked Hemi features twin Holley Dominator carburetors on top of a magnesium tunnel ram intake manifold. The Accel twin-plug distributor and wires are new old stock (NOS). (Photo Courtesy Denny Laube)

The Gary Hansen–built roll cage dominates the interior. A Hurst shifter handles the Hemi 4-speed transmission. (Photo Courtesy Denny Laube)

by a Powerglide transmission. Through mutual friends, Laube connected with Leal, who confirmed that the car was the real deal and agreed to build a correct 396 Hemi for the car.

Before Boutwell Customs applied the 1975-matching paint, the existing fiberglass fenders, hood, doors, and decklid needed to be replaced. As rules dictated in 1975, the only fiberglass part that was allowed in Modified Production was a hood scoop. Imagine the chore that it must have been to hunt down a snorkel scoop from the period. Laube had the same "fun" when it came to finding the correct unpolished Super Trick wheels.

As the restoration progressed, Leal took a keen interest in the project and pushed Laube to have the car completed in time for the Mopar Nationals at Columbus, which was just 60 days away. Leal would attend to see his old car, but Laube thought that it was an impossible task. Leal chuckled when he heard the excuses and reminded Laube that the car was initially built in 10 days. Was that the incentive Laube needed? I can't say for sure, but the car was completed in time for the Mopar Nationals to the delight of everyone, especially Leal.

The roll cage carries over into the trunk to stiffen the chassis. Mini wheel tubs, the battery, and a spare wheel for added weight are visible in the trunk. (Photo Courtesy Denny Laube)

The factory frame rails were narrowed for additional tire clearance. Leaf springs and fabricated ladder bars helped to control wheel hop. (Photo Courtesy Denny Laube)

CHAPTER SIX

SUPER STOCK AND STOCK ELIMINATOR

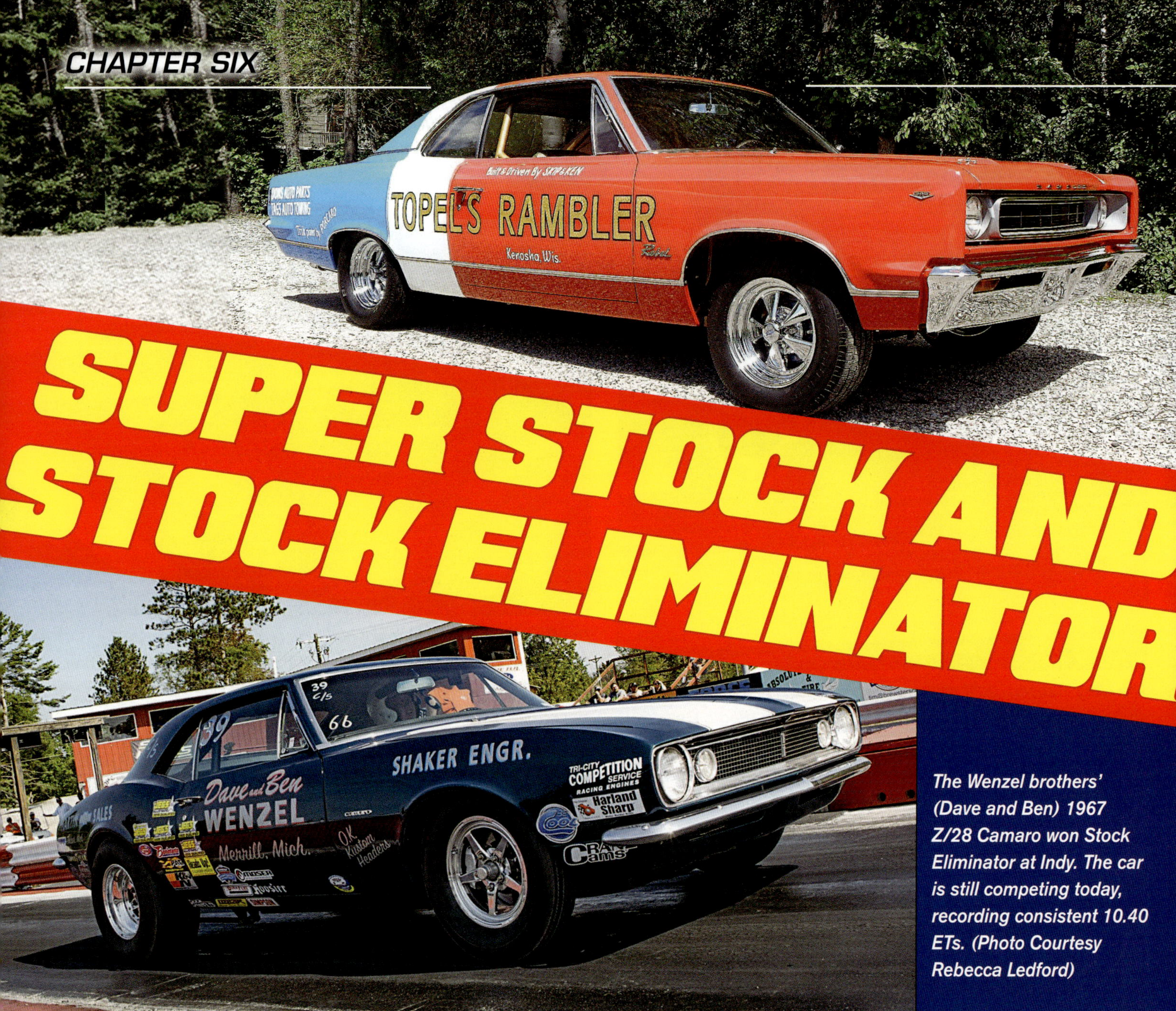

The Wenzel brothers' (Dave and Ben) 1967 Z/28 Camaro won Stock Eliminator at Indy. The car is still competing today, recording consistent 10.40 ETs. (Photo Courtesy Rebecca Ledford)

In 1967, Super Stock, which was initially a part of Stock Eliminator, became a stand-alone category. The new category initially consisted of 10 classes, ranging from SS/A through SS/EA. In 1972, the number of classes had reached 40 before reeling back to 32 in 1978. Unlike the Stock category, Super Stock rules were more liberal and permitted the use of any "stock configuration" intake manifold, any camshaft, and any size of slicks that fit the stock wheel wells.

When it comes to eliminator brackets, the Stock category has had higher participation numbers than anything else. Although Stock classes have been a part of drag racing since its birth about 75 years ago, it wasn't until the 1964 NHRA Nationals that Stock had its first eliminator program.

Top: In 2006, Fred Aherns bought this one-off, Topel-sponsored 1967 AMC Rebel. Then, he spent six years performing a ground-up restoration. This was the first Rebel to receive the combination of a 390-ci engine and 4-speed transmission. The car has no vehicle identification number (VIN) and was built without a radio, windshield wipers, and heater. Topel employee Skip Oettel built the 390 engine and drove the car in S/S competition through the latter 1960s. (Photo Courtesy Lou Costabile)

Ed Miller's World Champion Plymouth

Ed Miller became NHRA's first Super Stock World Champion after defeating the Camaro of Dick Arons at the World Finals in 1967. (Photo Courtesy William Wright)

The NHRA's first Super Stock World Champion was Ed Miller, who drove the *Miller & Guenther* (Kip Guenther) SS/A 1965 A990 Plymouth. In Plymouth jargon, the "A990" designation refers to the specially-built Hemi engines that were installed in 100 of these cars, but over time, enthusiasts attached the name to the complete package. The completed package consisted of cars picked from the assembly line and prepared specifically for drag racing.

Little was required of the new owners to prepare these cars for the quarter mile. The Hemi engines featured aluminum heads, a high-lift camshaft, a magnesium intake manifold, twin Holley 4-barrel carburetors, and tube headers. The remainder of the drivetrain was just as stout and consisted of an A833 4-speed transmission, (like the *Miller & Guenther* car had), or the heavy-duty TorqueFlite automatic transmission. An 8-3/4 rear end carried 4:56 gears and was supported by special leaf springs that shortened the wheelbase by 1 inch by mounting the housing forward.

Ed Miller's Plymouth had previously been campaigned by "Akron" Arlen Vanke. Miller partnered with Guenther in 1966 to help finance the operation. Miller won the Division 1 points championship to earn his place at the World Finals. Fellow division opponent Dick Arons was Miller's final-round opponent at the World Finals. The slower SS/EA Camaro proved to be no match, as Miller's SS/A Plymouth reeled him in on the top end and took the win with an 11.19 ET at 114.35 mph. Miller's win netted a $16,000 payday ($6,000 from the NHRA and $10,000 from George Hurst). Until that point, this was the largest payout for an eliminator win in NHRA history.

In 1968, Miller moved into a Hemi Barracuda and sold the world championship–winning Plymouth to Frank Elliott in Ontario, Canada. Elliott campaigned the car in B/MP. It switched hands a few more times and even spent a period as a street racer. It eventually found its way back to the states, where it was purchased in 1997 and restored by collector Don Fezell. In 2021, the Plymouth was sold through Mecum Auctions and now resides in a private collection.

Ed Miller's Plymouth was sold to Frank Elliott in Canada, where it competed in NHRA Division 1, B/MP with great success. (Photo Courtesy Rob Potter)

The Plymouth Rock II was preceded by a 1963 Max Wedge Plymouth. This one sat in Canada for years before Don Fezell brought it back to the United States in 1997 and restored it to the Miller & Guenther likeness. (Photo Courtesy Mecum Auctions)

The restored Plymouth sits on Cragar S/S rims. The front tires were from Jere Stahl, and the rear slicks were provided by Mickey Thompson. (Photo Courtesy Mecum Auctions)

There are no frills inside of this factory race car. The heater, radio, rear seat, and insulation were omitted. The lightweight bucket seats were installed at the factory. Ed Miller added the safety belt, Hurst shifter, and gauges. (Photo Courtesy Mecum Auctions)

Twin Holley 770-cfm carburetors are mounted on top of the Hemi. The factory-installed, solid-lift camshaft had 0.550 lift, which helped the engine produce an estimated 550 hp. (Photo Courtesy Mecum Auctions)

The lines of the 1965 Plymouth are difficult to beat. To aid traction, the battery was relocated to the trunk and replaced with a 95-pound truck unit. (Photo Courtesy Mecum Auctions)

Shaker Engineering Camaro

Driver Ron Kindle hazes the tires of the record-setting Camaro as he comes off the line at Michigan's Tri-City Dragway. Tri-City Dragway opened in 1966 and closed in 1978. (Photo Courtesy Herb Brinn)

Led by Jim Stevens, Shaker Engineering was founded during the early 1960s. The group consisted of five men who worked at Chevrolet's Bay City, Michigan, plant. These guys, the original "men in black," dressed in black (with black hats) and initially campaigned a black, 409-equipped B/S 1962 Impala. The group was well-known throughout the Northeast and was responsible for prepping several class-winning, and record-holding cars, including Ben and Dave Wenzel's 1967 Nationals–winning Camaro.

In late 1966, the Shaker team was down to just two members: Omer Lozo and Herb Brinn. Brinn heard that the 325-hp 396 would be added to the Camaro options list and placed his order. However, there was one problem: the Norwood plant (where East Coast Camaros were built) was on strike. Brinn, who was wanting the car for the 1967 racing season, couldn't wait. He turned to Bill Moser, the general manager of Chevrolet assembly plants and asked if he could get a Camaro built for him in California. Moser was a fraternity brother of Brinn's from General Motors Institute (GMI) and was happy to help out.

The Camaro was assembled in Los Angeles but couldn't be shipped to Bay City because it was in the Norwood district. The Camaro could be shipped as far as Chicago, which was where Brinn would have to pick it up. The Camaro was ordered for the purpose of drag racing, and the 376 miles that are on the car's odometer today were racked up during that trip from Chicago to Bay City.

The Camaro's third owner added the flames, making the Shaker Camaro *unrecognizable. The owner babied the car, taking great care of it. (Photo Courtesy Herb Brinn)*

As this car was to spend its life on the track, it was ordered with the bare minimum. It never had a radio, and is a column-shift car because a floor shift and console would have added unnecessary weight. All big-block 1967 Camaros came equipped with a right-side traction arm, but oddly, this one never received the bar. This was no concern to Brinn, who figured that he would have removed it anyway.

"I fabricated my own traction bars for the car, which are still on it today," Brinn said.

Backing the 396 was a Turbo-400 transmission, which

The Camaro has been beautifully restored, including the correct red nose stripe. The red and black were the colors of Shaker Engineering. (Photo Courtesy John Berglund)

initially was prepared by Bill Waddill, who was a GMI instructor and an advisor to GM's Hydra-Matic division. Back in the early days, the Camaro was run with a reverse shift pattern. Running in SS/EA, the NHRA rules required that the 396 have the factory Quadrajet carburetor, which had its downfalls. To overcome fuel delivery issues, Brinn instructed then-driver Ron Kindle to start in neutral and bring the revs up to 6,000 before slamming the shift lever into gear on the green light. It worked well until the NHRA banned the practice of neutral starts.

Kindle, who drove the Camaro through the middle of the season, put the Camaro on the map when he set the class record in May 1967 with a 12.13 ET. Brinn credited the Engle 0.564/0.581 solid-lift camshaft for really waking the car up.

Capable of high-11-second ETs, the Camaro earned enough division points through the season to qualify for the World Finals. With John Blackstock now behind the wheel, the Camaro qualified number one with a 12.12 ET. It was the only Super Stock car at the meet to run under its record. Blackstock easily won the first round, but an issue with the distributor caused a stumble. With rains threatening, Blackstock was marched back to the staging lanes, and the guys had no time to look at the issue. In the second round, the Camaro was a few tenths of a second slower and lost with a 12.30 ET.

Brinn grew tired of hauling the Camaro around the country, and in early 1968, he parked the car. His

Modern upgrades help to make this 396 NHRA class legal. The Camaro was last raced in 2020. Herb Brinn is hoping for more to come. (Photo Courtesy John Berglund)

Larry Sokol heats the tires as he prepares for another trip down Michigan's U.S. 131 tarmac. ETs in the 11.50s at 114 mph were common. (Photo Courtesy Herb Brinn)

The Camaro looks just as good on the inside as it does on the outside. The Camaro remains column shifted. Toggle switches for the transmission, fuel, fan, and water are mounted where the radio would have been. (Photo Courtesy John Berglund)

interest quickly turned to his second love, oval-track racing, and he went into business with Ed Howell. Later in 1968, he sold his trailer to fellow Michigan drag racer Dave Boertman, and in 1969, he sold the Camaro to ex-Shaker team member Frank Burrell. Burrell did little with the car, which was then sold to Steve Pischel. Pischel took great care of the car and never even got it wet. He made the biggest change to the Camaro when he removed the stickers and added flames.

In 2000, Brinn bought the Camaro back from Pischel and had the body taken down to bare metal before reapplying the tuxedo black paint and lettering. The red bumble bee stripe, which was a special request by Moser when the car was built back in February 1967, was also reapplied. The Camaro found its way back to the track in 2001, now with Larry Sokol at the controls, and was raced periodically through 2020. In addition to having "go," this Camaro also shows well. At the 2015 Muscle Car and Corvette Nationals (MCACN), the Camaro took gold in its class.

The flawless paint was applied by Lorne Drouillard, and Scott Shaver did the lettering. (Photo Courtesy John Berglund)

Rodekopf S/S AMX

Bob Smith prepared the Hurst-assembled AMX for Brian Rodekopf. Initial ETs were 11 seconds flat. (Photo Courtesy Todd Wingerter)

By 1968, American Motors Corporation's (AMC's) muscle car march was in full swing. That year, it introduced the AMX, which was a two-seater categorized as a poor man's sports car. AMC left little doubt as to the AMX's intended use by revealing the car in February 1968 at the Daytona Speedway. Any remaining doubt as to AMC's desires were removed in early 1969, when it released 52 Hurst-prepared AMXs for Super Stock competition.

NHRA rules stipulated that to compete in Super Stock, there had to be at least 50 units of a given model produced. Once dealer commitments were in, 52 Frost White AMXs were shipped to the Hurst facility in Ferndale, Michigan. Each AMX left Kenosha, Wisconsin, fitted with a 390 engine, a 2.64-first-gear BorgWarner 4-speed transmission, and a rear end that housed 4.44 gears and Henry's axles. Standard AMX equipment, such as the heater, windshield wipers, and radio were omitted, as was insulation and sound deadener.

Once in the hands of Hurst, the engines were pulled and disassembled, and J&E, 12.3:1 forged pistons and Crane modified cylinder heads were added. Twin Holley 650-cfm carburetors on an Edelbrock cross-ram manifold topped the engine. The camshaft remained stock, as it was known that racers would use their own preferred grind. A Mallory dual-point tachometer-drive distributor provided the spark, while Doug Thorley headers expelled the spent gases. Behind the engine was a Schiefer flywheel and a Borg & Beck 10-inch clutch. Protecting the driver was a Lakewood hydroformed bellhousing. Gear changes were controlled by a Hurst Competition Plus shifter with a reverse lockout.

Bill Rodekopf was a longtime AMC proponent with dealership experience dating back to the early 1950s, prior to when Hudson and Nash merged to form AMC. In 1967,

Though Brian Rodekopf dusted off the AMX and raced it on occasion between 1993 and 2009, the car retains the same appearance that it had when it debuted in 1969. (Photo Courtesy Mark Weymouth)

The 390 engine is just as it was when it was raced. In 1969, Brian Rodekopf recalled engine builder Bob Smith testing up to 15 different Sig Erson camshafts in the 390. (Photo Courtesy Mark Weymouth)

All Super Stock AMXs carried a charcoal-colored interior. Many of the cars left Hurst with the red, white, and blue exterior paint, which reportedly cost $73 extra. (Photo Courtesy Mark Weymouth)

Hurst modifications carried to the body and included the addition of a hood scoop and rear wheel openings that were stretched 3 inches for tire clearance. (Photo Courtesy Mark Weymouth)

local insurance adjustor and drag racer at heart Bob "Tree" Smith walked into the Rodekopf's showroom with a proposal that would put Rodekopf Rambler on the performance map. Smith proposed that Rodekopf sponsor a car that he himself would race and maintain it. It took nerve, but Smith was so thorough with his proposal that he convinced Rodekopf. The first drag strip venture was a bare-bones 1968 Javelin equipped with a 390 engine and a 4-speed transmission. In the fall of 1968, a Super Stock AMX replaced the Javelin.

The AMX arrived in April, and work began immediately. Smith recalls driving the car off the top deck of the transporter, as the driver was afraid to touch it. Once in the shop, Smith swapped out the camshaft. From there, the red, white, and blue paint was applied. The first trip to the home track of Kansas City International netted Smith an ET of 11 seconds flat at 128 mph. Built to run in the NHRA's SS/E class, the 390 was factored by the NHRA before it even spun a tire, going from the factory rating of 340 hp to 375. Eventually, the AMX was factored to 405 hp and forced to run in SS/C.

Smith drove the AMX through 1971, when economics saw Rodekopf's son Brian take over driving chores. By then, the car's reputation had been established, running deep into the 10s. Brian raced the AMX through the 1977 season. His best ET in the car was a 10.54.

In 1978, the AMX was retired. In its place, Brian teamed with fellow AMX Super Stock racer Clark Rand to campaign a Pro Stock Hornet. The Rodekopf AMX was placed in storage (in an underground limestone cave). There it sat, untouched in climate-controlled comfort for the next 16 years.

In 1993, Brian was convinced to dust off the AMX to compete with the Ozark Mountain Super Shifters. The rules were simple: no electronics, no power adders, and the cars had to be manually shifted. Brian prepped the AMX by rebuilding the Holleys and checking the compression. All was good. He installed a battery, plugs, and away he went. Brian ran a few races with the group and recorded 10.70 ETs before putting the AMX back into storage.

The AMX was shown many times afterward, and with the eye-catching paint that was applied in 1970, it always drew a crowd. In 2009, Brian made his last pass down the track in the car. Not long after that, the car was sold to Larry Weymouth, who owns it to this day. Weymouth has a soft spot for AMC performance cars and always had an eye for the Rodekopf AMX. It completely floored him when he received a call from Brian, who had pegged Weymouth as the next owner long before.

Weymouth has had to do very little to the car, and keeps it just as it was when it was last raced by Brian. It is stored in climate-controlled comfort and will remain so. Of the 52 Hurst AMX cars built, this one has been judged to be the most original.

Doug Davis competes in the **Rats Nest** *on a summer night in 1972 at Ohio's Edgewater Park Raceway. The Central Office Production Order (COPO) Camaro ran 11.20 ETs in SS/D class. (Photo Courtesy Bob Martin)*

The acronym COPO will make any Chevy enthusiast's heart race. A Central Office Production Order (COPO) was initially used when dealers ordered fleet of cars, such as taxicabs or police vehicles. By the later 1960s, the central office was being used for special order requests relating to performance, such as a fleet of L-72 equipped Camaros.

For those not up on their General Motors jargon, the L-72 is a 425-hp 427 engine. This engine was only installed in the Corvette and full-size Chevys. However, through the COPO system, 1,015 L-72 engines found their way into Camaros in 1969. Of this number, 822 were 4-speed equipped, and 193 had the Turbo-400 automatic transmission.

The COPO Camaro featured here, the *Rats Nest*, was purchased new from Ray Bryant Chevrolet in Dayton, Ohio, by a college student. Not being able to live with the poor gas mileage and standard steering, he sold the car after a few months. Doug Davis bought it and drove it briefly around his hometown before turning it into a dedicated quarter-mile car that competed in the NHRA's SS/D class.

Davis added the red, white, and blue *Rats Nest* paint and had Ault & James go through the 427 engine. Davis beefed up the driveline by adding aftermarket goodies from Schiefer, Hurst, and Lakewood. Ohio's Kil-Kare Raceway was Davis's home track, where he coaxed the Camaro to 11.20 ETs. He campaigned the car through 1973 and made a few trips to the NHRA U.S. Nationals before selling it to a gentleman named Daniel Knisely.

Over the next several years, the Camaro switched hands a few more times. Ralph Willis bought the car around 1978 and painted over the red, white, and blue paint with a nice black lacquer and gold stripes. The original 427 had previously been sold off, so a fresh 427 engine was installed. The Camaro gave up its M-22 Muncie transmission to another Camaro project and it was replaced by a Turbo-400. By the early 1980s, the Camaro was in the possession of D. J. Justice and showed only 15,000 miles on the odometer.

Jim Lammers, a coworker of Justice, always wanted a 1969 RS/Z-28 Camaro and started looking for one in 2017. However, the prices were generally more than he wanted to spend. He recalled a conversation that he had with Justice in the early 2000s. They talked about his Camaro at the time, but not being a real Z/28, Lammers didn't show much interest. The coworker retired a few years later, and Lammers lost contact with him.

The **Rats Nest** *turned into a good-looking street car that made the occasional quarter-mile jaunt. New old stock fenders were installed prior to the black paint. (Photo Courtesy Jim Lammers)*

In 2018, Jim Lammers bought the Camaro and restored it to LeMans Blue in the spring of 2021. In the fall of 2021, he modified it to the Rats Nest *configuration. In 2024, he returned it to stock. (Photo Courtesy Jim Lammers)*

Fast-forward 15 years and Lammers, still having not found a suitable RS/Z-28, reached out to the owner of the black Camaro through a mutual friend. Yes, he still had the Camaro, but he wasn't interested in selling it. They talked about the car, and Lammers told him that if he ever decided to sell it, to give him a call. For the next week, Lammers couldn't get the car out of his head. The next weekend, he called Justice to ask if he could come and have a look at it, figuring that he'd look, not like what he saw, and finally stop thinking about it.

Justice had mentioned years before in conversation with Lammers that he wondered if it might be a COPO car. He even had a local "car guy" come look it over, and he determined that it wasn't. Lammers did some research of his own on the criteria that makes a COPO Camaro to help determine whether this car was or wasn't one.

Looking over the car for the first time, Lammers could see that the mileage was true.

"The interior certainly looked the part, and the body was pretty rust free with just a few spots that looked a little funky in the rear inner wheel houses," Lammers said. "The rockers, floor, and trunk pans looked perfect. It had a few of the COPO signs I was looking for, [including] the disc brakes and big-block heater core, but [it] was missing the curved-neck radiator and 12-bolt rear end."

Lammers loved the car, and after a little friendly sales pressure and the right offer, the car was his.

The Rats Nest *Camaro looks like it could easily tear up the track once again. With the price of a restored COPO 427 Camaro well into the six figures, don't count on it ever happening again. (Photo Courtesy Tommy Lee Byrd)*

The Day 2 look of the Camaro was enhanced under the hood by the addition of the aftermarket air cleaner, rocker covers, and headers. (Photo Courtesy Tommy Lee Byrd)

Aside from the dash pad, the interior is all original. A Sun tachometer is mounted on the column, as are aftermarket gauges and a Hurst Line-Loc that are hidden in the photo. (Photo Courtesy Tommy Lee Byrd)

Once he was home, Lammers began tracing the cars history, and he made contact with each previous owner or their family. Sadly, Davis had passed away in 2006, but Lammers was able to reach out to his widow and their grown children. Lammers also contacted Camaro expert Jerry MacNeish, who verified that the Camaro was a genuine COPO car.

Jim and his brother Mike carried out the restoration, calling on Hausfeld Classics to complete the body and apply the factory LeMans Blue paint. Corvette Specialties built the fresh 427 engine. Behind it went the M-22 Muncie transmission and a 4.10-gear-equipped 12-bolt rear end. All of the parts that went into the Camaro were either original to the car, carried the correct date codes, or were new old stock (NOS).

Wanting the "as raced" appearance, Lammers had the car vinyl wrapped in *Rats Nest* guise. Back onto the car went the correct Fenton wheels on the front, the Ansen wheels on the back, Sun blue-line gauges, the Hurst Line Loc, Lakewood track bars, a scattershield, and a safety loop. Open headers with no exhaust system rounded out the drag-strip necessities. The reborn *Rats Nest* was ready to go by the fall of 2021.

In 2024, Lammers opted to restore the Camaro to showroom stock. The wrap and Day 2 parts were removed, and the GM parts were installed, including the exhaust and smog equipment. Lammers sold the Camaro in 2024 but has been left with great memories and new friends.

M&H Racemaster slicks fill the stock wheel housings. Those Lakewood "Traction... Action" bars are carryovers from the car's racing days. The 12-bolt rear end has 4.10 gears. (Photo Courtesy Tommy Lee Byrd)

The front and rear spoilers of the 1969 Camaro were added by the car's second owner. They have since been removed, as today, the Camaro appears showroom stock. (Photo Courtesy Tommy Lee Byrd)

Bill McGraw's Rod Shop Charger

Bill McGraw's 1971 Charger R/T was one of the most feared SS/E cars in the nation. It was capable of running well under the class ET mark of 11.10. (Photo Courtesy John Bober)

In 1968, Ohio drag racers Gil Kirk and Jim Thompson created the Rod Shop—a store that sold performance parts and had service at a great price.

Previously, Thompson had owned a different store that had the same name (the Rod Shop), but then he closed it to go to work for Jegs. After a little coaxing by Kirk, the pair formed a partnership and opened the new Rod Shop. They started with a shop in Columbus with the speed parts up front, and a well-equipped four-bay shop in the back. Kirk kept up his racing activities and campaigned a Modified Production 1968 Camaro, partnering with Bill McGraw, who worked as a mechanic for the Rod Shop.

By 1969, Kirk convinced several local Ohio racers to run under the Rod Shop banner. The sponsorship deal for the racers included engine building servicing and parts at a discount. The Rod Shop team's first national-event win came in 1970, when Dick Shoyer and his Anglia won Modified at the NHRA Summernationals. By the end of the 1970 season, the Rod Shop was sponsored by Chrysler. The deal necessitated that the Rod Shop would run all Dodges starting the 1971 season. One of those was a Hemi Charger R/T that was campaigned by Bill McGraw.

McGraw's Charger, according to research carried out by collector Todd Werner, is the first 1971 Hemi Charger produced. The car proved to be a perfect fit for NHRA SS/E. McGraw won class at Indy in 1971, recording an 11.24 ET at 123.62 mph to defeat the *Norris Ford* Mustang that was driven by Bud Shellenberger.

McGraw campaigned the Charger through 1971. Although he had success with the car and won the Division 3 points title, he didn't care for the Charger, according to the current owner John Bober. Although the car could easily run under the class record, hitting a reported best ET of 11.08, McGraw never set the class mark, stating that Chrysler never allowed him to, fearful that the car would be torn down and that the few not-so-legal modifications would be discovered—one of them being a slight engine setback.

In 1972, the Charger was sold to Bob Bond, and it

Bob Bond had success with the Charger, winning a division championship. He campaigned the car through 1979 before parking it. (Photo Courtesy Michael Pottie)

You couldn't miss the Rod Shop cars with their patriotic stripes. The paint on the doors, upper quarter panels, hood, and trunk is original. (Photo Courtesy John Bober)

repeated its division championship win. Bond raced the car until the 1979–1980 period before retiring. In 1982, Bond put the Charger up for sale. Jerry Getalaff got himself a great deal when he paid $5,000 to purchase the car. Getalaff, who was from Ohio, lived in Florida during the winter. He brought the Charger down with him, and one day, Mike Flynn, the owner of Hollywood Wheels spotted it in Getalaff's garage. Getalaff had done nothing with the car, keeping it how he bought it. Flynn worked as broker for collector Todd Werner, and

This engine is straight out of 1971. The Hemi could be shifted at 8,200 rpm due to a few cheater parts. Bill McGraw did try running in the SS/EA class with the Charger. (Photo Courtesy John Bober)

Responsible for the tire melting performance was a Jim Thompson–prepped Hemi, a Doug Nash transmission, and a 5.87-gear-equipped Dana rear end. All of those parts remain with the car today. (Photo Courtesy John Bober)

in 2002, a deal was made where Flynn and Werner bought it. Flynn hired RP Custom to repaint the sides of the car, returning it to the *Rod Shop* livery. The remainder of paint on the Charger remains as it was applied in 1971.

John Bober first laid eyes on the car in 2009, but it took until 2019 before he purchased it from Werner, who had bought out Flynn's interest in 2006. Bober has done little to the Charger beyond repairing the Stewart Warner mechanical tachometer and installing new fuel lines, valve cover gaskets, and the period-correct fender stickers.

The Charger shows just 82 miles on the odometer, and the engine has never been apart. It retains the original "Rat Roaster" intake manifold, AFB carburetors, cool can (a can that cools the fuel before it reaches the carburetors), rocker covers, and Mega-Blaster ignition. The Charger was built for speed and came out of Northland Dodge without power steering, power brakes, and a radio. The sound of the Hemi is all the music that is necessary.

A Hurst Super Shifter is visible as well as Stewart Warner gauges to monitor the Hemi. The interior, with just 82 miles on the odometer, is all original. (Photo Courtesy John Bober)

The McGraw/Rod Shop Charger has been judged to be the most original Super Stock car in existence. The wheel wells have been mini tubbed, and the springs were moved inboard for tire clearance. (Photo Courtesy John Bober)

Norris Ford Drag Club Mustang

Even in 1971, a Super Cobra Jet Mustang was a rare sight. The low-option car was ordered by Norris Ford specifically for drag racing. (Photo Courtesy Tim Orick)

Norris Ford, which is located in Dundalk, Maryland, supported its community drag racers and was home to one of the nation's largest Ford Drag Clubs. In 1970, it fielded its own car, a Super Cobra Jet Torino. In 1971, it added a special-order, Super Cobra Jet Mustang to its stable. Campaigning the two cars was a crew that consisted of club president Floyd Miller, Bunk Apperson, Albert Knell, Nelson Zanchetta, and Bud Shellenberger.

Shellenberger, the 1965 NHRA Nationals Top Stock champion, was the shop foreman at Norris and drove the Torino in NHRA competition during the 1970 season. In 1971, the reins were given to Zanchetta, and Shellenberger drove the Mustang.

The Mustang was special ordered by Norris Ford and optioned with drag racing in mind. Outside of the driveline, the SportsRoof model was a bare-bones car. Under the National Advisory Committee for Aeronautics (NACA)–scooped hood was the Super Cobra Jet 429. Underrated by the factory at 375 hp, the engine produced 480 ft-lbs of torque, had 11.3:1 compression, and was fitted with a 780 Holley carburetor, forged pistons, and four-bolt main caps. The *Norris Ford Drag Club* Mustang received a Doug Nash–prepped Toploader 4-speed transmission, and in place of the factory 4.11 gears, 4.30s were installed. Additional modifications to the 429 included an Offenhauser intake manifold, JR Headers, and a Lunati cam. Apparently, the team tested up to 15 different Lunati grinds in search of additional power.

Shellenberger drove the Mustang to a best ET of 10.90. At the NHRA Nationals in 1971, Shellenberger's 11.10 ET was good for runner-up in SS/E class. The results had the Mustang labelled as the fastest SS/E Ford in the nation.

In 1971, Norris Ford sold the Mustang and Torino a few weeks after Labor Day weekend, and like Ford Motor Company, ended its involvement in racing activities. Jim

The Norris Ford Drag Club *Super Cobra Jet Mustang is being hauled in style. (Photo Courtesy Tim Orick)*

The 1970 Torino was Norris Ford's first owned and operated drag car. Today, the same gentleman owns both the Torino and the Mustang. (Photo Courtesy Tim Orick)

Price purchased the Mustang, and for the next year, he continued to campaign it in SS/E.

The Mustang eventually ended up in Virginia. It wasn't heard from until it popped up in the mid-1980s at a few local car shows. In 2015, it appeared at a Ford show in Carlisle, owned by collector Don Fezell. The Mustang appeared as it did in 1971 but without the contingency stickers. The same year, the current owner of the Mustang, Henry Smith, located and purchased the Torino. When the Mustang showed up for sale at Mecum Auctions in 2017, Smith jumped at the opportunity to unite the two cars once again. Both cars are now back home in Maryland.

Through its four owners, the Mustang has never been registered. While Smith is putting the Torino through a full, rotisserie restoration, the Mustang required little and shows just 195 miles on the odometer. The missing contingency stickers were reproduced by Krazy Graphics in Pennsylvania. Mechanically, the Mustang has seen some upgrades, as Smith takes it to the track occasionally, where once again, the Mustang gathers 11-second time slips.

The Mustang has a history with Pennsylvania's Maple Grove Raceway, dating back to 1971. Current owner Henry Smith still puts the car through its paces on occasion. (Photo Courtesy Alan Aug)

The Mustang still has the original Wimbledon White paint that was sprayed in November 1970. The 429 engine has been modified by owner Henry Smith, and it produces wheels-up, 11-second ETs. (Photo Courtesy Tim Orick)

When it came to the original muscle cars, the Super Cobra Jet was Ford's last hurrah. Reportedly, only 53 of these engines found their way into Mustangs. (Photo Courtesy Tim Orick)

The Mustang's original interior was updated with modern features, including a tachometer, gauges, and a harness. The odometer shows only 195 miles. (Photo Courtesy Mecum Auctions)

This Mustang was built with drag racing in mind, and owner Henry Smith carries that tradition onward. Here, he warms the Firestones before another run. (Photo Courtesy Tim Orick)

Brock & Nelson '55 Chevy

The 1972 season was a great one for Larry Nelson and Duane Brock. By midsummer, their '55 Chevy had racked up enough wins to more than pay for itself. (Photo Courtesy Bob Martin)

In 1972, Larry Nelson and Duane Brock seemed to come out of nowhere to win the NHRA Summernationals with their SS/T '55 Chevy business coupe turned sedan (a back seat was added). Nelson hauled the car out of a scrapyard while he was stationed in Texas.

With Nelson at the wheel, the pair saw immediate success, winning division races, including a few against future Pro Stock legend Bob Glidden. Their Summernationals win came at the expense of Tony Cieri and his SS/Q 1965 Chevelle station wagon. In the final round, Nelson defeated Cieri with a record-setting 13.20 ET.

A week later, Nelson went to National Trail Raceway in Ohio, where he won the National Dragster Open. At the NHRA World Finals in Amarillo, Nelson qualified number two and battled his way to the final round, where he fell to the factory-backed Mopar of Dave Boertman. In trying to hold off the charge of Boertman, Nelson lowered the class record once again, this time to a 13.06 ET at 105.28 mph.

Brock and Nelson alternated between the sedan and a wagon through 1973, swapping the 265, 3-speed, and 12-bolt rear end, back and forth between the two so that they could compete in different classes.

Larry Nelson (left) was reunited with the Chevy in 2017. Although it was rough and he would have a lot of work to do, he was a happy man to have the car back. (Photo Courtesy Larry Nelson)

In 1974, Nelson went to work for Jegs and soon moved into an A/Super Modified Chevy II. The '55 sedan was sold to Joe and Paul Smith, a pair of brothers from New Hampshire. The two did little racing with the '55 and showed no real success with it. For several years, Nelson stayed in contact with Joe, who promised that if they'd sell the car, he would be the first person they contacted.

Fast-forward to 2017, and a friend of Nelson spotted the old Chevy for sale on a class racer

The Nantucket Blue paint (a factory color for a 1968 Chevy) was sprayed on the '55 Chevy by Tom Sondles after spending hours bringing the body back to life. Although it is difficult to see in this photo, lace covers the top. (Photo Courtesy Tommy Lee Byrd)

This car looks as good as it goes down the track. The restoration is show quality. The '55 has been turned into a Business Coupe, which means that there is no back seat and the rear side windows do not roll down. (Photo Courtesy Tommy Lee Byrd)

forum. Nelson was taken by surprise and immediately responded to the post. Sadly, Joe Smith had passed away, and Paul had no idea of the arrangement that his brother had made with Nelson. Although Nelson wasn't the first to respond to Paul's advertisement, he ended up purchasing the car after making a deal with fellow racer Lyn Smith, who had contacted Paul before Nelson.

The Chevy had been sitting for approximately 45 years, having last raced in 1979. Although the car was housed in a garage when Nelson went to retrieve it, it had spent several years sitting outdoors and was in rough shape. During this period, a strong storm had blown a tree over and onto the car's roof. According to Nelson, during the restoration, not a panel was left untouched. Under the car, a new chassis was slipped into place, as the original had been modified during its previous life as a Super Stocker to allow for the springs to be moved inboard for tire clearance.

Although the Chevy made a few passes at the drag strip in late 2023, Nelson wasn't satisfied with its performance and pulled the engine over the winter with plans to make some upgrades. A back injury sidelined Nelson for a few months, but he was able to get the car together in time for the Tri-Five Nationals in June 2024. There, he won the Junior Stock program by mimicking his 1972 performance with a best ET of 13.18. This brought to mind the old adage that says, "The more things change, the more they stay the same."

The 265-ci engine received a mix of new and period-correct parts. Sticking true to the Junior Stock rules of old, the 265 retains the factory intake and carburetor. (Photo Courtesy Tommy Lee Byrd)

Chris Sondles at Woody's Hot Rodz provided significant help during the restoration with new chrome and a new interior. The shifter is by Long and features a built-in line-lock button. (Photo Courtesy Tommy Lee Byrd)

The best ET with the current engine was a 13.14 at 98.38 mph. At the 2024 Tri-Five Nationals at Bowling Green, Larry Nelson and the '55 Chevy won Junior Stock Eliminator. (Photo Courtesy Tommy Lee Byrd)

Receiving power from the 265 engine is a two-step clutch, Jerico 4-speed transmission, and a 6.14-gear-equipped 12-bolt rear end. The trunk carries a fuel cell. (Photo Courtesy Tommy Lee Byrd)

B/FX F-100 XL

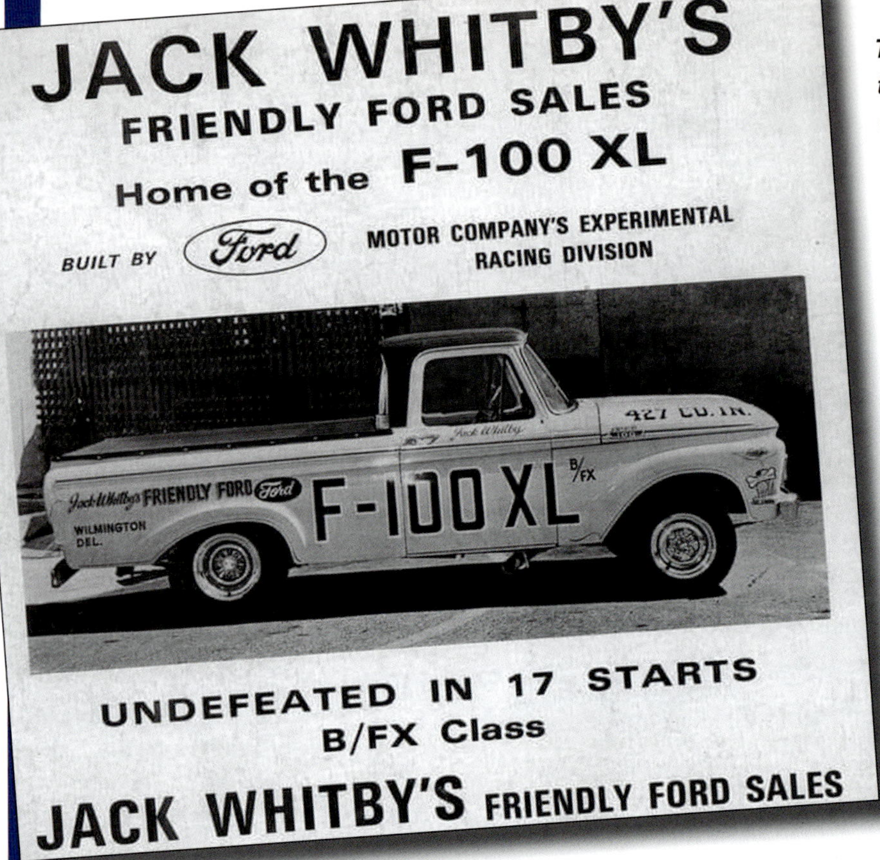

Though Ford offered copies of the 1963 **F-100 XL** *through its dealership network at an extra $3,400, no others were built. In late 1963, Jack Whitby sold the lone F-100 XL to Bill Naudain.*

Ford's foray into the world of organized drag racing wasn't limited to the use of sedans and coupes. In 1963, Ford's truck division looked to get in on the action as well. Funding was made available to have Dearborn Steel Tubing (DST) build a prototype drag truck based on the industry-leading F-100. This was the first of what the truck division hoped would be many race-ready F-100s available to the buying public in 1964.

Based upon research performed by Ford historian Charlie Morris, the F-100 XL, as it would be deemed, was built around a base, 6-cylinder-powered F-100. The first line of business was installing a 425-hp 427 low-riser engine and BorgWarner T-10 transmission. Out back, the truck was lowered by changing the factory mounting of the 4.86-gear-equipped 9-inch from the bottom side of the springs to the top side.

Rear-facing traction arms were fabricated by using heavy-duty Ford truck drag links and tie-rod ends. Shock absorbers were 50-50s in the rear and 90-10s up front. Both the front and rear springs were modified to aid performance. To aid in weight transfer, the fuel tank was moved from the cab to the rear of the bed, and the battery moved from the engine bay to the box, which was then covered by a tonneau cover. To accent the exterior's Sandshell Beige paint, the interior received red bucket seats, a console, and a steering wheel from a Falcon Sprint.

With a weight of 3,825 pounds, the truck fell into the NHRA's B/Factory Experimental category. Ford test driver and successful drag racer Len Richter helped work out the bugs before the controls were turned over to DST employee Jack "Skinny" Fuche. The F-100 XL made its debut at Michigan's Onondaga Dragway in early June. It reportedly won class and did so at another 16 tracks up and down the East Coast. On slicks measuring 15x9.00 in width, the truck produced a best ET of 12.72 at 108 mph. The truck was towed to Indy for the NHRA Nationals, but a parts failure brought the weekend to a quick end.

After repairs, it was sold to Jack Whitby of Friendly Ford in Wilmington, Delaware. As with many one-off race-only vehicles, the F-100 XL was received by Friendly Ford with just a certificate of origin. Whitby continued to race the truck, racking up the wins through the end of the season. At the end of the year, the truck was put up for sale. As it wasn't a production vehicle, Whitby had to go through the process of first registering it. Bill Naudain, who was tired of waiting on the 1964 Thunderbolt that he had ordered from Friendly Ford, purchased the truck.

The **F-100 XL** *performed double duty into the mid-1960s. Bill Naudain used the truck to not only haul his boat but also his farm equipment. (Photo Courtesy John Norris)*

The **F-100 XL** *looks right at home on the track. These days, it is displayed in its as-raced, unrestored condition by the current owner in Delaware. (Photo Courtesy John Morris)*

The twin-carbureted low-riser 427 fits easily into the engine bay. At some point, owner Bill Naudain may have swapped out the engine to try a SOHC 427. (Photo Courtesy Tammy Jefferson)

The interior of the **F-100 XL** *features a Ford Falcon console and bucket seats. Shortly after purchasing the truck from Friendly Ford, Bill Naudain swapped out the 4-speed transmission for a B&M Hydro Stick because he suffered from polio and had difficulties shifting. (Photo Courtesy Tammy Jefferson)*

Sometime after purchasing the truck from Whitby, Naudain began receiving letters from Ford attorneys stating that the truck wasn't legally his and that they wanted it back. It seems that Ford had no idea that Jack had registered the truck. With ownership papers in hand, Naudain ignored them. He continued to race the truck until around 1966, and even drove it on the street. He used it to fetch groceries, supplies, and even to tow his boat. In 1967, he retired the truck to his barn, hidden away from persistent lawyers.

In 2005, John Morris coaxed Naudain into cleaning up the truck and get it running again. The F-100 XL shows just 9,500 miles on the odometer, and it appears today just as it did 60 years ago. A refreshed 427 resides under the hood, and the old paint gleams with a coat of wax. Sadly, Naudain passed away in 2014, but Morris continues to show the truck, keeping the memories alive in Naudain's honor.

Coming off the line with the nose in the air and the tail dragging was once thought to be ideal for weight transfer. Note the tow-bar knuckles. This truck was flat-towed from track to track. (Photo Courtesy Tammy Jefferson)

With a little waxing, the original paint shines bright. The chrome rims are original. The battery is under the tonneau cover. (Photo Courtesy Tammy Jefferson)

1964 Plymouth *Hurri-Cain*

The Fred F. Cain Inc. 1964 Plymouth Savoy is 1 of 55 that was produced, and it was initially driven by Bob Cain. Low-11-second ETs were recorded. (Photo Courtesy David Cain)

With drag racing grabbing the attention of the nation's youth, the manufacturers (General Motors, Ford, and Chrysler) could not resist joining the fray. There was money to be made. "Race on Sunday, sell on Monday" became a popular concept. Each manufacturer offered exotic machinery, but none went to the extremes that Chrysler did. Its Max Wedge cars of 1962 and 1963 had the competition tearing their hair out. In 1964, Chrysler reintroduced the Hemi, and solidified its status as the performance-car leader.

The new 426 Hemi was a race-bred engine, which in 1964, found its way into 1955 Plymouths and 1955 Dodges, which were specially prepared factory lightweights. These cars were complete packages that were built with one goal in mind: squash the competition. The engine in each of these cars featured an aluminum cross-ram intake manifold that carried twin Holley carburetors. A transistorized ignition lit the fire, and tube headers expelled the gasses that were squeezed out by the 12.5:1 compression. Completing the driveline was an A-833 4-speed transmission, or in the case of the *Hurri-Cain*, a reverse-shift-pattern, TorqueFlite automatic transmission. The 8.75 rear end carried 4.56 gears that were mounted on heavy-duty springs.

The body of these 110 cars featured numerous lightweight components, including an aluminum front clip, bumper, and doors. The side glass was cut from Lexan, while the rear window was a thin, tempered piece. Stepping inside, there were no frills whatsoever—no armrests, visors, rear seat, or dome light. The two bucket seats were A-100 van units that were mounted on lightweight aluminum brackets. Of course, in a car such as these, there was no place for a radio, heater, insulation, or sound deadener.

The Plymouth Savoy *Hurri-Cain* was campaigned out of the Fred F. Cain Plymouth dealership in Wilmington, Massachusetts. Fred's son Bob campaigned the car in A/FX and raced up and down the East Coast, recording ETs in the low 11s. In 1968, Paul Wentworth took over the driving when the Cains moved into Funny Car. He drove the Savoy through 1970, running low-11-second ETs while competing in B/Modified Production.

After being sold, the Savoy passed through a few hands before ending up with Tim Hennessey in early 1981. Hennessey did a great job restoring the car with all of the parts that were available at the time. He sold the car in 1985, and it passed through a few more owners,

The initial restoration of the Hurri-Cain *was performed in the early 1980s by Tim Hennessey. Richard Boeye restored the car again in the 2009. (Photo Courtesy Woody Walcher)*

The heart of the Hurri-Cain *is the 426 Hemi, which was underrated at 425 hp. The chrome air-cleaner lid hides twin Holley carburetors. This car was built with hood pins. (Photo Courtesy Woody Walcher)*

In place of the rear, a cardboard trunk divider was installed along with and carpet that had no underlay. Note the lack of window cranks for the Lexan windows. (Photo Courtesy Woody Walcher)

Colorado's Nick Pfannenstiel is given credit for heading the restoration. Pfannenstiel matched the factory white paint and adding the correct Fred F. Cain *lettering. (Photo Courtesy Woody Walcher)*

It doesn't get much more plain than this. There is no radio, heater, or frills. Lightweight seats took the place of a heavier bench seat. (Photo Courtesy Woody Walcher)

Who would think that a factory race car would need a spare tire. This was installed to add weight where it was needed, as was the 80-pound battery. (Photo Courtesy Woody Walcher)

The color-matched steel wheels offset the paint nicely. American magnesium rims were installed on the front. (Photo Courtesy Woody Walcher)

including Major League Baseball player Reggie Jackson, before landing with Richard Boeye in 2009.

The restoration hobby had come a long way since the early 1980s, and many more reproduction parts had come on the market. Boeye hired Jim Zellner to perform a thorough restoration, reproducing correct factory markings and installing correct hardware that wasn't available in the 1980s. Nick Pfannenstiel reproduced the paint and lettering that remains on the car today.

The car is now with its 12th owner, Woody Walcher.

Les Ritchey's 1965 Fairlane

When Ford introduced the Mustang in mid-1964, it had no idea that sales would catch fire like they did. Within the car's first six months, Ford had sold 100,000 units. It was shortly after the car's introduction that the manufacturer decided that the Mustang would be the company's new performance flagship. Guys such as Gas Ronda and Les Ritchey, with their 427-equipped "pony cars," proved this to be a great decision. The Fairlane, which was Ford's performance leader in 1964, would take second stage.

The Fairlane was sponsored by Mel Burns Ford in Long Beach, California. At the time, it was one of the nation's largest Shelby dealerships. Carroll Shelby used the successful Fairlane in this advertisement.

In 1964, 100 "Thunderbolt" Fairlanes were produced by Ford. These were full-race, high-rise 427-equipped cars that produced 12-second ETs right out the door. In 1965, there were just two drag-race-specific Fairlanes built by Ford: one with the 427 that was campaigned by Darrell Droke in B/FX, and the other was built with the high-performance, 271-hp 289 and campaigned by Les Ritchey and Ron Root in Stock Eliminator.

The Ritchey Fairlane came down the assembly line with specific orders. It was built with no weight-robbing items, such as the radio, heater, insulation, sound deadener, or sealant. The weight reduction went as far as replacing the rear seat with a fiberglass part. Under the hood, the 289 was equipped with a 735-cfm Holley carburetor and an aluminum Shelby intake manifold. A Carter fuel pump fed the 289, and the spent gas was expelled through a set of Bellanger headers. A C-4 transmission and 9-inch rear end completed the driveline. With a weight of 3,100 pounds, the Fairlane fell into the NHRA's D/SA class.

Instead of giving the Fairlane to Ritchey, a contracted Ford driver, the car was sold to him for $1. This was common practice for Ford, as it absolved the company of any liability issues if they arose. Ritchey's shop, Performance Associates in West Covina, California, further prepared the Fairlane for its life on the track and added the Cragar wheels, gauges, a driveshaft safety loop, and rear-facing traction arms.

The Fairlane carried the sponsor name of Mel Burns Ford, which was located in Long Beach and was a predominant dealer for Shelby cars and parts. The Fairlane made its debut shortly after the NHRA Winternationals. While Ritchey manned his A/FX Mustang, his friend Ron Root drove the Fairlane during a regional meet at Pomona in April and won class with a 14.49 ET. In 1966, Root took possession of the Fairlane and campaigned it as the *Gendarme 4*.

When this Fairlane was bought by Alan Pound in 2008, there were no clues regarding its historical significance. Instead, the Fairlane showed years of neglect. (Photo Courtesy Alan Pound)

A&R Restoration, which is now A&R Collusion of Emroy, Texas, carried out the extensive restoration. Minor rust repair had to be carried out on one lower quarter panel. (Photo Courtesy Alan Pound)

Although the history is a little foggy regarding what happened to the Fairlane after Root sold it, it ended up in the hands of Cleat Gan in Texas. Gan was well-known in racing circles and rubbed elbows with the sport's leaders. He was a founder of the Kendig (Predator) carburetors, and used the Fairlane as a test bed. Gan raced the Fairlane at Southern California tracks until 1974, when he returned to his home state of Texas. Gan last raced the car in 1976 at Green Valley Raceway. In 2008, Gan sold the car to Alan Pound.

Pound heard of the car after being told about a nondescript warehouse in Lewisville, Texas, that stored several interesting cars. The cars he that discovered belonged to Gan, and the cars, along with some spare engines, were for sale. Pound, who operated A&R Restorations with Ronnie McEnturff, jumped in and bought a few cars and engines. Pound was given a heads-up by Gan to check the Fairlane, as it had some history. Through extensive research, Pound discovered the Fairlane's historic significance.

The Fairlane showed a little over 1,100 race miles on the odometer, and although it looked rough, it was actually in remarkable condition. Outside of the hood and trunk lid, all of the original body parts were used in the restoration. The engine wasn't in the car, but Pound discovered the short-block in with the engines that he had purchased from Gan. One cylinder needed sleeving, and a proper set of date-coded heads were

The restored silver blue Fairlane 500 is a site to behold. Alan Pound spent seven years completing the restoration, and no expense was spared. (Photo Courtesy Mecum Auctions)

The 289 eclipsed the factory rating of 271 hp with the addition of the Shelby intake manifold, 735 Holley carburetor, Ram-Air, Bellanger headers, and fine tuning by Les Ritchey. (Photo Courtesy Mecum Auctions)

Built for quarter mile action, this Fairlane offers no frills. There is no radio, no heater, and no insulation. The new blue and turquoise interior matches the original. (Photo Courtesy Mecum Auctions)

The extent to which Ford went to reduce weight in the Fairlane is amazing. The rear seat was made of formed fiberglass that was covered by the factory upholstery. (Photo Courtesy Alan Pound)

purchased from a seller in New York. Breathing through the factory ram tube is a correct 735 Holley and a Shelby intake. Today, the Fairlane retains its original C-4 transmission (that has been rebuilt) and 9-inch rear end.

In 2015, the rotisserie restoration was completed, and Pound debuted the car at the Muscle Car and Corvette Nationals (MCACN) later that year. Today, the one-of-one Fairlane is owned by a Gan family member.

An old hot rodder's trick of raising the rear of the hood helped with air movement. In this case, it also provided extra space for the hood to clear the carburetor covering. Note the rear-facing traction arms. (Photo Courtesy Mecum Auctions)

From any angle, this car is a knockout. The Fairlane is a one-of-one factory drag car that was built on a one-year-only bodystyle. The Cragar S/S wheels were a popular choice in 1965 and remain so today. (Photo Courtesy Mecum Auctions)

Tension '57 Chevy

Seen here in 1967 in Tulsa, Oklahoma, for the World Finals, the* Tension *Chevy of Don Stephenson earned numerous class wins and records through the 1970 season. (Photo Courtesy Chuck Connors)

No car dominated 1960s Stock class drag racing like the '57 Chevy. Five different V-8 engine options, three different transmission choices, and five different bodystyles ensured maximum penetration in multiple classes.

In 1963, Nebraska-based Don Stephenson jumped on the wagon early when he debuted his 210-model '57 Chevy, which was powered by the twin 4-barrel, 270-hp 283. Backing the potent little mouse motor was a 4-speed Muncie and a 5.13-geared rear end.

In 1967, the plain white Chevy received its *Tension* name. Apparently, Stephenson was visiting a bar, and on the bathroom wall, a sign stated that the best way to relieve tension was by having sex. It seems to be that Stephenson felt that drag racing a '57 Chevy Stocker was another good option.

Between 1963 and 1970, Stepheson competed in K/Stock and L/Stock and set class records six different times. On top of the massive number of event wins throughout NHRA Division 5, Stephenson hauled the Chevy to Pomona for the 1969 Winternationals, where he went home with the L/S class win, running a 13.24 ET at 103.80 mph.

Shown as it was discovered after sitting for approximately 30 years, the Chevy looked pretty rough and showed few signs of its past glory. Tony Beam had no idea what he had just purchased for $200. (Photo Courtesy Don Stephenson)

Stephenson raced the Chevy through 1969, but when the NHRA changed the rules for 1970, eliminating the 4-speed transmission in the '57 Chevy, Stephenson put the '57 up for sale. His only options would have been to run the cast-iron Powerglide or weak-kneed 3-speed standard—which, to Stephenson, was not an option.

Stephenson turned his attention to motocross, racing with his son for the Kawasaki and Suzuki factory race teams, while the *Tension* '57 passed through numerous owners, and was used as a street racer at one time.

The car fell off the radar for several years before being discovered and bought by Randy Dumond. Sadly, Dumond passed away around 2000, and his wife listed the car for sale. A cousin of the current owner, Tony Beam, discovered the car for sale and notified Beam, who was in the market for a '57 Chevy.

Beam bought the car, which at this point was little more than a body and chassis. Beam intended to turn it into a nice street car for his wife. He pictured the car painted red with a tan roof. Beam's wife liked the idea of Bel-Air inserts on the quarter panels, so he went scrounging the flea markets for a nice set.

When Beam was talking with one gentleman, who tried to talk him out of the idea, the gentleman inquired as to the car Beam had. Beam had no idea at this point that it was the *Tension* '57. However, Beam described the car to the gentleman, and that man knew exactly what Beam had. He had been trying to find the car himself for about 10 years, which was roughly the same amount of time that Beam owned it. Beam confirmed that it was the *Tension* when he sanded

Those who receive credit for restoring the look of the* Tension *are Dustin O'Brien, who applied the paint, and "Pudge" Grabil, who did the lettering on the car. (Photo Courtesy Tony Beam)

Aside from the aftermarket tachometer and gauges, the interior remains stock. A Turbo-400 transmission currently resides in the car. A proper 4-speed transmission will take its place in the near future. (Photo Courtesy Tony Beam)

Currently, the* Tension *is powered by a 350-ci engine. The not-so-legal Junior Stock parts include an aftermarket intake and carburetor. Period-correct changes are coming. (Photo Courtesy Tony Beam)

off paint from a fender and quarter panel, revealing the old lettering. This, to Beam's wife's dismay, resulted in a change of plans.

Around 2009, the restoration of *Tension* became serious. Outside of one quarter panel that needed a section replaced (after being hit by a runaway Altered-class car years before), the body was overall in pretty decent shape. Once the quarter panel was repaired, fresh white paint was applied by Dustin O'Brien, and the responsibility of lettering the car went to "Pudge" Grabil.

Powering the '57 today is a mildly worked-over 350. Currently in place of the 4-speed is a turbo transmission. As the 6-foot-7-inch Beam explained, they don't make these cars for tall people. There just isn't enough leg room for him to properly work the 4-speed. Beam does have the clutch pedals and a transmission, as well as seat brackets that will move the seat further back, and they will be installed when time permits.

Running the car at the Tri-Five Nationals in Bowling Green in 2023, Beam recorded a top speed of 99 mph.

The* Tension *'57 Chevy rides on timeless Cragar S/S rims on the front and "chromies" on the back. The rear bumper, side chrome, and grille bar are all new. The beltline trim, front bumper, and window chrome are untouched originals. (Photo Courtesy Tony Beam)

On the track, the* Tension *has run 13.94 ETs at 99 mph, which is slightly slower than the car's 1969 L/S record. Tony Beam figures that there's more to come. (Photo Courtesy Mark Fountain)

John Barkley's '57 Chevy

Few '57 Chevys are as recognizable as the one that was campaigned by John Barkley and Marv Ripes. Being a national event winner, record holder, and cover car makes it tough to forget. (Photo Courtesy John Eichinger)

Although history shows that the strongest Stockers came out of the East, no one can deny that the West had its share of top-notch performers, including Dave Kempton, Tom and Tim Neja, Cal Method, and John Barkley.

Barkley's first venture into the sport came in 1966 with a '57 Chevy wagon—a car he would race in partnership with Marv Ripes. In 1967, Barkley followed with the H/SA '57 Chevy sedan. With a Joe Allread 220-hp 283 under the hood, Barkley won class at the NHRA World Finals with a 14.74 ET.

At the 1968 NHRA Winternationals, Barkley defeated Jim McFarland in the Stock Eliminator final round. McFarland, who was the editor of *Hot Rod* magazine at the time, was driving a *Sox & Martin* 340-powered Barracuda. Barkley recalled that his closest race of the weekend came in the semifinals, where he faced fellow Southern California racer Bob Lambeck. Barkley was so wrapped up in winning rounds that he never realized he was in the semifinals until Lambeck pointed out to him that one of them was going to be in the final. Barkley went exactly a tenth of a second under his 14.60 dial to defeat Lambeck. A few months later, Barkley won the *Hot Rod* magazine meet at Riverside. All of a sudden, Barkley's '57 Chevy was one of the most feared Stockers in the nation. His reputation earned him a photo on the cover of *Car Craft* magazine's July 1968 issue.

A beckoning from Uncle Sam put a temporary halt to Barkley's racing activities. While stationed in Vietnam, he asked a few friends back home to sell the car for him. An advertisement placed in *National Dragster* magazine went unanswered. Barkley's old friend Ripes purchased the Chevy, feeling that it would be a great candidate for testing his new high-stall converter. Ripes used the combination to win Stock Eliminator at the 1970 NHRA Springnationals. Shortly after the win, he sold the Chevy to a gentleman in Illinois. Barkley resumed his racing activities upon his return to the United States and built a new '57 Chevy sedan.

The old '57 went through a few owners over the years, and it's believed that the car was raced in the Illinois area until sometime in the 1980s. As would be expected, several changes were made to the car over the years, including an engine swap and the addition of a 12-bolt rear end.

The car fell off the radar before showing up again around 1999 on an auction website. Barkley passed up on it and later kicked himself for doing so. He did his best to keep track of the car after that. It went through one repaint over the years, but the orange stripes that he

This is how the '57 sedan appeared when John Barkley bought it in 2016. It's surprising that none of the previous owners had changed the color over the years. (Photo Courtesy Phil Cooper)

The '57 Chevy is back on the track where it belongs. The car recorded consistent mid-14-second ETs, which proved that John Barkley still had the touch. (Photo Courtesy John Barkley)

applied in 1968 in his parents' garage remained original to the car.

In 2011, while attending the Street Rod Nationals, Barkley was surprised when his boss pointed out that his old car was in the Cragar booth. The owner at the time had a thing for old drag cars and had vinyl stickers applied that matched Barkley's originals from 1968.

In 2015, the '57 showed up at the Tri-Five Nationals, and it did so again in 2016. Barkley could no longer resist the urge to pursue the car. About a week after the Tri-Five Nationals, he made a deal with the owner and purchased the car. Living in California and the car being in Clarksville, Tennessee, Barkley had longtime friend Phil Cooper pick up the car for him and deliver it to St. Louis. From there, it hitched a ride with another friend to Arizona and then to California. The car arrived in the Golden State just in time for Ripes's surprise 80th birthday party.

Barkley readily admits that returning the car back to as it appeared in 1968 took the help of many. Tony Janes supplied a 283, which Bob Lambeck rebuilt. Janes also supplied a new Marv Ripes Powerglide that he had tucked away years before. Tom Ordway supplied

It's like stepping back in time. The tachometer and gauges monitor the 283 while an aftermarket shifter controls the Marv Ripes Powerglide transmission. (Photo Courtesy Tom Olsen)

Upgrades under the hood were made to ensure consistent, reliable performance. The dual master cylinder was installed to improve safety. The '57 still runs a generator. (Photo Courtesy Tom Olsen)

Surrounded by Junior Stock Chevys at the 2023 Tri-Five Nationals makes it look like 1968 all over again. (Photo Courtesy Tom Olsen)

numerous parts, including a gauge cluster and a steel front bumper to replace the fiberglass part that had been installed by the previous owner.

The Lambeck 283 was spun on the dyno before being installed in the car, and it produced 305 hp. That's a phenomenal number, considering the NHRA rated the engine at 215 hp. The decision was made to return to class racing. First things first, though. Due to a cam change, Barkley had to go through his existing combination. It took almost two years to sort it out, but he eventually got the car to the point where it ran a couple tenths of a second under his class index. Barkley entered an NHRA meet at Woodburn in 2022 and won his first round. That's all that Barkley was looking for.

Barkley parted with the '57 in 2024, feeling that it was spending too much time in the garage. The new owner, Jeff Kane, is loving the old Chevy. He made some upgrades in the name of safety to help ensure that the old Chevy lasts for many more years.

Hubert Platt's Cobra Jet Mustang

Hubert Platt's interest in all things Ford spanned back to his teenage years. His persistence and winning ways paid off when he earned Ford factory support in the mid-1960s.

In 1968, Ford hit a home run when it unleashed the 428 Cobra Jet Mustang. It had Holman-Moody-Stroppe prepare the initial six cars for the NHRA Winternationals in February. Hubert Platt fielded two of the Mustangs: one in SS/E and the other in C/SA. He made it to the Super Stock final in the one car, and missed class call in the Stocker.

Platt wrecked his Super Stock Mustang in a Fourth of July match race and upgraded the Stock-class Mustang to take its place. At the same time, the car received a 4-speed transmission and new paint, which consisted of black down one side and white down the other. Platt campaigned the Mustang through the end of the 1968 season before parting with it.

Although the trail of the Mustang gets a little fuzzy immediately after Platt, it ended up in the hands of Paul Corbin, whose father worked for Holman-Moody-Stroppe. Corbin painted the Mustang blue and white, and raced it for several years after partnering with Canadian Calvin Cowan. Eventually, the Mustang went to Canada, where it was given to Cowan. Cowan, of Didsbury, Alberta, ended up dying in a motorcycle accident, and the Mustang was inherited by his sister. She stored the car for 40 years and then gave it to her son.

This is how the Mustang appeared when it was discovered by current owner Peter Sitzler in 2021. It's amazing that these old race cars are still turning up. (Photo Courtesy Peter Sitzler)

Current owner Peter Sitzler got wind of the Mustang and made a deal to buy it in 2021.

For the most part, the Mustang was complete and surprisingly original. It showed just 195 miles on the odometer. Sitzler did most of the restoration of the car himself, leaving the body and paint to Kevin Wouters at Redline Custom Autobody in St. Albert, Alberta. Dave Dunbar did the lettering and pinstripes. Custom Automotive Specialties built the engine, which makes 460 hp on the dyno.

The fully restored, award-winning Hubert Platt Cobra Jet *Mustang resides in Canada. Nearly 60 years later, these Cobra Jet Mustangs are still a threat on the track. (Photo Courtesy Peter Sitzler)*

Chesrown Oldsmobile

Many people don't realize how involved Oldsmobile was in the sport of drag racing during the 1960s. Ron Garey helped to enlighten the masses when he won the NHRA Springnationals with his W-31-powered F-85.

Looking at Oldsmobile advertisements from 1968, it appears that the company was still trying to shake its stodgy "older man's car" image. In 1968, it was pushing its line of Cutlasses, starting with the 442, as "Youngmobiles." The W-series packages (W-30, W-31, and W-32) enhanced performance, and the youth of the day understood that. The W-30 and W-32 centered on the 400-ci 442, while the W-31 centered on the new-for-1968 350-ci engine. The W-31 package was available in the F-85 Sport coupe, Cutlass S Sport, Holiday coupes, Cutlass Supreme Holiday coupes, and Cutlass convertibles. The W-31 saw a release date of mid-January.

The heart of the package was the forced-air-induction-equipped 350, which drew in cool air from twin scoops below the bumper. The engine carried 10.5:1 compression and the same 308 duration, 0.474-inch-lift camshaft that was used in the 442's 400-ci engine. The heads were fitted with 2.00-inch intake valves and 1.625-inch exhaust valves and heavy-duty springs. The factory rated the W-31 at 325 hp and 390 ft-lbs of torque. Ron Garey's Chesrown Oldsmobile–sponsored F-85 is believed to be the first W-31 that left the Lansing Oldsmobile plant.

Garey was employed as a transmission specialist at Chesrown and had been racing a variety of cars for a few years. His most recent was a 1966 L69 tri-carbureted F-85. His success with the car caught the attention of Oldsmobile's Dale Smith, who headed the manufacturer's racing program. Smith set up Garey with one of the first Track-Pack packages that had been developed for the tri-carb 442s.

Although the W-31 was not released to the public until mid-January, Garey received his F-85 the first week of October 1967, with plans to have the car ready to run Stock Eliminator at the 1968 NHRA Winternationals. Tweed Vorhees, the current owner of the F-85, and a Chesrown employee at the time of delivery recalled the car arriving at the dealership on a single car carrier along with two spare engines.

According to Vorhees, Garey went through the engine, opening the bores 0.030 and filling them with Forgetrue pistons. He installed a Lunati "cheater" cam, cc'd the heads, installed Manley valves, and balanced the reciprocating parts. Elks Head Service out of Newark, Ohio, performed the machine work, including polishing the crank. The headers were already on the car when it arrived at the dealership. An aftermarket Schiefer clutch and 18-pound flywheel filled the scattershield. A slick-shifted Muncie transmission was backed by an

Roughly six weeks after the Winternationals, the body of Ron Garey's Chesrown F-85 was destroyed at Ohio's Hyde Park Drag Strip. (Photo Courtesy Tweed Vorhees)

The body and paint were completed by the crew at Buckeye Career Center, which is located in New Philadelphia, Ohio, and offers technical education. (Photo Courtesy Tweed Vorhees)

The Aaron Shipley–built engine is topped with the original intake and carburetor. When the engine is sorted, it should be capable of 11-second ETs. (Photo Courtesy Tweed Vorhees)

Oldsmobile 12-bolt rear end that was equipped with specially made 5.38 gears.

Suspension modifications included Moroso modified spindles, and ladder-style track bars out back that were devised by Garey. Each rear spring received an Air-Lift airbag. This was the combination that allowed Garey to win E/S at the Winternationals, defeating Bill Shrewsberry's Dodge Dart with a 12.90 ET at 107.01 mph.

A major setback occurred in late March when Garey had the misfortune of a rollover crash at the old Hyde Park Drag Strip. Although Garey suffered only a minor injury, the body of the car was destroyed. A call was made to Dale Smith, who arranged for Garey to receive a complete new body from the Fisher Body plant. The re-body job was completed, and the car, with the unscathed driveline, was back to racing in just over three weeks. At the NHRA Springnationals in June, Garey defeated John Dianna's Chevy delivery in the Stock Eliminator final with a 12.78 ET, which gave Oldsmobile its first national-event eliminator victory.

In 1969, Garey moved into a Smothers Brothers–sponsored Cutlass, and the F-85 was sold and campaigned by Jim Wheeler out of Remlinger Oldsmobile. Wheeler campaigned the car for the next few seasons before it was stripped

The owner couldn't wait to get the recently completed F-85 into the daylight. The paint colors are the proper factory Provincial white and a burgundy that was used for 1968 Oldsmobiles. (Photo Courtesy Tweed Vorhees)

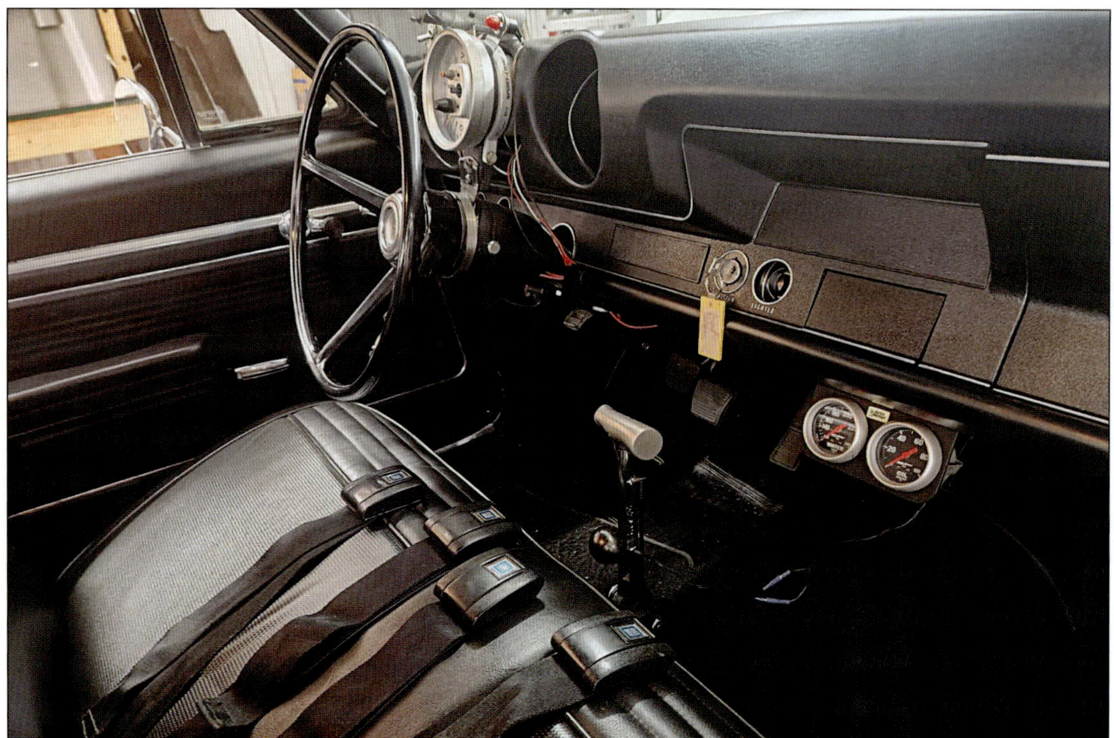

Since this F-85 sees time on the track, the interior is a combination of stock and race-ready components. The upholstery is the work of Roy Wizard. (Photo Courtesy Tweed Vorhees)

With the Keystone Klassic wheels and contingency stickers in place, the F-85 looks just as it did during the summer of 1968. (Photo Courtesy Tweed Vorhees)

of its performance goodies and sold on the dealer's used lot. Paperwork shows that the last time the car was registered and licensed was in Ohio in 1978.

In 2010, Vorhees was approached by a gentleman who said he knew of a *Chesrown* car that might be for sale. Vorhees was a little skeptical but gave the man his number and figured that he would never hear from him again. Months later, the gentleman called. The owner of the supposed *Chesrown* car was ready to sell. It took about three years to hammer out a deal, but finally, Vorhees hauled the car home in 2013.

A few telltale signs pointed to this being the car, things such as the extended Moroso spindles, the dash-mounted VIN plate (which was attached using regular rivets back when the body was switched), and the chassis that had the scars from the track bars that Garey had installed but were now long gone. Vorhees was finally able to confirm the VIN when a copy of the original ownership papers was found in the paperwork that had been hidden away for years.

The restoration was an ongoing process that took about 5 years to complete. Vorhees had Aaron Shipley's AKS Custom Engines build the 0.030-over 350, which used the forged crank from a 330-ci engine (350 cranks were iron), Speed Pro 0.030 "Stocker" pistons, 403 connecting rods, and a Joe Mondello flat-tappet cam to move the valves.

Where a Muncie transmission once rode, now resides a BorgWarner Super T-10. The rear end now holds 4.33 gears. All of the body work and paint was completed by Buckeye Career Center under the supervision of Jeff Newsome. The interior is made up of new and original parts, which were handled by Wizard Upholstery.

Hard Times Firebirds

Considering the number of wins of which Truman Fields deprived his competition, Hard Times *was an appropriate name for the Firebird. Propelling the car to record ETs was a Tom Ellison 400-ci engine. (Photo Courtesy Bill Truby)*

Truman Fields bucked the trend. Instead of racing a Chevy in Stock Eliminator, he chose a 1968 Ram Air 1 Firebird. To say that he succeeded where many others would have failed is an understatement.

In 1968, Truman and his brother Dennis returned home from serving in the United States military and marched down to Hartwell, Ohio's, Jake Sweeny Pontiac, where each of them bought a 400-ci Verdoro Green Firebird. Truman, knowing that his car was going directly to the drag strip, ordered it with a 4-speed and rear 4.30 gears. Dennis's Firebird was more sedate and would be used to tow the Fields Brothers' drag-racing effort.

Around 1970, Truman recalled Pontiac's Herb Adams and Tom Nell showing up at Edgewater and watching as the Firebird ran mid-11-second ETs. The pair all but accused Truman of cheating. Truman suggested that they show up the next week at Michigan, where he planned to run, and he'd prove that he wasn't. Truman set the record and Adams and Nell were there to watch tech teardown the Firebird and show the engine to be legal. A week later, Truman received an invite to go to Detroit. The Firebird ran two-tenths of a second under the existing record of 11.69.

Tom Ellison helped prep the Firebird's 400 engine, and Truman stated that the only real trick to assembly was to clean the cylinders from the bottom up, with the heads and main caps torqued in place. They found that the cylinders would distort when the heads were torqued down. Their method of cleaning up the cylinders eliminated this problem.

A 2.20-first-gear Muncie backed the engine—until it blew it apart and they built a slick-shifted unit to replace it. The factory-installed 4.30 gears were swapped out for 4.56 gears. Truman ran as steep of a gear as 4.80 with a taller tire. Over the years, the Firebird ran as a Ram Air 1 and Ram Air 2 car. The difference was in the heads, with the Ram Air 2 using refined round exhaust ports. In 1972, a change in NHRA rules to a pure stock format required Truman to run the Ram Air 1 heads. Under the new rules, he still he managed to post 12.0 ETs. Eventually, the NHRA factored the engine at 380 hp, which was 40 hp more than the factory rating.

Today, the first Hard Times *Firebird (there were three) is true to its 1973 form. The Motor Wheel rims are extremely rare today. (Photo Courtesy Mark Weymouth)*

In 1976, Truman traded the Firebird to Roy and Mike

The interior of the Firebird retains its drag flavor. Truman Fields ordered the car with a bench seat because it was lighter than a pair of bucket seats. (Photo Courtesy Mark Weymouth)

There were a reported 321 Firebirds built in 1968 with the Ram-Air 1 engine. Pontiac underrated the engine at 335 hp, and actual output was likely closer to 400 hp. (Photo Courtesy Mark Weymouth)

McKinney for their Stock-class 1968 Firebird and a motorcycle. The McKinneys weren't too impressed when Truman showed up five weeks later at Edgewater and ran a tenth of a second quicker than they did. A plan was devised that the two would run opposing classes to prevent butting heads. McKinney would run B/S with the Ram Air 2 setup, while Truman ran C/S with the Ram Air 1.

Truman saw his greatest success while campaigning the McKinney Firebird. He won NHRA World titles in 1982 and 1983, and in 1984, he was voted as *Car Craft* magazine's All-Star Drag Racing Team Stock Class Driver of the Year.

In 1993, Truman retired from his job with IBM. Free of continuously

The styling of the Pontiac distinguished it from the Camaro. This Firebird was a C/Stock drag car from Day 1. (Photo Courtesy Mark Weymouth)

Restoration of the Firebird was completed by Ross Gregory at Marquette Classics. Mark Weymouth and Vincent Impastato performed the drivetrain work. (Photo Courtesy Mark Weymouth)

being moved about by the company, Truman settled in Kentucky, and in 1994, he began racing again. The McKinney car remained in storage, and a new Firebird was purchased and raced in Pure Stock. It was this car that became the first Pure Stocker to break into the 11-second category. Today, Walt Hollifield of South Carolina owns this Firebird.

With all of the moves and life's distractions, Truman lost track of his original Firebird that he had traded to the McKinneys. In 2002, a friend of Truman's discovered the car in an old horse barn. The car was rough, having sat for some time. Truman purchased his old Firebird, even though the price went up when the seller realized who the buyer was. After completing the deal and extracting the car from the barn, Truman set to work on the restoration. The famed Dauber was called on to remove the McKinney colors and apply fresh Verdoro green. Meanwhile, Truman dug out all his old 1971, class-legal parts. Once it was completed, he ran an E/SA 11.70 on the class 12.05 standard.

Truman sold the original Firebird in 2010 to Jim Mino, who campaigned the car before it was sold to Walt Hollifield. In 2014, Hollifield sold the car to Mark Weymouth. Weymouth went through the Firebird from top to bottom and restored it back to its 1973 Indy-winning form. Being such a low-mileage car, only minor repairs to the body were necessary.

In 2011, Truman sold the McKinney Firebird to Todd Hoven. Hoven continues to campaign the car and has had plenty of success with it.

Todd Hoven runs his Firebird with the Ram Air II setup. He campaigned the car for a few years. Prior to 2015, it was lettered in the likeness of the **Hard Times.** ***(Photo Courtesy Todd Hoven)***

Smothers Brothers Oldsmobile

Jim Waibel's Smothers Brothers King Olds Cutlass S was prepared in a week and immediately set the G/S class record. Oldsmobile supported Waibel's racing through 1972. (Photo Courtesy Mashie Mihalko)

Dickie Smothers, who is one half of the controversial Smothers Brothers comedy team, was seriously into racing. This fact was not lost on Oldsmobile's Dale Smith or Carl Schiefer of Schiefer clutches. The two put their heads together and offered the brothers a sponsorship deal. If they put a team together, Oldsmobile would provide them with a string of 1969 W-Machines. It was a no-brainer deal for the Smothers, as they and their TV show would receive free publicity.

With GM's no-racing edict, Smith had little to no budget to work with, and anything that he did want to get to the racer had to go through the proverbial back door. Pete Kost, a member of the assembled team, recalled that Oldsmobile sponsored the brothers' television show, and the support (cash to the racers) was funneled through the show.

"We'd be at a national event, and a gentleman would walk up, hand us an envelope with money, wish us luck, and be on his way," Dickie said.

The envelopes contained $2,000.

The Smothers Oldsmobile team consisted of Kost (from Seattle), Willard Wright (Los Angeles) Ron Garey (Ohio), Berejik Olds (Boston), and Jim Waibel (Lakeland, Florida). Two Top Fuel teams were added: Florida's Don Garlits and California's Dwight Salisbury.

Oldsmobile provided the cars fresh off the assembly line and applied the Smothers Brothers' chosen colors. Looking for a driver in NHRA's Division 2, Smith contacted Buster Couch, the division director who suggested Waibel. Waibel's Cutlass S, which is one of just 26 W-31, 4-speed-equipped convertibles produced, was delivered to his door in Lakeland, Florida. The Cutlass was pulled from the assembly line carrying Saffron yellow paint before the Smothers crimson red, and stickers were applied.

Waibel had no problem making the Cutlass competitive. On its initial outing, the car ran below the H/S class record. Following the same philosophy he had when running his previous Chevys, the 350 Oldsmobile engine was built to minimum allowable specifications. As with other Oldsmobile racers who enjoyed the support of the manufacturer, anything he wanted was just a phone call away.

Dickie Smothers loved racing. He showed his interest in drag racing with this 1968 Cutlass. Although it was built to compete in the SS/F category, Smothers's Hollywood contract prevented him from racing in competition. (Photo Courtesy John Eichinger)

"I'd break a Muncie, call Dale Smith for another, and he would send two," Waibel said.

Waibel was instructed to never order parts, as Smith could pull them right off the assembly line, saving his limited Oldsmobile budget.

Waibel campaigned the Cutlass into 1970, taking an H/S class win at the 1970 NHRA Winternationals and then making an uneventful appearance at the inaugural Gatornationals. Shortly after that, Waibel turned

After 40 years of neglect, the Cutlass was in need of a complete overhaul. Thankfully, it had spent its life in Florida and rust wasn't a major issue. (Photo Courtesy Jeff Kane)

Living not far from Garner Customs & Restoration in Florida, Dick Smothers stopped by to see the progress. (Photo Courtesy Jeff Kane)

The Cutlass is shown at the 2022 Philadelphia Concours d'Elegance. The car won best-in-class honors. (Photo Courtesy Jeff Kane)

the car over to King Olds, per his contract agreement. Prior to doing so, the race W-31 was yanked, and in its place, went a bone stock 350. King Olds wasted little time in prepping the car for its used lot. The stickers were ground off, and yellow paint was sprayed on, not wasting any time to paint the doorjambs.

The Cutlass spent the next approximately 40 years on the streets of Florida before once again turning up on a used car lot. There, the car was spotted by an old crew member of Waibel's, Jimmy Johnson, who recognized the traction bars that he himself had welded on. Johnson contacted Waibel and bought the car at his request. Waibel's intentions were to restore the Cutlass to how it was when he raced it. However, time catches up.

In 2018, current owner Jeff Kane struck up an online conversation with Waibel's son, Jeremy. Kane, who had no idea he was talking to the son of Jim Waibel, was looking for a '57 Chevy fuel-injection unit that Jeremy said his father had. At some point, Kane asked if he was related to Waibel, and Jeremy said that Jim was his father. It turned out that Waibel had several parts for sale—and maybe even one of his old race cars. Kane, a Chevy man from way back, remembered Waibel's Junior Stock Chevys from the 1960s and had gotten his hopes up that the car may be one of Waibel's old '57 cars. He was disappointed to learn that it was the *Smothers Brothers* Oldsmobile. However, the more that he looked at photos of the car, the more it grew on him.

Plans were made for Kane and his then-future-wife, Brenda, to fly down from their home in Delaware to pick up the fuel-injection unit and have a look at the Cutlass. The injection unit he liked, and Jeremy said that he wouldn't take less than $500 for it. I think Kane surprised him when he said he wasn't going to pay that for it, as it was worth a lot more. When it came to the Cutlass, it was Waibel's wife, Margaret, who asked what

The spotless engine bay is a reflection of the work performed by the crew at Garner Customs & Restoration. The 350 engine was rebuilt by Aron Shapley. (Photo Courtesy Jeff Kane)

The underside of the Cutlass is clean. Remnants of the car's drag racing days are the air-lift bag inside the coil spring and the original traction arms. (Photo Courtesy Jeff Kane)

Legendary Auto Interiors provided the reproduction upholstery for the Cutlass. Dickie Smothers's stamp of approval is noted on the inside of the glove-box door. (Photo Courtesy Jeff Kane)

he would do with it if they were to sell it to him. Kane responded that he would restore to just how it was when Waibel raced it. That was the answer that the Waibel's were looking for. Others had wanted the car, but because of its rarity, their plans were to restore it to showroom stock condition. That's not what the Waibel's wanted.

The restoration got off to a slow start, but with Waibel running into medical issues, Kane, with a promise to be kept, got busy in 2021. At the suggestion of friend Bruce Ponti, Kane reached out to Garner Customs & Restoration in Florida. A deal was made to restore the Cutlass, and once again, it was headed to Florida. Kane set a deadline of March 2022, as his desire was to debut the car at the NHRA Gatornationals. When the track opened in 1970 for the inaugural Gators, the Cutlass was the first car to go down the track. However, Garner did him one better. The shop wanted to debut the car at the 2021 Muscle Car and Corvette Nationals (MCACN) in November, which was six months away.

The fact that the Cutlass spent its life in Florida paid off, as the only real rust on the car was a few spots on the lower quarter panels that were handled by the more-than-competent hands of Butch Lloyd. The rest of the car was pretty rough, though, as it did spend several years resting outdoors.

A lot of favors were pulled and asked, to meet the 2021 deadline. Rick Bedford prepped the chassis and driveline, while Ken Garner and his crew got busy on the body and interior. Aaron Shapley built the engine, and Legendary Interiors stepped up and prioritized the Cutlass. The first time that Kane and his now-wife, Brenda, laid eyes on the restored car was at its MCACN debut. A stunned reaction would be an understatement. Although, there was nothing like the smile on Waibel's face when he saw and heard the car at the Gatornationals in 2022.

The beach and the sunset provide a great back drop for the King Olds. *This is the only known Smothers car that still exists. (Photo Courtesy Jeff Kane)*

Von-Wil Mustang

Imagine cracking a garage door to find this. It is a Boss 302 with only 198 miles on the odometer, which is a dream come true. (Photo Courtesy Randy Saba Collection)

When Houston, Texas, resident Bob Justice ordered his Boss 302 Mustang from Von-Wil Ford in June 1969, he had but one thing in mind: drag racing. This Boss had no options—not even a radio.

Justice wrangled a sponsorship deal out of Von-Wil Ford, who performed all of the drag-racing prep work on the Mustang. Justice's intentions were to run in the NHRA Stock category, where the Mustang fit into the F class. The category allowed for minimal modifications, but with the race-ready 302, few modifications were necessary. Right from Dearborn, the engine came equipped with a 780 Holley carburetor, 2.23-inch intake valves, 10.5:1 compression, and a 0.477-inch-lift solid camshaft. It was greatly underrated at 290 hp.

The modifications that were made at Von-Wil Ford is unclear, but it is known that headers were added, a blueprinted cam installed, and the Ford rev-limiter, which limited the Boss engine to 6,150 rpm was removed. A 5.14 rear gearset was installed, as were fabricated track bars and Gabriel HiJacker shocks. Up front, a set of Cure Ride drag shocks were installed. Tragically, Justice was only able to make a few passes on the car, recording a best ET of 13.04 at Eastex Dragway before his untimely death.

Justice's grieving wife pushed the Mustang into the family's air-conditioned garage, and there it remained for the next 38 years, untouched, collecting dust, and stockpiling items that the family set aside. The car showed just 198 miles on the odometer.

In 2008, the family was ready to sell the Mustang. The car was advertised through a broker, and the car was purchased by Illinois resident Dick Jones. It then went to a collector in Michigan, who sold it in November 2017 to its current owner, Randall Saba, in Colorado.

Being stored in a climate-controlled garage, the only things replaced were rubber parts that suffered dry rot. The interior received a cleanup and remains just as Ford produced it. The Acapulco Blue paint remains all original and was washed and given a buff. No touchups were necessary. The heads on the 302 were pulled just to ensure that the cylinders were clean, and they were.

Although the Autolite "High Performance" battery still sat in the original tray, it no longer held a charge, so a new one was installed to fire the car. Yes, the engine does sound sweet! On the rare occasion when the car is shown, the Autolite battery is installed. The Mustang remains to be one of the best all-original cars ever to be discovered.

The paint, and flat hood on this Boss Mustang are all original. The rims were painted gold by the original owner to match the lettering. (Photo Courtesy Randy Saba)

The "Pony Tail" lettering was applied for the Von-Wil Ford dealership, which was the sponsor and is still in business today. The Mustang features period-correct M&H slicks on the rear and Goodyear tires on the front. (Photo Courtesy Randy Saba)

This is just as the engine appeared in 1969. The only changes necessary were to replace the dry-rotted rubber parts and the Autolite battery. The smog equipment was removed by the original owner. (Photo Courtesy Randy Saba)

The Light Blue Corinthian interior remains unchanged from 1969. Aftermarket add-ons include the Motorola tachometer and a Hurst Competition Plus shifter. (Photo Courtesy Randy Saba)

The original owner, Bob Justice, would be as surprised as anyone to know that his Mustang was preserved. On occasion, the car is shown to amazed crowds. (Photo Courtesy Randy Saba)

One-Owner Chevelle

Initially campaigned as a C/Stocker, this Chevelle had no problem getting air under the front tires. It's difficult to see, but the rear filler panel was painted using the lace technique. (Photo Courtesy Jerry Frailey)

A Monaco Orange 1969 Chevelle sure catches the eye. Pack it with a 375-hp 396, Muncie transmission, and a 4.10 rear gear, and the competition was sure to catch a good view of the taillights. Jerry Frailey bought this Chevelle new while earning $2 an hour working in Janesville, Wisconsin. He has managed to hang onto the car to this day.

Frailey's plan from the outset was to race the Chevelle, so the first modifications saw him add Mickey Thompson headers. As a dual-purpose car, a low-restriction, chambered exhaust system was added. To get the 396 into its power range quicker, the 4.10 gears were swapped out for 4.88s. Torq Thrust wheels were wrapped in M&H slicks. Sponsorship came way of the Union 76 station that was operated by his dad. By coincidence, the Monaco Orange matched the Union 76 color perfectly.

Frailey's first pass down the Union Grove track netted him a trophy. Running in C/Stock, he was consistently in the low-12-second ET range. By the early 1970s, Frailey, wanting to go faster, was eyeing Super Stock. He added an aftermarket intake, carburetor, solid engine mounts, roller rockers, and Accel and Mallory ignition components. A Mr. Gasket vertical-gate shifter moved the Muncie transmission, which was now equipped with a 2.64 Liberty first gear. The 12-bolt rear saw its 4.88 gears swapped for 5.38s. These changes put the Chevelle well into the 11s.

In late 1975, with the Chevelle showing just 20,000 miles on the odometer, Frailey rebuilt the 396 and sent the Chevelle out for a narrowed rear end and wheel tubs to mount 14-inch-wide Firestones. It took until 1977 to get the car back, and when it was done, the chassis was not going to handle the power of the built 396. Frailey recalled that the work was quite crude by today's standards, as back then, all they had to work with were blow torches and a stick welder. Unsure of what to do, Frailey moved the Chevelle into his garage, and there it sat for the next 34 years.

In 2011, Frailey pulled the Chevelle out of its long slumber and hauled it to TLC Restorations in Milton, Wisconsin, where work was performed to make the Chevelle driveable once more. Work included locating a replacement 1969 Chevelle and 12-bolt housing. The search led them to Arizona, where a rust-free donor car was located. Back in Wisconsin, the donor car gave up its chassis, wheel tubs, and rear

Today, the Chevelle features its original paint. Experts guess that no more than a handful of Monaco Orange L78-powered Chevelles were built in 1969. (Photo Courtesy Robert Rippberger)

Owner Jeff Frailey restored the Chevelle using Day 2 parts. (Photo Courtesy Robert Rippberger)

The underside of this Chevelle is immaculately clean. (Photo Courtesy Robert Rippberger)

With a little more than 20,000 miles on the Chevelle, the interior has survived quite nicely. The carpet is the only item that was replaced. The original carpet had been cut for the roll cage. (Photo Courtesy Robert Rippberger)

The filler panel on this SS 396 Chevelle never received the standard, factory-applied matte black finish. Jeff Frailey applied the black paint himself. (Photo Courtesy Robert Rippberger)

Aside from spots on the bottom of each quarter panel behind the wheel, the paint on the Chevelle is original. (Photo Courtesy Robert Rippberger)

seatback support. A correct-code 12-bolt rear end was located and installed along with the correct 4.10 gears. Since Frailey retained pretty much all of the original parts that he had removed from the Chevelle, they all went right back on. Under the hood, the engine block is the correct CE-code Chevrolet replacement for the car. In addition, the original heads and accessories were attached to the block.

Liking the idea of making passes on the Chevelle once again, Frailey set the car up in typical street/strip fashion and has recorded ETs in the 11s on that rare occasion that he has taken the car to the track.

Super Cobra Jet *Witch Doctor*

Torino Cobras weren't common to see at the track. Keith Garner took an underrated package in the Super Cobra Jet 429 Torino and made it a winner. (Photo Courtesy Greg Garner)

Doctor Keith Garner knew his way around a Ford order form. In 1970, when he went looking for a car that would blow the doors off the competition, he chose the Torino Cobra with the Super Cobra Jet (SCJ) 429 Drag Pack option.

What this $155 option gave Garner was a bulletproof SCJ 429 fitted with goodies, such as a 780-Holley carburetor, 4-bolt mains, forged pistons and rods, a solid-lifter cam, and an oil cooler. The transmission options were either a beefed-up C-6 or the 4-speed. Out back, the only option was a Detroit locker that was stuffed with a 3.91, or 4.30 gear. The 429 was rated at a questionable 375 hp. Super Stock magazine tested one in stock trim, street tires and all, and recorded a 13.62 ET in the quarter mile. Garner would work his magic and vastly improve on this ET.

Garner ordered the Torino through McFayden Ford in Omaha, Nebraska. Seeing that it was going to be a double-duty car, he ordered it with a few creature comforts: power steering, power brakes, an AM/FM stereo, and power windows. The car was delivered by train to Omaha, and shortly after being unloaded from the rail car, it was stolen! Six months later, it was found unscathed in an Omaha warehouse, showing just six miles on the odometer. Given the option, Garner went ahead with his purchase.

Garner street raced the car a bit but found that the Super Cobra Jet 429 markings scared off the competition, so he removed the script from the shaker scoop and traded the 429 fender emblems for 351 markings. In 1971, he took the Cobra to the racetrack for the first time and won a class trophy. That was all it took to get him hooked. In late 1973, with 62,000 miles showing on the odometer, the Torino became the *Witch Doctor*, a dedicated drag car.

With the change, the Torino went on a bit of a diet. The shaker hood and scoop came off, the heater, and radio were removed, the power steering came off, and the power disc brakes were replaced with manual drum brakes. Garner wasn't happy when he was informed that the shaker hood and scoop were stolen from the body shop that did the changeover to a flat hood. Today, outside of the hood, and a spot on the upper left quarter panel, the paint is all original. The quarter panel needed a touch-up after one of

Greg Garner raced the car through 1982 on tracks throughout the Midwest, racking up wins at North Star Dragway in Minnesota, Thunder Valley Dragway in South Dakota, and Kearney Dragway in Nebraska. (Photo Courtesy Greg Garner)

Greg Garner, who was 8 years old at the time, came up with **The Witch Doctor** *name and logo, lifting it from a Donruss "Odd Rods" sticker. John Beyke of Beyke Signs in Hastings, Nebraska, applied the graphics.*

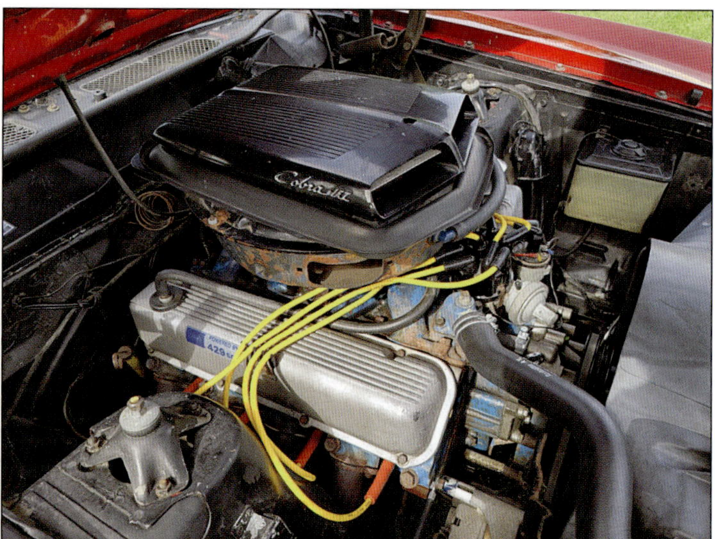

The Super Cobra Jet 429 was available only in 1970 and 1971. This one was bored 0.030-over by the original owner and has not been rebuilt since that time. Photo Courtesy Mike McClaflin)

The interior remains completely original and very clean. Bucket seats, the console, and power windows were just a few options that were selected. The tachometer is on the right, where it's easy to read. (Photo Courtesy Mike McClaflin)

Fewer than 1500 Super Cobra Jet Torinos were built in 1970. This one retains almost all of its original Medium Red paint. (Photo Courtesy Mike McClaflin)

Garner's street races, when a losing competitor kicked the car and dented it.

Garner raced the *Witch Doctor* through 1979 before giving up the seat to his son, Greg. To call the car dominant would be an understatement. It was the Kearney Dragway points champion and the Nebraska Stock Champion from 1972 through 1975 and again in 1977. In addition, in each of those years, the Torino held class records.

After 1982, the Garners retired the *Witch Doctor*. Looking to expand their

In 1970, the Torino was voted **MotorTrend** *magazine's Car of the Year. It's easy to see why. Stylist Bill Shenk was responsible for the design. (Photo Courtesy Mike McClaflin)*

horizons, the Garner Racing Team campaigned a fresh pair of Stockers: a U/S 1977 Oldsmobile Starfire (driven by Keith) and an N/SA 1979 Malibu (driven by Greg). The pair raced the two cars in NHRA and IHRA competition all over the United States before retiring at the end of 1994.

The *Witch Doctor* was put into storage before being sold to a forgotten party in the late 1990s. In 1999, the car passed through Mecum Auctions and was purchased by Roger Shinn. In 2001, the current owner, Steve McClannahan, bought the Torino from Shinn. McClannahan's intention was to strip the car of its lettering and build a nicer version of the 1970 429 Torino GT that he had in high school. However, that idea quickly fell by the wayside because, "The car was just to cool the way it was," McClannahan said.

Knowing the car's history and how unique it is, McClannahan, to the delight of the public, shows it on occasion. When it's not in the public eye, the *Witch Doctor* spends its time in a climate-controlled garage to ensure that it remains just as cool as it was when it was first labelled with the name in 1973.

Epilogue

There's an old advertisement that states, "You've Come a Long Way, Baby." Well, such is the sport of drag racing. The cars that are featured in this book show us just how quickly the sport evolved in a short period.

Props go out to the caretakers of these cars who have taken the time and energy to preserve history. It's no small feat to maintain or restore an old race car, considering how difficult parts are to find and the fact that most of the cars here were used, abused, and discarded as "just cars."

I want to give special word of thanks to those who have re-created cars. Although this book does not include re-creations, there are plenty that have been built that are just as nice (and some are even nicer) as the original. They stir the memories just as the original cars did.

In 2014, CarTech released the book *Drag Racing's Quarter-Mile Warriors: Then & Now*. It was in 2024 that the book you are now holding was initiated. At the rate in which these original, surviving, and restored drag cars are coming out of the woodwork, there may be a third volume in the future. In the meantime, there are plenty of events and museums that showcase these beautiful cars. It's well worth the time to attend an event or visit a museum.

Finally, let's not forget the annual series of nostalgia events. Pro Stock, Gasser, Modified, and Super Stock shows are filling bleachers, as those with the same feel for yesterday are creating more and more tributes to the cars of the past and racing the wheels off of them.